MARK AS STORY

MARK AS STORY

An Introduction to the Narrative of a Gospel

THIRD EDITION

David Rhoads
Joanna Dewey
Donald Michie

Fortress Press
Minneapolis

MARK AS STORY
An Introduction to the Narrative of a Gospel
Third Edition

Cover design: Joe Vaughan
Interior design: PerfecType, Nashville, TN

Library of Congress Cataloging-in-Publication Data
Rhoads, David M.
Mark as story : an introduction to the narrative of a gospel /
David Rhoads, Joanna Dewey, Donald Michie. — Third ed.
p. cm.
Includes bibliographical references.
ISBN 0-8006-3160-9 (alk. paper)
1. Bible. N.T. Mark—Criticism, Narrative. I. Dewey, Joanna, date– .
II. Michie, Donald, date– . III. Title.
BS2585.2.R46 2012
226.3'066—dc21 99-12061
CIP
The paper used in this publication meets the minimum requirements of American
National Standard for Information Sciences – Permanence of Paper for Printed
Library Materials, ANSI Z329.48-1984.
Manufactured in the U.S.A. AF-3160
22 21 20 19 18   10 11 12 13 14 15 16 17 18 19

Dedicated to the community of biblical scholars
who have so enriched our lives and our work.

Contents

Chapter 5. The Characters I: Jesus 99

Chapter 6. The Characters II: The Authorities, the Disciples, and the Minor Characters. 117

Preface to the Third Edition

The primary purpose of all three editions of this book is the same: to serve as an introduction to the Gospel of Mark *as a story*. We are not so much trying to give an interpretation of Mark—though of course we do that—as we are endeavoring to show how narrative analysis can illuminate a text, using Mark as our example. The approach followed in the successive editions of this book has come to be known in biblical studies as narrative criticism—the analysis of formal features of narrative such as tone, style, narrator, setting, plot, character, and rhetoric. Despite the explosion of new literary approaches and other developments in the past three decades, there remains the need for a basic introduction to biblical narrative, particularly one that incorporates relevant insights from new developments. So the purpose and the approach of this edition as well as its intended audiences remain the same.

In the second edition, the book was substantially rewritten throughout, with no page remaining unchanged. We did not think that this third edition required as thorough a revision. We affirm our analysis of Mark's story in the second edition. Nevertheless, there are three areas in which significant advances in our thinking make this new edition relevant and timely: Mark as oral/aural composition; the importance of the cosmic dimensions of Mark's story; and the Roman imperial context as a key to understanding the world within Mark's narrative. We wish to say a word about each of these three developments.

Mark as an Oral/Aural Composition

It has become clear that Mark's story was presented from memory, told all at one time, probably in houses, in marketplaces, at meals, at evening gatherings, and at synagogue-like assemblies. In modern English, it takes about two hours to recount Mark's Gospel, not an unusual length of time for an ancient storyteller to recall or for an ancient audience to embrace.

Recent New Testament research has recognized that first-century Mediterranean societies were predominantly oral/aural cultures in which probably no more than three to five percent of the people were able to read or write. So, for the people of the time, the Gospel of Mark *was* the oral performance they experienced. We do not use the word *performance* here in any artificial sense of actors simply playing a part or people simply putting on a show. Rather, we use it to emphasize that the stories were told in lively and meaningful ways. Mark was also performed in this way, we assume, by committed followers of Jesus using all their best storytelling skills to enable others to hear about Jesus, to understand the presence of the rule of God, and to become people who follow Jesus in spite of opposition and risk.

As such, the written text of the Gospel of Mark functioned as a script for storytelling, much as a script functions for a play or sheet music for a musical performance. We cannot imagine a musicologist studying the score of a symphony without hearing a performance of it. Nor can we imagine a dramatist studying the script of a play without ever seeing the play. So also we now need to take seriously the performance nature of the biblical writings, including the Gospel of Mark.

Ancient storytellers brought out the dynamics of the story in their telling, putting their stamp on the story, and shaping it to each particular audience. The performer used voice, volume, pace, gestures, facial expressions, and bodily movement to express an interpretation of the story and to engender certain impacts on different audiences. The performance would stimulate the audience's imagination and bring out the emotion, the humor, and the irony of the story. In short, ancient communities experienced the Gospel embodied in a performer. This makes a difference in how we think of Mark as a story: The narrator is now a live person, the settings are places in the storytelling space, the characters are brought to life dramatically, the suspense and drama of the plot are conveyed by the storyteller, and the communal audience is engaging the story and interacting with it. The connection between the story world and the real world is also more immediate because of the audience's relationship with the one telling the story.

Our focus in this book remains on the story itself rather than on its performance. After all, whether performed by an ancient storyteller or read silently by a modern reader, Mark is a *story*—and a powerful one at that. Nevertheless, our interpretations have been influenced by our work on oral narrative in antiquity. As such, we now refer to the Gospel of Mark as an oral/aural "composition" and the author as a "composer." We refer to those who experienced the story as a communal "audience" or as "hearers" instead of as readers.

To assist in making the oral nature of Mark's story more immediate to those who study it, we have added appendix 3, which contains some exercises designed to assist readers in learning and performing episodes from Mark's Gospel. For resources on the orality of biblical writings, see www.biblicalperformancecriticism.

org. For resources on storytelling, see also the Network of Biblical Storytellers at www.nbsint.org.

The Importance of the Cosmic Dimensions of Mark's Story

In this edition, we place greater emphasis on the way in which Mark depicts the rule of God moving toward a universal realm encompassing all of creation. The cosmic conflict between God and Satan is foundational to all the other conflicts in the narrative. Through Jesus, these cosmic conflicts get played out with natural forces, Judean* and Roman authorities, the disciples, and those who come to Jesus for healing. The cosmic conflict—and God's assured victory in the near future— are not "background." Rather, they are integral to the story, both to the characters in the story and to the audience hearing it.

As a result of our emphasis on the cosmic conflict, we shift the interpretive center of gravity from the end of the story to the beginning of the story. Scholars have tended to think of Mark as a "passion narrative with an extended introduction." This view places the death of Jesus as the key watershed event. By contrast, we focus on the cosmic shift that occurs at the opening of the story with the arrival of the rule of God. This arrival of God's rule—the heavens opening, the defeat of Satan in the desert, and the announcement by Jesus—is the key watershed event in the narrative world. Mark, then, may be described as "the arrival of the rule of God with an extended denouement"—that is, all events in the story are manifestations and consequences of God's activity in establishing God's reign.

This shift in focus to the beginning of the narrative does not diminish the power and climactic force of the execution of Jesus—an event that reveals more fully the nature of God's reign and that seals a covenant with all who would embrace God's rule. Nevertheless, the shift does place the entire narrative firmly in the broader framework of God's activity in establishing God's rule over all of life.

The Roman Imperial Context

For Mark's early audiences, the power and destructive force of the Roman Empire would have been burned into the memories of audiences, because Mark's story was composed in the immediate aftermath of the Roman-Judean War of 66–70 CE, a war in which, in response to rebellious forces in Israel, the Roman legions invaded Israel and brought devastation down through the villages of Galilee and

---

*To be historically accurate and to avoid contributing to modern anti-Semitism, instead of the terms *Jews* and *Jewish*, which could refer to all Jews at all times, we are using the proper first-century designation *Judeans* to refer to those in the ancient Mediterranean region who belonged ethnically and religiously to the people of Israel, whether inside or outside the land of Israel.

Judea, besieging Jerusalem until both the city and the temple lay in ruins, and cru-
cifying and enslaving its people. To Mark's audiences, the Roman Empire spelled
domination and destruction.

It has become clear to us that just as surely as the Judean Jesus as son of God
is rooted in the traditions of Israel and the God of the Judeans, so also Jesus and
the rule of God are portrayed in Mark as an alternative to the Roman emperor and
the Roman Empire. In the opening words, Jesus is named the chosen son of God, a
title held by emperors. The rule of God is not like Roman rule. For Mark, the rule
of God represents a new social order of care for the vulnerable, of mutual service
rather than domination, and of self-giving for others—even to enduring persecution and execution rather than resorting to violence. Mark's vision is the arrival
of God actively involved in the world through Jesus and his followers, ultimately
leading all people and all nations and all creation to fulfillment.

To bring home the power of this story in Mark's real world, we have added a
case study in the conclusion that imagines a concrete scenario in which the Gospel
is proclaimed to a gathered audience in Palestine shortly after the Roman-Judean
War. This case study suggests how the Gospel might have been heard by those
experiencing it.

These three themes represent our ongoing study of Mark's Gospel and are
reflected in the concluding bibliography of selected works available since the
publication of the second edition. We have chosen to leave the endnotes as they
were in the second edition.

In the course of our work on this edition, we have become even more acutely
aware of the importance of story for our lives as individuals and for our shared
life together. Next to the basic needs for physical survival, story is essential to life.
It is how we make sense of our lives. Shared stories hold a community together.
We are immersed in such cultural, national, and global stories. We interpret our
personal lives as being in the middle of a story that has a beginning and strains
toward a conclusion. Reading the stories of others makes us aware of our own
stories, enables us to question them, and gives us an opportunity to embrace new
stories, even to undergo transformation and renewal. And so we invite you to
consider the Gospel of Mark.

We are grateful to our colleague Mark Allan Powell for contributing an afterword, new to this third edition, on the thirtieth anniversary of its first appearance.
It offers an appreciation of the contribution *Mark as Story* has made to Gospel
studies, and it traces different streams of narrative criticism into the present. We
are grateful to Neil Elliott, acquiring editor at Fortress Press, for his encourage-
ment and support of this project. We remain delighted to be part of the academy of
scholars, who contribute in interesting and generative ways to the study of biblical
literature and early Christianity.

The Gospel of Mark as Story

When we enter the story of the Gospel of Mark, we enter a world of conflict and suspense, a world of surprising reversals and strange ironies, a world of riddles and hidden meanings, a world of subversive actions and political intrigues. And the protagonist—Jesus—is most surprising of all.

The Gospel of Mark deals with the great issues—life and death, good and evil, God and Satan, triumph and failure, human morality and human destiny, and the nature of authority in the life of a nation. It is not a simple story in which virtue easily triumphs over vice, nor is it a collection of moral instructions for life. The narrative offers no simple answers but tough challenges fraught with irony and paradox: to be most important, one must be least; nothing is hidden except to become known; those who want to save their lives must lose them.

Within the story, characters may think they understand their situation only to discover their expectations overturned: the disciples follow Jesus expecting glory and power, only to find a call to serve and the threat of persecution; the authorities judge Jesus in order to preserve their traditions and authority, but they only bring judgment on themselves; the women come to anoint the dead Jesus, only to discover he is among the living.

Not only is the story itself full of mysteries and ironies, but the composer has told the story in order to transform the audience and to be a means to help bring about the rule of God. The composer of this story has used sophisticated storytelling techniques, developed the characters and the conflicts, and built suspense with deliberateness, telling the story to generate certain insights and responses in the audience. The ending has a surprising twist that leads the audience to reflect on their own relation to the drama. As a whole, the story seeks to shatter the customary way of seeing the world and invites hearers to embrace another, thus impelling them to action.

The Historical Context of the Gospel of Mark

We know little about the composer of Mark's Gospel or about the first hearers. The Gospel was unsigned and undated and contains nothing that attests explicitly either to its geographical location or to the specific circumstances of its earliest performances or even to the gender of its originator.[1] Nevertheless, for convenience, we will continue to refer to the composer as "Mark."[2]

Two major proposals have emerged about the origin of Mark's Gospel. Some scholars accept a tradition from the second-century church leader Papias, who attributed this Gospel to a certain John Mark,[3] "an interpreter of the apostle Peter" who wrote down the traditions about Jesus but "not in the right order." These scholars place the origin of Mark's Gospel in Rome in the mid- to late 60s CE, some thirty years after the death of Jesus and shortly after the execution of Peter and the harsh persecution of Christians in Rome by Emperor Nero.[4]

Other scholars doubt the accuracy of the Papias tradition. They argue that a study of Mark, taken by itself apart from any traditions about it, suggests no connection between the anonymous composer and the apostle Peter. These scholars locate this Gospel in or near Palestine, usually in a rural context, perhaps Galilee or Syria. They date the Gospel during or just after the Roman-Judean War of 66 to 70 CE—a revolt by Israel against Roman domination that resulted in the catastrophic defeat of Israel by the Roman legions and the destruction of Jerusalem and the Judean temple.[5] We favor this view.

There are also differences among scholars about whether the composer was a Judean or a Gentile, whether he came from the peasant class, and whether he had some education. Most scholars think Mark wrote to a community or communities composed of both Judeans and Gentiles, even as he drew upon the traditions of Israel to shape his narrative. Some argue that Mark intended for the story to be told to many different audiences across a wide geographical area.[6]

There is general agreement that the composer addressed people who faced rejection and persecution in their mission to spread the word about Jesus and the rule of God. The narrative suggests that persecution came from both the Judean and the Roman authorities. Mark composed his Gospel, in large part, in order to give people courage to live for the rule of God despite opposition and threat.

What Type of Story Did Mark Compose?

What were some of Mark's aims in the Gospel? Mark clearly was inviting people to put faith in the good news about the arrival of the rule of God and the way of life that the rule of God entailed. In so doing, he was leading them to become followers of Jesus. He was also warning them about the imminent culmination of the rule of God over nations and people. And, as we have suggested, he was seeking to empower followers in the face of conflict and persecution.

What genre or type of story does the composer tell in order to generate such a significant impact on hearers? Again, scholars are not in agreement. Some see similarities to Greco-Roman literature—ancient biography, Greek tragedy, popular novellas, or storytelling in the mode of ancient rhetoric. Others compare the Gospel with Judean literature—an "apocalypse" revealing the secrets of the end-time, an enigmatic parable, a midrashic commentary on the Hebrew Bible, or a writing in the mode of a Hebrew Bible narrative. Mark's Gospel may be a mixed genre. Many suggest that Mark has created a new type of composition, a gospel—a narrative acclamation of the "good news" of the rule of God: what God has done and will do through Jesus of Nazareth and those who follow him.[7]

Whatever Mark intended, he has surely produced a narrative that makes a claim upon hearers. This claim is strengthened by the fact that his story concerns real people, is based on actual events, and makes predictions about future events. And Mark has apparently brought all his storytelling capacities to bear on this task.

The Coherence of Mark's Narrative

Using a variety of oral sources and perhaps a growing oral narrative, Mark has created a story with settings and events and characters. So we might ask: How does Mark's Gospel fare as narrative? How unified or coherent is it?

At first glance, Mark's narrative may seem very spare, with many gaps and breaks. However, it is important to observe that narratives in general are a lot like matter: They feel solid to the touch, but they are really composed mostly of empty space.[8] Thus to a greater or lesser degree, every narrative has gaps—unexpressed assumptions, inconsistencies, lack of resolution, and so on. Many such gaps in Mark are of the kind inherent in any narrative, because of the selective nature of description and the limitations of using words to portray people, places, events, and the meaning of life. So the point is not whether Mark has gaps, but rather: How successful has the composer been in creating a coherent experience of a unified world? Does the story hang together? Is it consistent?

Our study reveals Mark's narrative to be of remarkably whole cloth.[9] The narrator's point of view is consistent. The plot is coherent: Events that are anticipated come to pass; conflicts are resolved; prophecies are fulfilled. The characters are consistent from one scene to the next. Oral techniques of storytelling such as recurring designs, overlapping patterns, and interwoven motifs interconnect the narrative throughout. There is also a consistent thematic depiction of the human condition, faith, God's rule, ethical choices, and the possibilities for human change. The unity of this Gospel is apparent in the integrity of the story it tells, which gives a powerful overall rhetorical impact. Mark's complex artistry has been compared to an intricately composed "fugue" or to an "interwoven tapestry."[10]

Given the unity of Mark's story, it is clear that some gaps in Mark are intentional. There are gaps due to rhetorical strategies that create suspense, puzzlement, and an open ending; gaps due to a spare style that is suggestive rather than exhaustive in description; and gaps due to the episodic nature of a narrative designed for oral performance. There are additional unintentional gaps for twenty-first-century audiences that are due to our lack of knowledge that Mark and his first-century audiences possessed—knowledge we no longer share but which we must construct in order to understand the story.

Because the Gospel of Mark is a coherent narrative with a powerful impact, it is important to experience the narrative as a whole. Those who first experienced the Gospel of Mark would have heard the whole Gospel proclaimed to them in groups on single occasions. They undoubtedly were engaged by the drama of the story, experienced the tension of the conflicts, identified with the characters, and felt suspense about the outcome. Emerging from the experience of Mark's story world, they were perhaps able to see the world around them in a new way and to have new possibilities awakened in them.

Unfortunately, in our time, we usually encounter Mark's Gospel in bits and pieces—as verses quoted apart from their context or as episodes read at worship. This is similar to hearing quotations from a Shakespearean play without ever having seen the whole play. To get the full impact of Mark's story, we need to experience it in its entirety. Therefore, we encourage people to read or hear all of Mark at one time.

The Story World

As a coherent narrative, Mark's Gospel presents us with a "story world," a world that engages and grips us, a world such as we experience when we get "engrossed" in reading a novel or experiencing a theatrical play.

As a way to grasp the notion of a story world, consider the experience of seeing a film: The images and sounds on the screen draw us into another world, a world with its own imaginative past and future and its own universe of values. For a time, it seems as if we are no longer sitting in a movie theater or our own living room but are immersed in a different time and place, sharing the thoughts and emotions of the characters, undergoing the events they experience. In a sense, then, this story world has a life of its own, independent of the actual history on which the film might be based.

Clearly, we as viewers are engaging with a film through the filter of our own experiences, making our sense of this world as it unfolds before us. Nevertheless, depending on the power of the film and its relation to our lives, we may come away from the experience with a deeper understanding of life or a new sense of purpose or a renewed capacity for courage and creativity or with a different view of current events. We have entered another world, and it has changed us. Reading stories has the same power as seeing films, and in reading we participate even more fully, because as readers we ourselves visualize the world suggested by the words we read.

The same dynamics would be true for ancient audiences experiencing a performance of Mark's Gospel. The Gospel would be especially powerful because it was a story close to their life world; it depicted events of momentous importance to them, and it related directly to them and their circumstances. The ancient audiences would be experiencing Mark's *version* of these events *told in such a way* as to have a particular impact on them and to result in changed attitudes and actions.

As such, when we approach Mark as a work that creates a story world, we see that the statements in Mark's narrative refer to the people, places, and events *as portrayed in the story*.[11] Just as a film may be a version of historical events, so also Mark is a version of historical events. Although Jesus, Herod, the high priests, and the Roman procurator Pilate were real people, they are, in Mark, nonetheless characters portrayed in a story. The desert, the synagogue, and Jerusalem are settings as depicted in the story world. The exorcisms, the journeys, the trial, and the execution are events depicted in the story world. The ancient performers of Mark drew their audiences into this story world. It is this story world that is the subject of our study. *Thus, unless otherwise identified as helpful background information from the general culture of the first century, all subsequent references to people, places, and events refer only to the story world inside Mark's narrative.*

Guidelines for Reading Mark as a Story

It is important to seek to understand a story on its own terms rather than to have it say what we want it to say. For modern readers seeking to understand Mark's Gospel on its own terms as a narrative, the following four guidelines may be helpful.

First, as we have suggested, read Mark as story rather than as history. For if we look through Mark as a window into history, we will think first of the historical figure Jesus rather than of Mark's *portrayal* of Jesus. If we look through the story, then, if there is something we do not understand, we may think that Mark omitted something about Jesus from his narrative, and we will go looking to other sources to find the answer. By contrast, if we look at Mark as a portrayal of characters, settings, and events as they are presented to us *in the narrative*, then, if there is something we do not understand, we will reread Mark carefully to find within the story itself the basis for clarity.

Second, read Mark independently from the other Gospels. In narrative study, we cannot legitimately use the other Gospels to "fill out" or to "fill in"—as a way to explain or elaborate Mark's story. For example, if we read Mark's story in light of the birth narratives from Matthew or Luke, we have already significantly changed Mark's story, because Mark does not contain these events. Or if we read an episode in Mark in light of details given about the same episode in one of the other Gospels, we will have changed Mark's story. Mark's story is complete in itself apart from the other Gospels—which are themselves also, in the same sense, self-contained stories about Jesus. Consider, for a time, treating Mark's Gospel as if it were the only story we know about Jesus.

Third, avoid reading modern cultural assumptions into Mark's first-century story. We bring to our reading many assumptions from the Western postindustrial, electronic, and individualistic age that are radically different from first-century assumptions. Because Mark is a first-century narrative, it is important to use social and cultural patterns from the first century as a basis for understanding Mark's story—in the same way that we need to know about the language, customs, and culture of the sixteenth century in order to understand the plays of Shakespeare.

Fourth, avoid reading modern theologies about Jesus back into Mark's story. We may bring to our reading of Mark our own image of Jesus, for example, Jesus as "meek and mild," in the words of the hymn. Yet Mark's Jesus is neither meek nor mild. Or we may read into Mark's story later doctrines about the Trinity or the two natures of Christ. Or we may think of Jesus' death in Mark as an atoning sacrifice for sins to be forgiven. Or we may think that the rule of God is only about individual salvation rather than a vision for the transformation of nations and all creation. Since these ideas are not present in Mark, however much they do or do not represent historical or religious truth, they should not be used to interpret Mark.

These four guidelines are really not possible to carry out in any absolute way, given the nature of texts and our own subjectivity. Nevertheless, our continual efforts to work at these guidelines will bear fruit as we seek to understand Mark's narrative on its own terms.

A Narrative Method for Interpreting Mark

How do we unpack a narrative to understand what it means and to see how it works? We can point to five key features of narrative for analysis—narrator, setting, plot, character, and rhetoric.

Narrator refers to the way the story gets told—the voice of the storyteller, point of view, the overarching beliefs and ethical norms of the narrative, the manner of address and tone of the narrative, as well as the storytelling techniques in the narrative. The narrator is not the author/composer, but a device the composer uses to get the story told.

Setting refers to the contexts within the story—the depiction of the cosmos, the social and political world of the story, as well as the specific temporal and spatial contexts in which events take place.

Plot involves events—their order in the narrative, sequential relations, turning points and breakthroughs, and the development and resolution of conflicts.

Characters are the actors in the story—their identity and place in society, their motives and drives, their traits, their ways of relating to each other, their disclosure in the plot, as well as the changes and developments that take place in the characters as a result of the action.

These first four features of narrative represent basic features of an overall view of life. The narrator manifests the beliefs and values of the story. The setting provides the possibilities and limitations within which people live out their lives. The plot represents a particular expression of movement from past to present to future. The characters reveal a view of human nature reflected in individuals and communities. Together these four features in a narrative constituting a way of viewing the world that readers and hearers might consider for their own lives.

Finally, the fifth element of narrative is *rhetoric*, which refers to the various ways an author or composer may use the combined features of narrative to persuade readers and hearers to enter and embrace the world presented by the narrative. As such, it is not enough to ask what a narrative *means*. We must also ask what a narrative *does* to change its audiences. A study of the rhetoric of Mark identifies how the narrative may transform its audiences.

To understand fully the dynamics of rhetoric, it is necessary to explain the concept of an "ideal audience." In the conclusion of our study, we will imagine the responses of one possible real audience of Mark's Gospel. However, throughout our study, we will be using the construct of an ideal audience or ideal hearers. For example, we will often mention how the narrator leads audiences or hearers to respond in certain ways to various aspects of the story world. In most cases, these references are not to actual audiences, since it is not possible to predict the responses of actual audiences.

Hence, in order to speak about the rhetorical impact of Mark's story, we employ the hypothetical concept of an ideal audience. The ideal audience is an imaginary construct with all the ideal responses *implied by* the narrative itself, as best we can construe it. It is the audience that the narrator seeks to create and shape in the course of telling the story. Constructing a portrait of an ideal audience is a matter of inferring from each phrase in the narrative how an audience is being led to react and how these implied responses accumulate to generate an overall impact on an audience. We modern readers of Mark can track these implied responses in part by attending to what we may infer as ideal responses of ourselves as *ideal readers*.

We do not intend for our study of these five features of narrative to fragment the story, for we will be looking at the whole story from each of these different perspectives. Nor do we mean for our interpretation to be an abstract substitute for the story itself. We do not want to reduce the story to a moral or a message or a summary, for then it is no longer a story. A story is not just a vehicle for an idea, such that the story can be discarded once one has the idea.[12] Rather, our goal is to enhance the experience of the story as a story. Looking at these features of story can help us grasp the story more fully. For it is only in the reading and the hearing of the story itself that we experience its magic and its capacity to change us.

CHAPTER 1

The Gospel of Mark

Introduction to the Translation

The translation that follows is set out as a short story without chapter and verse designations, so that readers may experience the narrative as an integrated whole.[1] The paragraph divisions mark a shift in scene, a change of speaker, or the end of a conflict. Punctuation often serves to establish connections in the narrative and to emphasize the developing action. None of these features appears in the early manuscripts, and so it is the work of translators to provide what they consider appropriate to the meaning and impact of the language. We have translated so as to bring out the drama of the story, as we see it, from the original Greek language.[2]

We have based this translation on a standard reconstruction of the original Greek text. The earliest copies of Mark in handwritten manuscript form have been lost to us, and our only extant copies are from a time several centuries later than when Mark first composed his Gospel. Early copies of Mark from the first century have not survived. At this early stage, no two copies would have been alike. Scholars have sought to reconstruct Mark's original wording by assessing the variations found in the later extant copies.[3] This reconstructed text is the text upon which we depend for our translation.

Mark's Gospel ends with the shocking and powerful line, "And they [the women at the grave] said nothing to anyone at all, for they were afraid." Some Greek manuscripts have variant endings that briefly extend the story and bring the Gospel to different conclusions. However, scholars generally consider the line just quoted to be the actual last line of the original manuscripts of the Gospel. Most contemporary translations print the variant endings in a footnote or with the observation that "the earliest manuscripts do not have these endings."[4] The original ending is a powerful finale to Mark's story and has significant implications for interpreting the whole drama. This ending of Mark is the ending we honor with our translation.

Translators strive to capture the meaning and impact of the original language. Yet every translation is an interpretation, reflecting choices in which some meanings and connotations are captured and others are lost. This translation is a word-for-word style of translation, in contrast to a translation of dynamic equivalence or a paraphrase.[5] We have tried to find single words or brief phrases that most faithfully render the Greek words. Furthermore, because Mark composed his story about Jesus in the everyday language of the first century, we have used everyday English words for the translation.

We have tried to select words that are appropriate to the atmosphere, character traits, conflicts, and emotions in Mark's story. Often we have avoided overused words, such as *kingdom*, *repentance*, *forgiveness*, and *parable*. Instead, we have chosen words with nuances from the Greek not always highlighted, such as *rule of God*, *turning around*, *pardon of sins*, and *riddles*. Where formal names have a meaning in the Greek, we have conveyed that meaning in English, such as the Decapolis as the "Ten Cities," the Christ as "the anointed one," and Peter as "Rock." That is how they would have been heard in the Greek language of the first century.

Our choice of words takes into account the context of the whole story. Most translations render the same recurring Greek word differently from episode to episode. For example, the recurring Greek word *hodos* is rendered "way," "journey," or "road" at various places in the same translation. Similarly, *paradidōmi* is rendered "arrested," "handed over," "delivered up," and "betrayed." Thus readers of these English translations cannot see the verbal motifs that are part of the Greek. By contrast, wherever possible, we have translated the same recurring Greek word with the same English word, so that today's readers can see such verbal motifs recurring as they do in the Greek.[6] Repetitions of the same word would have echoed as motifs in the hearing of audiences in the first century.

Two additional word choices need comment. First, we have translated the word *kardia*, the Greek word for heart, as "mind" as in "hardness [or rigidity] of mind." For ancients, the heart was not considered the seat of the emotions but the place of thought and will; so "mind" is a closer English equivalent. Second, we have translated the Greek word *Ioudaioi* as Judeans rather than Jews, as in "king of the Judeans." This is a more literal translation, and it helps to clarify that the story came from the first century and that these are characters in Mark's story world.[7]

Also, we have sought to be faithful to most elements of the Markan oral style, even when they seem awkward—word order, the frequent use of participles, the recurring use of the word *and* to introduce sentences, the various functions of the imperfect tense, the emphatic pronouns (rendered in italics), the emphatic negatives, and formulaic phrases.[8] We have also translated so as to reflect oral stylistic devices such as the two-step progressions, various forms of repetition, concentric structures, and narrative asides, all of which contribute to the suspense and drama of the story.

Finally, we have retained the male gender preference for the depictions of God and Satan in Mark's story.[9] At the same time, we have appropriately translated the inclusive meanings of Mark's gender language for people, rendering the masculine *anthrōpos* as "human," "humans," or "humanity" instead of "man," "men," or "mankind." In so doing, we have retained Mark's plays on words, such as the play on words between "humans" and "the son of humanity" and the contrast between thinking in "God's terms" and thinking in "human terms." Also, we emphasize the inclusive meaning of Mark's singular masculine pronoun by rendering it in the plural "they" or "all who" or with the pronouns "whoever" or "any." These inclusive translations are faithful to the composer's creation of a story that urges audiences to welcome all people.

The Gospel of Mark

The beginning of the good news about Jesus the anointed one, the son of God, was just as it is written in Isaiah the prophet:
> "Look, I am sending my messenger ahead of you,
>> who will pave your way,
> the cry of one shouting in the desert,
>> 'Prepare the way of the lord.
>> Make his paths straight.'"

It was John baptizing in the desert and proclaiming a baptism of turning around for pardon of sins. And the whole Judean countryside and all the Jerusalemites were going out to him and being baptized by him in the Jordan River, publicly admitting their sins.

And John was wearing camel's hair with a leather band around his waist, and he was eating grasshoppers and wild honey. And he was proclaiming, saying, "After me is coming one stronger than I am, the strap of whose sandals I'm not worthy to stoop down and untie. *I* baptized you with water, but *he* will baptize you with holy spirit."

And it happened—in those days Jesus came from Nazareth of Galilee and was baptized in the Jordan by John. And coming up from the water, immediately he saw the heavens being ripped open and the spirit like a dove coming down onto him. And there was a voice from the heavens, "You are my beloved son. I delighted choosing you."

And immediately the spirit drove him out into the desert, and he was in the desert forty days tested by Satan. And he was among the wild animals, and the angels were serving him.

Now after John was handed over to prison, Jesus came into Galilee proclaiming the good news about God, and saying, "The right time is fulfilled, and the rule of God has arrived. Turn around and put faith in the good news."

And going along by the Sea of Galilee, he saw Simon and Andrew the brother of Simon casting nets in the sea, for they were fishermen. And Jesus said to them, "Come after me, and I'll make you become fishers for people."

And immediately leaving the nets they followed him. And going ahead a little further, he saw James the son of Zebedee and John his brother in the boat preparing the nets. And immediately he called them. And leaving their father Zebedee in the boat with the hired workers, they went off after him.

And they entered into Capernaum. And immediately on the sabbath he entered into the synagogue and began teaching. And people were astounded by his teaching, for he was teaching them as one having authority and not like the legal experts.

And immediately in their synagogue was a man with an unclean spirit. And it screamed out, saying, "What do you have against us, Jesus Nazarene? Did you come to destroy us? I know who you are—the holy one of God."

And Jesus rebuked it, saying, "Shut up, and get out of him!" And the unclean spirit, convulsing the man and crying in a loud cry, came out of him.

And everyone was so astonished that they were arguing among themselves, saying, "What is this? A new teaching with authority? He gives orders even to the unclean spirits and they obey him." And the report about him immediately went out everywhere, into the whole surrounding countryside of Galilee.

And immediately coming out of the synagogue they went into the house of Simon and Andrew with James and John. Now Simon's mother-in-law was lying down with a fever, and immediately they told him about her. And approaching her, he grasped her hand and raised her up. And the fever left her and she began serving them.

Now when it was evening, after the sun set, people were bringing to him all the sick and the demon-possessed. And the whole city was gathered at the door. And he healed many who were sick with various illnesses and he drove out many demons. And he would not let the demons talk, because they knew him.

And early in the morning, while still quite dark, he arose, came out, and went off to a desert place and was there praying. And Simon and those with him tracked him down and found him and said to him, "Everyone's seeking you."

And he said to them, "Let's go elsewhere, to the next villages, so I might proclaim there too, for that's why I came out." And he went proclaiming in their synagogues, in all Galilee, and driving out the demons.

And a leper came to him, pleading with him, falling on his knees and saying to him, "If you want to, you can make me clean."

And moved by compassion, Jesus stretched out his hand and touched him and said to him, "I want to. Be cleansed!" And immediately the leprosy went from him, and he was made clean.

And becoming harsh with him, immediately Jesus drove him out and said to him, "See that you say nothing to anyone at all, but go show yourself to the priest and make for your cleansing the offering Moses prescribed, as testimony to them."

But going out he began to proclaim freely and to spread the word, so that Jesus was no longer able to enter openly into a city but was outside, in desert places. And people kept coming to him from everywhere.

And entering back into Capernaum after some days, it was reported that he was in a house. And so many people gathered that there was no longer room, not even places at the door. And he was speaking the word to them.

And some came bringing to him a paralytic carried by four of them. And not being able to take him to Jesus because of the crowd, they unroofed the roofing where he was. And digging through, they let down the mat on which the paralytic was lying. And seeing their faith, Jesus said to the paralytic, "Child, your sins are pardoned!"

Now some of the legal experts were sitting there and thinking in their minds, "Why does this man talk like this? He blasphemes! Who can pardon sins except God alone?"

And immediately aware in his spirit that they were thinking like this within themselves, Jesus said to them, "Why are you thinking these things in your minds? Which is easier, to say to the paralytic, 'Your sins are pardoned,' or to say, 'Rise and take up your mat and walk'? But so you may see that the son of humanity has authority to pardon sins on the earth"—he said to the paralytic—"I tell you, rise, take up your mat and go off to your house!"

And he rose and immediately taking up the mat he went out in front of everyone, so that they were all astounded and glorified God, saying, "We never saw anything like this."

And he went out again beside the sea, and the whole crowd came to him and he was teaching them. And passing by, he saw Levi the son of Alphaeus sitting at the toll-tax booth. And he said to him, "Follow me." And rising, he followed him.

And it happened—Jesus was reclining to eat in his house, and many tax collectors and sinners were reclining with Jesus and his disciples, for there were many of them and they were following him.

And the legal experts of the Pharisees, seeing that he was eating with the sinners and tax collectors, said to his disciples, "Why is he eating with the tax collectors and sinners?"

And hearing it, Jesus said to them, "Those who are well have no need for a physician, but those who are sick do. I came not to call righteous people, but sinners."

And John's disciples and the Pharisees were fasting. And people came and said to him, "Why are the disciples of John and the disciples of the Pharisees fasting, but your disciples aren't fasting?"

And Jesus said to them, "Can the attendants of the bridegroom fast while the bridegroom is with them? As long as they have the bridegroom with them, they can't fast. But the days will come when the bridegroom will be taken from them, and then they will fast in that day.

"No one sews a patch of unshrunk cloth onto an old cloak. Otherwise the patch pulls from it, the new from the old, and the rip gets worse. And no one puts fresh wine into old wineskins. Otherwise the wine will burst the wineskins, and the wine is destroyed along with the wineskins. Instead, put fresh wine into new wineskins."

And it happened—Jesus was going through the grain fields on the sabbath, and his disciples began to make a way picking the heads of the grain. And the Pharisees said to him, "Look, why are they doing what is illegal on the sabbath?"

And he said to them, "Haven't you ever read what David did when he had a need, when he and those with him were hungry? How he entered into the house of God when Abiathar was high priest and ate some of the consecrated bread, which it is illegal for anyone to eat except the priests, and he also gave some to those who were with him."

And he said to them, "The sabbath was made for humanity, and not humanity for the sabbath. So, the son of humanity is also lord over the sabbath."

And he entered again into the synagogue, and a man was there who had a withered hand. And they were watching Jesus closely whether he would heal him on the sabbath, so they might bring charges against him. And he said to the man who had the withered hand, "Rise, to the center!"

And Jesus said to them, "Is it legal on the sabbath to do good or to do evil? To restore a life or to put to death?" And they kept quiet.

And looking around at them with anger, grieved at the hardening of their minds, he said to the man, "Stretch out your hand." And he stretched it out, and his hand was made new. And going out, the Pharisees immediately held a council with the Herodians against Jesus, how they might destroy him.

And Jesus withdrew with his disciples to the sea, and a huge number from Galilee followed—also from Judea and from Jerusalem and from Idumea and across the Jordan and around Tyre and Sidon—a huge number, having heard what he was doing, came to him.

And he told his disciples to keep a little boat waiting for him because of the crowd, so they would not press him. For he healed so many people that any who had afflictions would fall on him in order to touch him. And the unclean spirits, when they saw him, would fall down before him and scream, saying, "You are the son of God." And he would rebuke them sharply not to make him known.

And he went up onto the mountain and summoned those whom he wanted, and they went off to him. And he made twelve so they might be with him and he might send them out to proclaim and to have authority to drive out the demons.

And he made the twelve. And Simon he nicknamed "Rock," and James the son of Zebedee and John the brother of James he nicknamed "Boanerges," which means "sons of thunder," also Andrew and Philip and Bartholomew and Matthew and Thomas and James the son of Alphaeus and Thaddeus and Simon the Canana-ean and Judas Iscariot, who also handed him over.

And he went to a house and again such a crowd came together that they were not even able to eat bread. And when his family heard, they came out to seize him, for they were saying, "He's out of his mind."

And the legal experts who came down from Jerusalem were saying, "He's possessed by Beelzebul," and, "He drives out the demons by authority of the ruler of the demons."

And summoning them, he began to talk to them in riddles: "How is Satan able to drive out Satan? If a rule is divided against itself, that rule isn't able to stand. If a house is divided against itself, that house will not be able to stand. And if Satan really did rise up against himself and was divided, he is not able to stand but is at an end. Yet surely no one is able to enter into the house of the strong one and plunder his goods, unless first he bind the strong one, and then he will plunder his house.

"Amen I tell you, everything will be pardoned the children of humanity, their sins and whatever blasphemies they blaspheme, but whoever blasphemes against the holy spirit won't ever obtain a pardon but is guilty of a sin to eternity"—because they had been saying, "He has an unclean spirit."

His mother and his brothers came, and standing outside, they sent someone to him, calling for him. And a crowd was sitting around him, and they said to him, "Look, your mother and your brothers are outside seeking you."

And answering them, he said, "Who are my mother and my brothers?" And looking around at those seated about him in a circle, he said, "Look, here are my mother and my brothers! For those who do the will of God, *they* are my brother and sister and mother."

And again he began to teach by the sea. And such a huge crowd gathered about him that he climbed into a boat and sat out on the sea, and the whole crowd was by the sea on the land. And he was teaching many things in riddles.

And he was saying to them in his teaching, "Hear! Look! The sower came out to sow. And it happened in the sowing that some seed fell beside the way, and the birds came and ate it up. And other seed fell on the rocky ground where there was not much soil, and immediately it sprouted up because the soil had no depth. And when the sun rose, it was scorched, and because it had no root, it withered. And other seed fell among the thorn plants, and the thorns came up and strangled it, and it did not yield fruit. And other seeds fell on the good soil, and they yielded fruit, coming up and growing, and produced thirty and sixty and a hundred per measure!" And he said, "Whoever has ears to hear, let them hear."

And when he was by himself, those around him with the twelve were asking him about the riddles. And he said to them, "To you has been given the mystery about the rule of God, but to those outside everything comes in riddles, so that looking they look and don't see,

and hearing they hear and don't understand.

Otherwise they might turn and be pardoned!"

And he said to them, "You don't understand this riddle? And how will you get the other riddles? The sower sows the word. Now there are those beside the way where the word is sown, and when they hear, immediately Satan comes and takes away the word sown in them. And there are those sown on the rocky places, who upon hearing the word immediately receive it with joy. And they don't have root in themselves but are short-lived. Then when oppression or persecution comes because of the word, immediately they stumble. And others are those sown among the thorns. Those are the ones who have heard the word, and the worries of the age and the lure of wealth and the desires for other things come in and strangle the word, and it is without fruit. And there are these sown on the good soil, who hear the word and receive it and produce fruit—thirty and sixty and a hundred per measure."

And he said to them, "Is the lamp brought to be put under the measuring basket or under the bed? Isn't it to be put on the lampstand? For nothing is hidden except to be made known, and nothing is secret except to come into the open. If any have ears to hear, let them hear."

And he said to them, "Look at what you hear. By what measure you measure out, it will be measured out to you and increased for you. For to those who have, more will be given them. And from those who do not have, even what they have will be taken from them."

And he said, "The rule of God is like this: A man sows the seed on the ground, then sleeps and rises night and day, and the seed sprouts and lengthens, he doesn't know how. On its own, the earth produces fruit—first a stalk, then a head, then a ripe grain in the head. And when the fruit delivers up its yield, immediately he sends out the sickle because the harvest stands ready."

And he said, "To what shall we compare the rule of God? Or into what riddle should we put it? It's like a grain of the mustard weed, which when sown on the ground is smallest of all the seeds on the earth. And when it is sown, it grows up and becomes the largest of all shrubs and makes such large branches that the birds of heaven are able to nest in its shade."

And with many such riddles he was telling the word to them, as they were able to hear it. And he did not talk to them apart from riddles, but privately for his own disciples he would unravel everything.

And on that day, when evening came, he said to them, "Let's go over to the other side." And leaving the crowd, they took him along as he was, in the boat, and other boats were with him.

And a fierce squall of wind came up, and the waves were dashing up into the boat, so that already the boat was filling. And Jesus was in the stern on the cushion sleeping. And they roused him and said to him, "Teacher, don't you care we're about to be destroyed?"

And rising, he rebuked the wind, and he said to the sea, "Silence! Shut up!" And the wind stopped, and there was a great calm.

And he said to them, "Why are you such cowards? Don't you have faith yet?"

And they were frightened with great fear and were saying to each other, "So who is this that even the wind and the sea obey him?"

And they came to the other side of the sea, to the countryside of the Gerasenes. And when Jesus got out of the boat, immediately he was met from the graves by a man with an unclean spirit who had his dwelling among the graves. And no one was able to bind him any longer, not even with a chain, because he had been bound often with fetters and chains, but the chains had been broken by him and the fetters torn apart, and no one was strong enough to subdue him. And throughout every night and day, among the graves and in the mountains, he would scream and slash himself with stones.

And seeing Jesus from a distance, he ran and did obeisance to him, and screaming in a loud voice, he said, "What do you have against me, Jesus son of the most high God? I'm putting you on oath, by God—don't torment me!"

For Jesus was saying to him, "Unclean spirit, come out from the man!"

And Jesus asked him, "What's your name?"

And he said to him, " 'Legion' is my name, because we are many." And he began pleading wildly with Jesus not to send them outside the country.

Now there beside the mountain a large herd of pigs was feeding. And the unclean spirits pleaded with him, saying, "Send us to the pigs so we might enter into them." And he let them.

And coming out, the unclean spirits entered into the pigs, and the herd, about two thousand, charged down the bank into the sea and drowned in the sea.

And those who had been feeding the pigs fled and reported it in the city and in the fields. And people came to see what it was that had happened. And they came to Jesus and saw the demoniac, the one who had been possessed by the "Legion," sitting, clothed, and in his right mind, and they were frightened.

And those who had seen it recounted for them how it had happened to the demoniac and about the pigs. And they began to plead with Jesus to go away from their territory.

And as Jesus was climbing into the boat, the demoniac began pleading with him that he might go with him. And Jesus did not let him, but instead said to him, "Go off to your house, to your family, and report to them what the Lord has done for you and how the Lord showed you mercy." And he went off and began to proclaim in the Ten Cities what things Jesus had done for him, and everyone was amazed.

And when Jesus had crossed in the boat back over to the other side, a huge crowd gathered around him, and he was by the sea. And one of the synagogue leaders came, Jairus by name. And seeing Jesus, he fell at his feet and pleaded urgently with him, saying, "My little daughter is near death. Come, lay hands on her so she might be restored and live." And Jesus went off with him, and a huge crowd was following him and pressing him.

And there was a woman who had had a flow of blood over the course of twelve years, and she had endured many things under the care of many physicians and spent everything she had and not been helped at all but rather was getting worse. And hearing about Jesus, she came from behind in the crowd and touched his cloak, for she had been saying, "If I touch just his clothes I'll be restored." And immediately the source of her bleeding dried up, and she knew in her body that she had been healed of the affliction.

And immediately aware in himself of the power that had gone out from him, Jesus turned around in the crowd and said, "Who touched my clothes?"

And his disciples said to him, "You're looking at the crowd pressing you, and you say, 'Who touched me?'" And Jesus kept looking around to see who had done this.

And the woman, frightened and trembling, having realized what had happened to her, came and fell before him and told him the whole truth. And he said to her, "Daughter, your faith has restored you. Go off in peace and remain free of your affliction."

While he was still speaking, people came from the house of the synagogue leader, saying, "Your daughter died. Why bother the teacher any longer?"

But Jesus, overhearing the word spoken, said to the synagogue leader, "Don't become afraid. Only have faith."

And he did not let anyone follow along with him, except Rock and James and John the brother of James. And they came to the house of the synagogue leader, and Jesus saw a commotion with great sobbing and wailing. And entering he said to them, "Why are you making a commotion and sobbing? The little child did not die, but is sleeping." And they began jeering at him.

And driving everyone out, he took along the father of the little child and the mother and those with him, and he went in where the little child was. And grasping the hand of the little child he said to her, "*Talitha koum,*" which is translated, "Little girl, I tell you, rise."

And immediately the little girl rose and began walking, for she was twelve years old. And they were immediately stunned with great astonishment. And he ordered them strictly to let no one know about this, and he told them to give her something to eat.

And he went out from there and came to his hometown, and his disciples followed him. And when sabbath came, he began to teach in the synagogue.

And many hearing him were stunned, saying, "Where did *he* get all these things? And what is the wisdom given to *him* that such works of power come about through his hands? Isn't this the woodworker, the son of Mary, a brother of James and Joses and Judas and Simon? And aren't his sisters here with us?" And he was a stumbling block to them.

And Jesus said to them, "A prophet doesn't lack honor except in his hometown and among his family and in his house." And he was not able to do there even one work of power, except that he laid his hands on a few ill people and healed them. And he was amazed at their lack of faith.

And he began going around the surrounding villages teaching. And he summoned the twelve and began to send them out two by two, and he was giving them authority over the unclean spirits, and he was ordering them to take nothing on the way except a walking stick only—no bread, no beggar's bag, no coins in the belt, but to strap on sandals and not wear two tunics.

And he was saying to them, "Wherever you enter into a house, stay there until you come out from there, and whatever place doesn't receive you or hear you, go out from there and shake off the dust under your feet as testimony against them." And going out, they proclaimed that people should turn around, and they were driving out many demons and anointing with oil many ill people and healing them.

And King Herod heard about Jesus, for his name was becoming known. And people were saying, "John the baptizer has been raised from the dead, and that's why the works of power are working in him." Others were saying, "He's Elijah." And others were saying, "A prophet like one of the prophets." But when Herod heard, he said, "The one I beheaded, John, he was raised."

For Herod himself had sent out and seized John and bound him in prison on account of Herodias, the wife of Philip his brother, because Herod had married her. For John had been saying to Herod, "It's not legal for you to have the wife of your brother."

Now Herodias was holding a grudge against John and wanted to put him to death, but she was not able to, for Herod was afraid of John, knowing him to be a just and holy man, and was carefully protecting him. And when he heard him, he was greatly puzzled, but he was glad to hear him.

And an opportune day came when Herod on his birthday held a banquet for his greatest leaders and the military officers and the most important people of Galilee. And when Herodias's own daughter entered and danced, she delighted Herod and those reclining to eat with him. The king said to the little girl, "Ask of me whatever you want, and I'll give it to you." And he swore an oath to her, "Whatever you ask of me I'll give you, up to half of my kingdom!"

And she went out and said to her mother, "What should I ask for?"

She said, "The head of John the baptist."

And entering immediately with haste before the king, she asked, saying, "I want you to give me right now on a plate the head of John the baptizer."

And the king became profoundly sad, but because of the oaths and those reclining to eat he did not want to refuse her. And immediately sending for an executioner, the king ordered him to bring John's head. And going off, he beheaded him in the prison and brought his head on a plate and gave it to the little girl, and the little girl gave it to her mother. And when John's disciples heard, they came and took his corpse and placed it in a grave.

And those who had been sent out gathered around Jesus and reported to him all that they had done and taught. And he said to them, "You come privately to a desert place and rest awhile." For so many people were coming and going that the disciples did not even have an opportunity to eat. And they went off in the boat to a desert place privately.

And many people saw them going and recognized them and ran together there on foot from all the cities and arrived ahead of them. And getting out of the boat, Jesus saw a huge crowd, and he had compassion on them, because they were like sheep without a shepherd, and he began to teach them at length. And since it was already a late hour, his disciples approached him and said, "The place is a desert and it's already a late hour. Disband them, so they might go off to the surrounding fields and villages and buy themselves something to eat."

And answering, he said to them, "*You* give them something to eat."

And they said to him, "Are we to go off and buy two hundred denarii worth of bread and give it to them to eat?"

He said to them, "How many loaves have you? Go see."

And finding out, they said, "Five, and two fish."

And he ordered them to have everyone recline group by group on the green grass. And they reclined to eat by companies of a hundred and of fifty.

And taking the five loaves and two fish, looking up to heaven, he blessed and broke the loaves and gave them to his disciples to set before them, and he had them distribute the two fish to everyone, and everyone ate and was filled. And the disciples took up twelve baskets full of scraps and leftover fish, and there were five thousand people who ate the bread.

And immediately he compelled his disciples to climb into the boat and go on ahead to the other side, toward Bethsaida, while he himself disbanded the crowd. And taking leave of the crowd, he went off to the mountain to pray.

And when evening came, the boat was in the middle of the sea, and he was alone on the land. And seeing them straining at the rowing, for the wind was against them, about the fourth watch of the night, he went toward them, walking on the sea. And he wanted to go past them, but when they saw him walking on the sea, they thought, "It's a ghost!" and screamed out, for they all saw him and were terrified.

Immediately he spoke to them and said to them, "Take courage. I am. Don't be afraid." And he went up to them, into the boat, and the wind stopped. And they were completely stunned within themselves, for they had not understood about the loaves. Rather, their minds were hardened.

And crossing over to the land, they came to Gennesareth and docked. And when they got out of the boat, people immediately recognized Jesus and ran around that whole region and began to carry the sick on their mats to wherever they heard he was. And wherever he entered, into villages or into cities or into fields, they would place the sick in the markets and plead with him that they might touch just the fringe of his cloak. And as many as touched it were restored.

And the Pharisees and some of the legal experts came from Jerusalem and gathered around him. And seeing that some of his disciples were eating bread with defiled, that is, unwashed, hands—for the Pharisees and all the Judeans do not eat unless they wash their hands up to the elbows, thus observing the tradition of the elders, and they do not eat anything from the market unless they purify it, and there are many other traditions that they have received to adhere to, such as cleansings for cups and pitchers and kettles—the Pharisees and the legal experts asked him, "Why don't your disciples walk according to the tradition of the elders, but instead eat bread with defiled hands?"

He said to them, "How well Isaiah prophesied about you hypocrites, as it is written,

> 'This people honors me with the lips,
>   but their minds are far away from me.
> In vain they worship me,
>   teaching teachings that are human teachings.'

Having abandoned the ordinance of God, you adhere to the tradition of humans."

And he said to them, "How well you nullify the ordinance of God in order to establish your tradition! For Moses said, 'Honor your father and your mother,' and 'Whoever pronounces misfortune on father or mother must surely die. But *you* say, 'If a man says to his father or mother, "Whatever might have been a benefit to you from me is *corban*" ' "—that is, devoted to God—"you no longer allow him to do anything at all for his father or mother, thus annulling the word of God by your tradition that you handed on. And you do many other things like this."

And summoning the crowd again he said to them, "Hear me everyone and understand. There is nothing from outside people that by going into them is able to defile them. Instead the things that come out from people are the things that defile people."

And when he entered into a house away from the crowd, his disciples were asking him about the riddle. And he said to them, "Don't *you* understand this either? Don't you see that nothing entering into people from the outside is able to defile them, because it doesn't enter into their minds but into their stomachs and goes on out into the latrine?"—thereby pronouncing all foods clean.

He said, "What comes out from people, *that* is what defiles people. For from inside, from the minds of people, come the evil designs—sexual immoralities, thefts, murders, adulteries, expressions of greed, malicious acts, deceit, amorality, envious eye, blasphemy, arrogance, reckless folly. All these evils come out from inside and defile people."

Now from there he arose and went off to the territory of Tyre. And entering into a house, he wanted no one to know about him, but he was unable to escape notice. Rather, a woman whose little daughter had an unclean spirit immediately heard about him, came, and fell at his feet. Now the woman was Greek, a Syrophoenician by birth, and she asked Jesus to drive the demon from her daughter.

And he said to her, "Let the children be satisfied first, for it isn't good to take the bread for the children and throw it to the little dogs."

But she answered and said to him, "Yes, lord, and the little dogs down under the table eat some of the little children's crumbs."

And he said to her, "Because of this word, go on off—the demon has gone out of your daughter!" And going off to her house, she found the little girl thrown on the bed and the demon gone out.

And coming back out of the territory of Tyre, he went through Sidon to the Sea of Galilee, up the middle of the territory of the Ten Cities. And people brought to him a deaf and tongue-tied man and pleaded with Jesus to lay his hand on him.

And taking him off from the crowd privately, Jesus thrust his fingers into his ears and with spittle touched the man's tongue. And looking up to heaven, he groaned and said to him, "*Ephphatha*," which means, "Be opened!" And immediately his ears were opened and the binding of his tongue was loosed, and he was talking clearly.

And Jesus was ordering them to tell no one, but the more he was ordering them, the more they insisted on proclaiming it. And people were utterly astounded, saying, "He's done everything well. He even makes the deaf hear and the mutes speak."

In those days when again there was a huge crowd and they did not have anything to eat, Jesus summoned the disciples and said to them, "I have compassion for the crowd because already for three days they've stayed with me, and they don't have anything to eat. And if I disband them hungry to their houses, they'll become faint on the way, and some of them have come from a distance."

And his disciples answered him, "How will anyone be able to satisfy these people with bread here in a desert?"

And he asked them, "How many loaves have you?"

They said, "Seven."

And he ordered the crowd to recline on the ground. And taking the seven loaves, giving thanks, he broke them and gave them to his disciples to distribute, and they distributed them to the crowd. And they had a few little fish. And blessing them, he told the disciples to distribute these also. And people ate and were satisfied, and the disciples took up seven baskets full of scraps. Now there were about four thousand people, and Jesus disbanded them.

And immediately climbing into the boat with his disciples, he went to the district of Dalmanoutha. And the Pharisees came out and began to argue with him, seeking from him a sign from heaven, testing him. And groaning deeply in his spirit, he said, "Why does this generation seek a sign? Amen I tell you, surely a sign won't be given to this generation." And leaving them, he embarked again and went off to the other side.

And the disciples forgot to take bread, and except for one loaf they did not have any with them in the boat. And he was giving them orders, saying, "Beware! Look out for the leaven of the Pharisees and the leaven of Herod."

And they began discussing among themselves, "We don't have bread."

And becoming aware of this, he said to them, "Why are you discussing that you don't have bread? Don't you understand or comprehend yet? Are your minds hardened? Having eyes don't you see, and having ears don't you hear? And don't you remember, when I broke the five loaves for the five thousand people, how many baskets full of scraps did you take up?"

And they said to him, "Twelve."

"When I broke the seven loaves for the four thousand, how many handbaskets full of scraps did you take up?"

And they said, "Seven."

And he said to them, "Don't you understand yet?"

And they came to Bethsaida, and people brought to Jesus a blind man and pleaded with him to touch him. And taking hold of the hand of the blind man, he led him outside the village. And spitting onto his eyes, laying his hands on, he asked him, "Do you see anything?"

And looking up, he said, "I see people, but they look like trees walking."

Then Jesus again laid hands on his eyes, and the man looked intently and was made new and saw everything clearly. And Jesus sent him to his house, saying, "Don't enter into the village."

And Jesus and his disciples went out to the villages around Caesarea Philippi. And on the way he asked his disciples, saying to them, "Who do people say I am?"

They told him, saying, " 'John the baptist,' and others say, 'Elijah,' but others, 'One of the prophets.'"

And he answered them, "But who do *you* say I am?"

Rock answered and said to him, "*You* are the anointed one."

And he rebuked them to tell no one about him, and he began to teach them, "It's necessary for the son of humanity to endure many things and be rejected by the elders and the high priests and the legal experts and be put to death and after three days rise." And he was speaking the word plainly. And taking him aside, Rock began to rebuke him.

But Jesus, turning and seeing his disciples, rebuked Rock, and said, "Get behind me, Satan, because you're not thinking in God's terms but in human terms."

And summoning the crowd along with his disciples, he said to them, "If any want to follow after me, let them renounce themselves and take up their cross and follow me. For all who want to save their lives will lose them, but all who will lose their lives for me and the good news will save them. For what does it profit people to acquire the whole world and forfeit their lives? For what would people give in exchange for their lives? For all who are ashamed of me and my words in this adulterous and sinful generation, also the son of humanity will be ashamed of them when he comes in the glory of his Father with the holy angels."

And he said to them, "Amen I tell you, there are some of those standing here who will definitely not taste death before they have seen the rule of God come in power."

And after six days, Jesus took along Rock and James and John and brought them up to a high mountain privately by themselves. And he was transformed before them, and his clothes became dazzling, intensely white, like no launderer on earth is able to whiten. And Elijah appeared to them with Moses, and they were talking with Jesus.

And Rock responded and said to Jesus, "Rabbi, it's good *we* are here. We should set up three shelters—one for you and one for Moses and one for Elijah." For he did not know how to respond, for they were so frightened.

And a cloud came overshadowing them, and there was a voice from the cloud, "*This one* is my beloved son. Listen to him!" And suddenly, looking around, they no longer saw anyone except Jesus alone with them.

And while they were coming down from the mountain, Jesus ordered them to recount to no one what they had seen until after the son of humanity had risen from the dead. And they seized on this word, arguing among themselves what "risen from the dead" meant. And they asked him, saying, "Why do the legal experts say that it's necessary for Elijah to come first?"

And he said to them, "If Elijah comes first to put everything right, then how is it written about the son of humanity that he is to endure many things and be scorned? On the contrary, I tell you that Elijah has already come, and they did to him whatever they wanted to, just as it's written about him."

And coming to the disciples, they saw a huge crowd around them and legal experts arguing with them. And immediately on seeing him, the whole crowd was astonished and began running up and greeting him.

And he asked them, "What are you arguing about with them?"

And someone from the crowd answered him, "Teacher, I brought my son to you because he has a mute spirit. And wherever it takes hold of him, it hurls him down, and he foams at the mouth and grinds his teeth and stiffens up. And I told your disciples to drive it out, and they weren't strong enough."

He answered them and said, "O faithless generation, how long am I to be with you? How long am I to put up with you? Bring him to me." And they brought the boy to him. And upon seeing Jesus, the spirit immediately convulsed the child, and he fell to the ground and was writhing about, foaming at the mouth.

And Jesus asked his father, "How long has it been happening like this to him?"

He said, "From childhood, and often it has thrown him even into fire and into water in order to destroy him. But if you're able to do anything, have compassion on us and help us."

Jesus said to him, "'If you're able?' Everything is possible to one who has faith."

Immediately the father of the boy screamed, and said, "I have faith. Help my lack of faith."

Seeing that a crowd was running together, Jesus rebuked the unclean spirit, saying to it, "Mute and deaf spirit, *I* order you: Get out of him and don't ever enter into him again." And screaming and convulsing him repeatedly, it came out.

And the boy became so like a corpse that most were saying, "He died." But Jesus grasped his hand and raised him up, and he rose.

And when Jesus entered into the house, his disciples asked him privately, "Why weren't *we* able to drive it out?"

And he said to them, "It isn't possible for anyone to drive out this kind except by prayer."

And going out from there, they were passing through Galilee, and Jesus did not want anyone to know it, for he was teaching his disciples, and he was telling them, "The son of humanity is to be handed over to human hands, and they will put him to death, and three days after being put to death he will rise." But they did not understand what he said, and they were afraid to ask him.

And they came to Capernaum, and when he was in the house, he asked them, "What were you discussing on the way?" But they kept quiet, for on the way they had been discussing with each other who was greatest.

And sitting down, he summoned the twelve and said to them, "If anyone wants to be most important, that person will be least of all and servant of all."

And taking a little child, he stood her in their midst, and putting his arms around her, he said to them, "All who receive one such little child in my name receive me, and all who receive me receive not me but the One who sent me."

John said to him, "Teacher, we saw someone driving out demons in your name, and we tried stopping him because he wasn't following us."

And Jesus said, "Don't stop him, for there is no one who will do a work of power by my name and very soon after be able to pronounce misfortune on me. For all who are not against us are for us. For all who offer you a cup of water based on a name, because you are under the anointed one, amen I tell you, they will definitely not lose their reward. And all who cause one of these little ones who have faith to stumble, it would be better for them if instead a large millstone had been hung around their neck and they'd been thrown into the sea.

"And if your hand causes you to sin, cut it off! It's better for you to enter into life maimed than with two hands to go off into Gehenna, to the unquenchable fire. And if your foot causes you to sin, cut it off! It's better for you to enter into life lame than with two feet to be thrown into Gehenna. And if your eye causes you to sin, tear it out! It's better for you to enter into the rule of God with one eye than with two eyes to be thrown into Gehenna, where their maggot doesn't die and the fire isn't quenched.

"For everyone will be salted with fire. Salt is good, but if salt becomes no longer able to preserve, how will you restore it? Have salt among yourselves, and be at peace with each other."

And arising from there, he went into the region of Judea, beyond the Jordan. And again crowds gathered around him, and as was his custom, again he was teaching them. And Pharisees approached and asked him if it were legal for a husband to dismiss his wife, testing him.

He answered and said to them, "What did Moses order you?"

They said, "Moses allowed him to write up a notice of divorce and to dismiss her."

Jesus said to them, "Because of your calloused minds he wrote this ordinance for you, but from the beginning of creation, God made them male and female. For this reason a man will leave his father and mother, and the two will be as one flesh, so that they are no longer two but one flesh. So, what God has yoked together, no human is to separate."

And in the house again, his disciples were asking him about this. And he said to them, "Whoever dismisses his wife and marries another commits adultery against her. And if that woman having dismissed her husband marries another, she commits adultery."

And people were bringing little children to him so he might touch them, but the disciples rebuked them. Now when Jesus saw it, he got angry and said to them, "Let the little children come to me. Don't stop them, for the rule of God belongs to such as these. Amen I tell you, whoever does not receive the rule of God like a little child will definitely not enter into it." And putting his arms around them, laying his hands on them, he was blessing them all.

And as he was setting out on the way, a man ran up and knelt before him and asked him, "Good teacher, what should I do to inherit life eternal?"

Jesus said to him, "Why do you call me good? No one is good except God alone. You know the ordinances: Don't murder, don't commit adultery, don't steal, don't testify falsely, don't defraud, honor your father and mother."

He said to Jesus, "Teacher, all these I have kept from my youth."

And Jesus, looking at him intently, loved him and said to him, "*You* lack only one thing. Go sell whatever you have and give to the poor, and you'll have a fortune in heaven, and come follow me." But becoming dejected at this word he went away sad, for he had a lot of property.

And looking around, Jesus said to his disciples, "How hard it will be for those who have possessions to enter into the rule of God." And the disciples were amazed at his words.

Jesus again answered and said to them, "Children, how hard it is to enter into the rule of God. It's easier for a camel to go through the eye of a needle than for a wealthy person to enter into the rule of God."

But they were completely stunned, saying among themselves, "Then who can be saved?"

Looking at them intently, Jesus said, "For humans it's impossible, but not for God, for everything is possible for God."

Rock began saying to him, "Look, *we* left everything and have followed you!"

Jesus said, "Amen I tell you, there is no one who has left a house or brothers or sisters or a mother or a father or children or fields for me and for the good news who does not receive a hundred times as many now, in this time, houses and brothers and sisters and mothers and children and fields—with persecutions—and in the coming age life eternal. But many who are most important will be least and the least most important."

Now they were on the way going up to Jerusalem, and Jesus was going ahead of them, and they were dazed, and those who were following were afraid. And again taking aside the twelve, he began to tell them the things that were about to happen to him: "Look, we're going up to Jerusalem, and the son of humanity will be handed over to the high priests and the legal experts, and they will condemn him to death and hand him over to the Gentiles, and they will mock him and spit on him and flog him and put him to death, and after three days he will rise."

And James and John, the sons of Zebedee, approached him, saying to him, "Teacher, we want you to do for us whatever we ask of you."

He said to them, "What do you want me to do for you?"

They said to him, "Give us a place to sit, one at your right and one at your left in your glory."

Jesus said to them, "You don't know what you're asking for. Are you able to drink the cup that I am about to drink or to be baptized with the baptism by which I am about to be baptized?"

They said to him, "We're able."

Jesus said to them, "The cup I am about to drink you will drink, and with the baptism by which I am about to be baptized you will be baptized, but to sit on my right or left is not mine to give; rather, it is for those for whom it has been prepared."

And when the other ten heard, they began to get angry at James and John.

And summoning them, Jesus said to them, "You know that those considered to be rulers over the Gentile nations lord over them and their great ones exert authority over them, but it's not to be like this among you. Instead, whoever wants to be great among you will be your servant, and whoever wants to be most important among you will be a slave of all. For even the son of humanity came not to be served, but to serve and to give his life as ransom for many."

And they came to Jericho. And as he was coming out from Jericho with his disciples and a large crowd, the son of Timaeus—Bartimaeus, a blind beggar— was sitting beside the way. And hearing that it was Jesus the Nazarene, he began to scream, and say, "Son of David! Jesus! Show me mercy!"

And many were rebuking him to be quiet, but he was screaming all the louder, "Son of David! Show me mercy!"

And stopping, Jesus said, "Summon him."

And they summoned the blind man, saying to him, "Take courage, rise, he's summoning you." And throwing off his cloak, he jumped up and came to Jesus.

And answering him, Jesus said, "What do you want me to do for you?"

The blind man said to him, "*Rabboni*—for me to see again."

And Jesus said to him, "Go off, your faith has restored you." And immediately he saw again, and he began following Jesus on the way.

And when they came near to Jerusalem, to Bethphage and Bethania at the Mountain of the Olives, he sent two of his disciples and said to them, "Go into the village opposite you and immediately as you're entering into it you'll find a donkey colt tied up on which no one has ever sat. Untie it and bring it. And if anyone says to you 'Why are you doing this?' you say, 'The lord has need of it and will send it back here immediately.'"

And they went off and found a colt tied up at a door outside on the street, and they untied it. And some of those standing there said to them, "What are you doing untying the colt?"And the disciples told them just as Jesus had said, and they let them take it.

And they brought the colt to Jesus, and they threw their cloaks on it, and he sat on it. And many people spread their cloaks onto the way, and others spread leafy branches cut from the fields. And those going ahead and those following were screaming,

"Hosanna!
     Blessed is the one coming in the name of the Lord!
     Blessed is the coming rule of our father David!
Hosanna in the highest places!"

And he entered into Jerusalem, into the temple, and after looking around at everything, the hour being already late, he went out to Bethania with the twelve.

And on the following day, after coming out from Bethania, he was hungry. And seeing from a distance a fig tree in leaf, he went to see if, perhaps, he might find figs on it. And coming to it, he found nothing except leaves, for it was not the right time for figs. And responding, he said to it, "May no one any longer ever eat fruit from you again."And his disciples heard him.

And they came into Jerusalem. And entering into the temple, Jesus began to drive out those selling and those buying in the temple, and he upended the tables of those changing money and the chairs of those selling doves, and he would not let anyone carry anything across the temple. And he began teaching and saying to them, "Isn't it written, 'My house shall be called a house of prayer for all the Gentile nations'? But *you* have made it a lair for bandits."

And the high priests and the legal experts heard, and they began seeking how they might destroy him. For they were afraid of him. For the whole crowd was astonished at his teaching. And when evening came, they went outside the city.

And passing by early in the morning, they saw the fig tree withered from its roots up. And remembering, Rock said to Jesus, "Rabbi, Look! The fig tree you cursed has withered!"

And answering, Jesus said to them, "Have faith in God. Amen I tell you, all who say to this mountain, 'Be taken up and thrown into the sea' and do not doubt in their mind but have faith that what they say will happen, it will be so for them. Therefore, I tell you, regarding everything you pray for and ask for, have faith that you have gotten it, and it will be so for you. And whenever you stand praying, pardon whatever you have against anyone, so that your Father in the heavens might also pardon you your offenses."

And they came back into Jerusalem, and while Jesus was walking in the temple, the high priests and the legal experts and the elders came to him and said to him, "By what authority are you doing these things? Or who gave you this authority to do these things?"

Jesus said to them, "I'll ask you one question. Answer me, and I'll tell you by what authority I do these things. Was the baptism of John from heaven or from humans? Answer me."

And they began discussing among themselves, saying "If we say, 'From heaven,' he'll say, 'Then why didn't you put faith in him?' But if we say, 'From humans'"—they were afraid of the crowd, for everyone held that John really had been a prophet.

And answering Jesus, they said, "We don't know."

And Jesus said to them, "Neither am *I* telling you by what authority I do these things."

And he began to tell them in riddles. "A man planted a vineyard and put a hedge around it and dug out a pit for the wine vat and built a watchtower and leased it out to farmers and went away. And he sent a slave to the farmers at the right time to get from the farmers some fruits of the vineyard. And taking him, they beat him and sent him away empty-handed. And again he sent to them another slave, and that one they struck on the head and dishonored. And he sent another, and that one they put to death. And many others, some they flogged and some they put to death. Still he had one more, a beloved son. He sent him to them last, saying, 'They will have respect for my son.' But those farmers said to each other, 'This one is the heir. Come on, let's put him to death and the inheritance will be ours.' And they took him and put him to death and threw him outside the vineyard.

"So what will the lord of the vineyard do? He'll come and destroy the farmers and give the vineyard to others. Haven't you ever read this writing?

'That stone which the builders rejected
　　has become the cornerstone.
This came from the Lord
　　and it is astonishing in our eyes.'"

And they began seeking how to seize him, but they were afraid of the crowd, for they knew that he had told the riddle against them. And leaving him, they went off.

And they sent to him some of the Pharisees and the Herodians to catch him in his words. And coming they said to him, "Teacher, we know that you are truthful and do not defer to anyone, for you don't look to human reactions but truthfully teach the way of God. Is it legal to give a tribute payment to the emperor or not? Should we give or not give?"

And seeing their hypocrisy, he said to them, "Why are you testing me? Bring me a denarius so I might see it." They brought one.

And he said to them, "Whose image is this, and whose inscription?"

They said to him, "The emperor's."

Jesus said to them, "What belongs to the emperor give back to the emperor, and what belongs to God give back to God." And they were utterly amazed by him.

And Sadducees, who say there is no resurrection, came to him and asked him, saying, "Teacher, Moses wrote for us, 'If someone's brother dies and leaves behind a wife but doesn't leave a child, then his brother is to take the wife and raise up a descendant for his brother.' There were seven brothers, and the first took a wife and when he died he did not leave behind a descendant. And the second took her, and he died without leaving behind a descendant. And the third did likewise. None of the seven left behind a descendant. Last of all, the wife died too. In the resurrection, when people rise, whose wife will she be, for the seven had her as a wife?"

Jesus said to them, "Aren't you misled because of this—you don't know either the writings or the power of God? For when people rise from the dead, they neither marry nor are given in marriage, but are like angels in heaven. And as for the dead, that they rise, haven't you read in the scroll from Moses, in the passage about the bush, how God spoke to him, saying, 'I am the God of Abraham and the God of Isaac and the God of Jacob'? God is not a God of dead people but of living people. You are greatly misled."

And one of the legal experts approached, heard them arguing, saw how well Jesus answered them, and asked him, "Which is the most important ordinance of all?"

Jesus answered, "The most important is: 'Hear, Israel, the Lord our God is the only Lord, and you shall love the Lord your God with your whole mind and with your whole life and with your whole intelligence and with your whole strength.' The second is this: 'You shall love your neighbor as yourself.' There is no other ordinance greater than these."

And the legal expert said to him, "How well you say truthfully, teacher, that he is the only one and there is no other beside him, and to love him with the whole mind and with the whole understanding and with the whole strength and to love the neighbor as oneself is much more than all the whole burnt offerings and sacrifices."

And seeing that he had answered wisely, Jesus said to him, "You are not far from the rule of God." And no one dared to question him further.

And speaking up while teaching in the temple, Jesus said, "How do the legal experts say that the anointed one is a son of David? David himself said by the holy spirit,

'The Lord said to my lord,
"Sit on my right,
   while I put your enemies
   down under your feet."'

David himself calls him 'lord,' so how is he his son?" And the huge crowd heard him gladly.

And in his teaching, he said, "Look out for the legal experts who want to walk about in flowing robes and who want formal greetings in the markets and the most important seats in the synagogues and the most important places at the banquets, the ones who eat up the houses of the widows and for appearance offer long prayers—*they* will get the most severe judgment."

And sitting down opposite the treasury box, he was observing how the crowd was putting coins into the treasury. And many wealthy people were putting in large amounts. And one poor widow came and put in two lepta, which make a quadrans.

And summoning his disciples, Jesus said to them, "Amen I tell you, this poor widow put in more than all those who put into the treasury box, for everyone else put in out of their surplus, but this woman out of her need put in everything she had, her whole living."

And as he was coming out from the temple, one of his disciples said to him, "Teacher, look! What stones! And what buildings!"

And Jesus said to him, "You see these great buildings? Definitely not a stone will be left upon a stone here that will not be pulled down."

And while he was sitting on the Mountain of the Olives, opposite the temple, Rock and James and John and Andrew were asking him privately, "Tell us, when will these things be? And what will the sign be when all these things are about to be brought to an end?"

And Jesus began to tell them, "Look out that no one mislead you. Many will come in my name saying, 'I am,' and mislead many. Now when you hear battles and reports of battles, don't be alarmed. It's necessary for these things to happen, but it's not yet the end. For nation will rise against nation and realm against realm. There will be earthquakes in various places. There will be famines. These are the beginning of birth pains.

"And you look out for yourselves. They will hand you over to sanhedrins, and you will be beaten in synagogues, and you will stand before governors and kings on account of me, as testimony to them. And it's necessary first for the good news to be proclaimed to all the Gentile nations. And when they lead you away, handing you over, don't be anxious ahead what you should say. Rather, say what is given to you in that hour, for *you* won't be the ones speaking, but the holy spirit. And brother will hand over brother to death, and a father his child, and children will rise up against parents and put them to death. And you will be hated by everyone because of my name. But those who endure to the end will be saved.

"Now when you see the 'desolating horror' standing where it's necessary that it not stand"—let the public reader understand—"then those in Judea are to flee to the mountains. Whoever is on the rooftop is to come down without entering to get something from the house. And whoever is in the field is not to turn back to get a cloak. How awful it will be for those who are pregnant and those nursing a child in those days. Pray that it not happen in winter. For those days will be an oppression the like of which has not happened from the beginning of creation that God created until now and definitely will not happen again. And if the Lord had not cut short the number of days, no flesh would be saved. But because of the chosen ones whom God chose, God cut short the days.

"And then if anyone says to you, 'Look, here is the anointed one! Look, there!' don't put faith in it. For false anointed ones and false prophets will rise up and give signs and portents to lead astray if possible the chosen ones. But you look out. I've told you everything ahead.

"However, in those days after that oppression,
'the sun will be darkened,
        and the moon won't give its light,
    and the stars will be falling from the heavens,
        and the powers in the heavens will be shaken.'
And then people will behold the son of humanity coming on clouds with great power and glory. And then he will send out the angels and gather the chosen ones from the four winds, from the ends of earth to the ends of heaven.

"Now from the fig tree learn the riddle. When its shoots have already become tender and it is sprouting leaves, you know that summer is near. So also you, when you see these things happening, you know that he is near, at the doors. Amen I tell you, this generation will definitely not pass away before all these things happen. Heaven and earth will pass away, but my words will definitely not pass away.

"But about that day or the hour, no one knows it, neither the angels in heaven nor the son, except the Father. Look out! Stay awake! For you do not know when the right time will be. It's like a man off on a trip, on leaving his house and giving authority to his slaves, to each their work, he also ordered the doorkeeper to keep watch. So, keep watch, for you do not know when the lord of the house is coming, whether in the evening or at midnight or at the rooster crow or early in the morning. Otherwise, he might come unexpectedly and find you sleeping. And what I say to you, I say to everyone. Keep watch!"

Now the Passover and the festival of Unleavened Bread were two days away. And the high priests and the legal experts were seeking how to seize Jesus by deceit and put him to death, for they were saying, "Not during the festival or there will be a riot of the populace."

And Jesus was reclining to eat in Bethania at the house of Simon the leper, and a woman came with an alabaster flask of very expensive pure nard ointment. Breaking open the alabaster flask, she began pouring ointment on his head.

But some were angry among themselves, "Why has this ointment been wasted? For this ointment could have been sold for more than three hundred denarii and the money given to the poor." And they were harsh with her. But Jesus said, "Let her be. Why are you giving her trouble? It's a good work she has worked for me. For the poor you always have among you and whenever you want you're able to do good for them, but you won't always have me. What she was able to do, she did. She anointed my body ahead for the burial. Amen I tell you, wherever the good news is proclaimed in the whole world, what this woman did will also be told, as a remembrance of her."

And Judas Iscariot, the one of the twelve, went off to the high priests to hand Jesus over to them. When they heard, they rejoiced and promised to give him silver. And he began seeking how at some opportunity he might hand him over.

And on the first day of the festival of Unleavened Bread, when it was customary to slaughter the Passover lamb, his disciples said to him, "Where do you want us to go off and prepare for you to eat the Passover meal?"

And he sent two of his disciples and said to them, "Go off to the city, and a man bearing a jar of water will meet you. Follow him, and where he enters, you tell the master of the house, 'The teacher says, "Where is my guest room where I am to eat the Passover meal with my disciples?"' And he'll show you a large upstairs room furnished and ready, and you prepare for us there."

And the disciples went out and came into the city and found things just as he told them, and they prepared the Passover meal.

And when it was evening, he came with the twelve. And while they were reclining and eating, Jesus said, "Amen I tell you, one of you will hand me over, one eating with me."

And they began to be sad and to say to him one by one, "Surely not I?"

He said to them, "One of the twelve, the one dipping bread with me in the same bowl. The son of humanity goes just as it is written about him, but how awful for that human by whom the son of humanity is handed over. Better for *him* if he had not been born."

And while they were eating, he took bread, blessed it, broke it, and gave it to them, and said, "Take it. This is my body."

And taking a cup, offering thanks, he gave it to them, and they all drank from it. And he said to them, "This is my blood of the covenant that is about to be poured out for many. Amen I tell you, I will not drink any longer from the produce of the vine until that day when I drink it new in the rule of God."

And after singing a psalm, they went out to the Mountain of the Olives. And Jesus said to them, "You will all stumble, because it is written,

'I will strike the shepherd,

and the sheep will be scattered.'

But, after I'm raised, I'll go ahead of you to Galilee."

Rock said to him, "Even if everyone else stumbles, at least *I* won't."

And Jesus said to him, "Amen I tell you, today, this night, before the rooster crows twice, *you* will renounce me three times."

But he kept saying wildly, "Even if it's necessary for me to die with you, I'll definitely not renounce you." And they were all saying the same thing.

And they came to a place with the name Gethsemane, and he said to his disciples, "Sit here while I pray."

And he took along with him Rock and James and John, and he began to be alarmed and anguished, and he said to them, "My life is profoundly sad to death. Stay here and keep watch."

And going ahead a little, he fell to the ground and began praying that if it were possible the hour might pass away from him, and he said, "*Abba,* Father, everything is possible for you. Take this cup away from me, yet not what *I* want but what *you* want."

And he came and found them sleeping, and he said to Rock, "Simon, are you sleeping? Weren't you strong enough to watch a single hour? Keep watch, all of you, and pray that you don't come to a testing. The spirit is eager, but the flesh is weak."

And again going off, he prayed saying the same word. And again coming back, he found them sleeping, for their eyes were very heavy and they did not know what to answer him.

And he came a third time and said to them, "Are you going to sleep through and keep resting? It's over! The hour has come! Look, the son of humanity is about to be handed over to the hands of sinners. Rise! Let's go! Look, the one handing me over has arrived."

And immediately, while he was still talking, Judas, one of the twelve, approached and with him a crowd with swords and clubs from the high priests and the legal experts and the elders.

Now the one handing him over had given them a signal, saying, "The one I kiss, that's him. Seize him and lead him away under security."

And coming, immediately he went up to him and said, "Rabbi!" and kissed him. And they put hands on him and seized him. But one of those standing by drew his sword, struck the slave of the high priest, and cut off a little piece of his ear.

And responding, Jesus said to them, "Did you come out with swords and clubs as against a bandit to capture me? Day after day I was among you in the temple teaching and you didn't seize me—but so the writings might be fulfilled."

And leaving him, the disciples all fled.

And a certain young man was following him wearing only a linen cloth around his naked body, and they tried to seize him. But leaving the linen cloth behind, he fled naked.

And they led Jesus off to the headquarters of the high priest, and all the high priests and the elders and the legal experts assembled. And Rock followed him from a distance, on inside into the courtyard of the high priest. And he was sitting together with the guards and warming himself in the firelight.

Now the high priests and the whole Sanhedrin were seeking testimony against Jesus in order to put him to death, but they were not finding any. For many were testifying falsely against him, and their testimony did not agree.

And some rose and testified falsely against him, saying, "We ourselves heard him say, '*I* will pull down this sanctuary made with hands and in three days build another not made with hands.'" But even on this point their testimony did not agree.

And rising to the center, the high priest asked Jesus, saying, "Aren't you answering anything at all? What are these people testifying against you?" But he kept quiet and did not answer anything at all.

Again the high priest asked him and said to him, "Are *you* the anointed one, the son of the Blessed One?"

Jesus said, "I am,
> and you will all behold the son of humanity
>> sitting on the right hand of Power
> and coming with the clouds of heaven."

The high priest, tearing his vestments, said, "What further need have we for witnesses? You heard the blasphemy! How does it appear to you?" And they all condemned him to be deserving of death. And some began to spit on him and to cover his face and hit him and say to him, "Prophesy!" And the guards began beating him.

And Rock was down in the courtyard when one of the servant girls of the high priest came by and, seeing Rock warming himself, looked closely at him and said, "*You* were with the Nazarene Jesus, too."

But he renounced him, saying, "I don't know or understand what you're talking about." And he went outside to the courtyard entryway, and a rooster crowed.

And the servant girl saw him and again began to say to those standing nearby, "This man is one of them." But again he renounced him.

And after a little while, those standing by said again to Rock, "You really are one of them, for you're a Galilean too."

But he began to put himself under a curse and to swear an oath, "I don't know this man you're talking about!"

And immediately for the second time a rooster crowed, and Rock remembered the saying, how Jesus had said to him, "Before the rooster crows twice, you will renounce me three times." And lurching off, he began sobbing.

And immediately, early in the morning, the high priests held a council with the elders and legal experts and the whole Sanhedrin, bound Jesus, took him away, and handed him over to Pilate. And Pilate asked him, "Are *you* the king of the Judeans?"

Answering him, he said, "*You* say so."

And the high priests were bringing many charges against him. And Pilate again asked him, saying, "Aren't you answering anything at all? Look how many charges they're bringing against you!" But Jesus no longer answered anything at all, with the result that Pilate was amazed.

Now at festivals it was his custom to release for them one prisoner whom they requested. Now the one called Barabbas was bound in prison with the insurrectionists who had committed murder in the insurrection. And coming up, the crowd began to ask Pilate to do as he customarily did for them.

Pilate answered them, saying, "Do you want me to release for you the king of the Judeans?" For he knew that the high priests had handed him over out of envy. But the high priests had stirred up the crowd to ask him instead to release Barabbas for them.

Pilate again responded and said to them, "Then what should I do with the one you call 'king of the Judeans'?"

They screamed back, "Crucify him!"

Pilate said to them, "Why, what evil did he do?"

But they screamed even louder, "Crucify him!"

Pilate, wishing to do the satisfactory thing for the crowd, released Barabbas to them. And after flogging Jesus, he handed him over to be crucified.

The soldiers led him away inside the courtyard, which is a praetorium, and they called together the entire cohort. And they put a purple cloak on him, and weaving thorn branches into a crown, they set it on him.

And they began to greet him, "Hail! King of the Judeans!" And they were beating him over the head with a reed staff and spitting on him, and getting on their knees, they were doing obeisance to him. And when they had mocked him, they took the purple cloak off him and put his own clothes back on him and led him out to crucify him.

And they drafted someone passing by, coming in from a field, Simon the Cyrenian, the father of Alexander and Rufus, to take up his cross. And they brought Jesus to the place Golgotha, which means "Place of a Skull." And they tried giving him wine drugged with myrrh, but he did not take it.

And they crucified him,

> and they divided up his clothes,
>
> casting lots for them, who might get what.

Now it was nine in the morning when they crucified him. And the inscription of the charge against him was inscribed: The King of the Judeans. And with him they crucified two bandits, one on his right and one on his left.

And those passing by were blaspheming him, wagging their heads and saying, "Ha! The one who is about to pull down the sanctuary and build one in three days! Get down off the cross and save yourself!"

In the same way also the high priests with the legal experts were mocking him to each other and saying, "He restored others, but he can't save himself. Let the anointed one, the king of Israel, get down now off the cross, so we might see and have faith!" And those being crucified along with him were ridiculing him.

And when it was noon, darkness came over the whole land until three. And at three Jesus cried out in a loud cry, *"Eloi! Eloi! Lema sabachthani?"* which means,

> "My God! My God!
>
> Why did you abandon me?"

And some of those standing by heard it and said, "Look, he's calling Elijah!" And someone ran, filled a sponge with cheap wine, put it on a reed staff, and offered him a drink, saying, "Let him be! Let's see if Elijah comes to take him down."

And Jesus let out a loud cry and died.

And the curtain of the sanctuary was ripped in two from top to bottom.

Now when the centurion who was standing in front of him saw how he died, he said, "Truthfully, this man was son of God."

Now there were also women watching from a distance, among them Mary the Magdalene, and Mary the mother of James the younger and of Joses, and Salome, who had been following him and serving him when he was in Galilee, and many other women who had come up with him to Jerusalem.

And because evening had already come and it was a preparation day, which is the day before the sabbath, Joseph from Arimathea, a respected member of the council who was himself also expecting the rule of God, coming and taking courage, went in to Pilate and asked for the body of Jesus.

Now Pilate was amazed that he had died already, and summoning the centurion, he asked him if he had been dead long. And finding out from the centurion, he granted the corpse to Joseph.

And buying linen cloth, taking him down, Joseph wrapped him in the cloth and placed him in a grave that was hewn out of the rock, and he rolled a stone up against the door of the grave. Mary the Magdalene and Mary the mother of Joses were observing where he was placed.

And when the sabbath passed, Mary the Magdalene and Mary the mother of James and Salome bought aromatic oils so they might go and anoint him.

And very early in the morning, on the first day after the sabbath, they were going toward the grave, just as the sun came up.

And they were saying to each other, "Who will roll the stone away from the door of the grave for us?" And looking up, they saw that the stone had been rolled away, for it was very large.

And entering into the grave, they saw a young man sitting on the right, wearing a white robe, and they were completely alarmed.

He said to them, "Don't be alarmed. You're seeking Jesus the Nazarene who was crucified. He was raised! He's not here! Look, the place where they put him! But go tell his disciples, even Rock, 'He's going ahead of you to Galilee. There you will behold him just as he told you.'"

And coming out, they fled from the grave, for they were trembling and stunned, and they said nothing to anyone at all, for they were afraid.

CHAPTER 2

The Narrator

S tories that share the same basic content can be told in many ways. Each author or composer will have a different style of narrating, a different point of view, and different objectives in telling a story. One way, therefore, to get at the distinctiveness of a story is to explore the dynamics of storytelling. Because the narrator of a story represents the sum total of the author's choices in getting a story told, we will deal with the key categories of storytelling under the rubric of the narrator: the role of the narrator (or storyteller), point of view, style and tempo, patterns of storytelling, and other narrative features.

The Role of the Narrator

Narrator is a literary term for the storyteller of a narrative.[1] In a literary work, the narrator is not the author but the teller that is embedded in the narrative itself. It is a rhetorical device the author uses to get the story told and to get it told so as to have a certain effect on the audience. In texts that are read silently, the narrator is actually more like a function than a character, and yet it is helpful to think of the narrator as a figure with strategies and beliefs who addresses an audience.

Stories have different kinds of narrators. The narrator may be a character in the story, either a protagonist or a minor character. Such first-person or "I" narrators are common. Mark Twain, for example, has Huck narrate *Huckleberry Finn*. Such narrators are limited. Huck, for example, can tell only what he himself has seen or heard, what he—but no other character—is thinking, and what his own limited values and experiences enable him to understand.

Other kinds of narrators are "third-person" narrators, unidentified voices who are in the narrative but external to the story, that is, a voice telling the story but not one of the characters in the story being told. A reader is not usually aware of such a third-person narrator any more than one is aware of a movie camera while watching a film, because the focus is not on the narrator but on the story. Third-person narrators can vary. A narrator with "objective omniscience" tells only what can be seen and heard. A narrator with "limited omniscience" also tells thoughts and feelings, but only those in the mind of the protagonist. A narrator with "unlimited omniscience" is able to tell anything about the story world, including what is in the mind of any character at any time and place. Most ancient stories, including Homer's *Odyssey* and *The Gospel of Mark*, are told by a narrator with unlimited omniscience.

The narrator of Mark's Gospel as a literary composition is a third-person narrator who does not figure as a character in the events of the story world. Such a narrator is not bound by time or space and is therefore able to be a presence in every scene, invisible to the characters and capable of being anywhere to "recount" the action. Mark's narrator is also omniscient, showing inside views of the thoughts, feelings, and perceptions of the characters. Sometimes the narrator turns from the telling of the story itself to give "asides" to the readers and is thereby also able to guide them by giving them privileged information. Exploring these characteristics will reveal how the omniscient narrator of Mark's story shapes and affects the reader in the experience of the story.[2]

When we consider the Gospel of Mark as a performance, some of the dynamics of the role of narrator change. Now the role of the narrator is played by a real person who brings the story to life before an actual audience. Here the role of the narrator embedded in the text is acted out by a performer with inflection, volume, emphasis, and pace, along with gestures, movement, and facial expressions. An ideal performer would perform so as to reflect faithfully the narrator's strategies and beliefs as implied by the narrative.

Assuming that the real-life performer is faithful to the role of narrator as embedded within the text, the same basic literary traits of the narrator of Mark we discuss below will also be applicable to a performance. Nevertheless, there will be differences: The performer/narrator will perform the narrator's role and also act out all the characters. In contrast to a silent reading of the narrative, in which the narrator is virtually invisible to the reader, in oral telling, the narrator is always visible, omnipresent to the audience. Indeed, part of an audience's response to a story such as Mark's that makes a claim on the audience will depend on the audience's evaluation of the real-life performer—is he or she credible or not? A performer will indeed have a social location, and his or her promotion of the standards of judgment in the story may be more or less prominent. The style and tempo evident in the story will be played out in various ways by a performer. Further, the performer will make use of performance techniques to bring out the oral strategies in the text—so as to generate certain effects on the audience.

We now turn to the traits of the narrator as implied by the story and to the oral patterns of storytelling, all of which will help to clarify for modern readers the role of the narrator.

The narrator speaks from outside the story world

Because Mark's narrator is not a character in the story, there is no identity, social location, or place in time specified for the narrator. The narrator simply begins the story in the past tense and proceeds to tell it without drawing attention to the act of narration itself. In a literary work, this effacing of the narrator's identity and presence enables the narrator to assume a position of authority in relation to the story being recounted. Because a reader is generally unaware of the narrator, the reader tends to accept the narrator's authority as a reliable guide through the story.[3] This obscuring of the narrator's presence also enables the narrator to place the focus on the events being narrated, thus enabling the reader to feel immersed in the story while actually being outside it. In a performance, however, in which the role of the narrator is assumed by a performer, the narrator is not effaced and the audience will likely be more immersed in the story.

The narrator is not bound by time or space

Unlike a character-narrator, Mark's omniscient narrator is not limited by time. The narrator knows the whole story being told, including the imaginative past and the imaginative future of the story world. The narrator can at any point relate something that happened earlier in the story (such as John's death) or tell what will happen later in the story (such as Judas handing Jesus over).

Nor is Mark's narrator limited by space. This narrator knows what happens everywhere. As such, the omniscient narrator can depict not only public events but also what happens privately in a house or on a boat, not only when Jesus is with someone but also when he is alone. The narrator can tell what happened at the grave, even though the women flee and tell no one. For the most part, the narrator depicts scenes in which Jesus is present, but the narrator can shift to other settings, for example, to the high priests' plotting against Jesus or to Rock's renouncing Jesus.

The narrator narrates the story with a temporal and spatial immediacy as one present to recount what is occurring in each successive episode of the story, with a sense of "here and now."[4] Because the audience experiences the story as the narrator tells it, the audience too has the sense of being present to witness these events of the story world.

Mark's narrator is omniscient

The omniscient narrator of Mark's story can narrate the words, actions, thoughts, or states of mind of the characters. A way to contrast the role of an omniscient narrator with a first-person narrator is to retell any episode in Mark from the point of view of a character in the episode, using "I" or "we" as appropriate. This will reveal the unlimited knowledge of an external, third-person narrator, because no character knows enough about the other characters or the events to be able to tell the whole story as the omniscient narrator has told it.

Mark's omniscient narrator can describe the inner feelings of the characters—their compassion, anger, fear, sadness, amazement, and love. The narrator tells when characters are dazed, stunned, puzzled, pleased, terrified, or dejected. The narrator also tells the audience what the characters are thinking, for example, that the opponents think Jesus is a blasphemer or that Pilate knows the high priests are envious. The narrator explains why characters do things and when characters do not understand and when they do not know what to say. The narrator even reveals that the disciples' minds are hardened when neither the disciples nor Jesus are aware of it. Mark's inside views are brief and undeveloped, yet they clearly show the unlimited omniscience of the narrator.

This knowledge of the omniscient narrator leads the audience to trust the narrator as a reliable guide in the world of the story. Reading or hearing the story from the narrator's point of view gives the audience an advantage over the characters in the story, because the audience knows what other characters are thinking and what other characters are doing.

The narrator guides by means of "asides"

At points throughout the story, the narrator seems to pause and—ever so briefly—address the audience more directly by providing commentary on the story, commentary that is not part of the events themselves and that often includes information not available to some or all of the characters in the story.

Sometimes the aside is an abrupt break in the syntax of the sentence. For example, after Jesus explains the riddle about what defiles, the narrator gives an aside, commenting that Jesus was "thereby pronouncing all foods clean." When Jesus prophesies to his disciples about the "desolating horror," the narrator abruptly comments, "let the public reader understand" (thus alerting the one performing Mark publicly before an audience to understand the significance of this phrase as a reference to the desecration of the holy temple). In performance, these asides draw attention to the narrator, if only in very brief and limited ways.

Other asides that provide explanations about the story world fit smoothly into the flow of narration. For example, the narrator explains that "defiled hands" are unwashed hands and that Sadducees do not believe in resurrection. Often the narrator translates the meaning of Aramaic words. Also, the narrator comments on actions or statements, often with an explanation introduced by the conjunction "for." The narrator explains that a little girl raised from the dead was able to walk, "for she was twelve years old," and that the fig tree had no fruit on it, "for it was not the right time for figs."

These explanations, along with the inclusion of details such as foreign words and customs, make the story seem more realistic and authentic. Also, when the narrator turns aside from recounting the story to comment directly, the narrator establishes a rapport by taking hearers into confidence and by assuring them in subtle ways that they are not forgotten. The audience comes to depend on the narrator to provide reliable commentary on the story. In this way, the narrator's increasing influence over the hearers' responses encourages them not only to receive the story but also, more importantly, to embrace the demands presented by the story and to accept the difficult meanings that the story is showing.

The narrator gives the audience privileged knowledge

Another way the narrator creates a close relationship with the audience from the very first words is by letting them know the secret of Jesus' identity, that he is "the anointed one, the son of God." Furthermore, the narrator lets the hearer see the private vision of the spirit that Jesus has at his baptism, hear the voice of God naming him "son," and accompany Jesus to the desert, where he endures testing by Satan. The hearers are on the inside, "in the know," about Jesus, in contrast to the characters in the story, who do not know Jesus' identity. The hearers are placed in a position of privilege, and they know from the start the authority that Jesus' words will bear throughout the story.

Such a situation creates tension and suspense, leading the audience to wonder: How will the authorities respond when they find out that Jesus acts as God's choice for the anointed one? Will the disciples ever figure out who Jesus is? And what will happen when they do? Hearing Mark's story for the first time is like watching a Hitchcock film in which the viewer is aware of a threatening situation at the opening of the film, then nervously watches the unsuspecting characters in the story become aware of the situation for themselves.

As the story develops, hearers are led to be close to or distant from various characters.[5] For example, hearers are led to side with Jesus (knowing who he is) and to distance themselves from the authorities (who do not know who he is and who oppose him). The narrator leads them to be both close to and distant from the disciples at different times and in different ways throughout the story. In the first half of the story, the audience watches the disciples struggle to figure out who Jesus is. Then, halfway into the story, when Rock realizes that Jesus is the anointed one, the disciples finally grasp what the audience has known from the start. The experience of being in the narrator's confidence for the first half of the story has given the audience assurance in dealing with Jesus' new and disturbing teachings, presented in the second half of the story—teachings about Jesus' commitment to service, his impending rejection and death, as well as the potential consequences for following Jesus. In relation to these new teachings, the audience is not at an advantage over the disciples, because they learn about them at the same time the disciples do.

The divulging and withholding of knowledge enable the Markan narrator to guide what the audience knows and when they learn it. By so doing, the narrator shapes their openness to embrace this story.

The Narrator's Point of View

Point of view refers to the perspectives present in a narrative. The narrator controls the overarching point of view of the story. At the same time, the narrator presents the differing points of view of the characters in the course of telling the story.[6]

The narrator is not neutral

When a narrator is omniscient, audiences tend to be unaware of the narrator's biases, values, and conception of the world and therefore tend to trust the narrator as a neutral, "objective" teller of the events. But the narrator is not neutral. Rather, the narrator functions like the director of a film, who is responsible for the presentation of the whole story. Viewers observe the scenes and characters from the director's arrangement and perspective, although they never see the director. Similarly, the narrator in literature presents the story with certain words that betray a particular perspective, in a certain order, and with various rhetorical techniques. The omniscient narrator is always there at the reader's elbow, shaping responses to the story—even, and perhaps especially, when the reader is least aware of it. In performance, the narrator's point of view expressed in the person of a performer will be more apparent.

To become aware of the point of view of the narrator when reading Mark's story, imagine this story about Jesus being retold by a narrator whose sympathies lie with the Pharisees and the high priests. It would be a very different story. Although the same basic content of the story would remain, the words chosen to describe the events would change and foster a very different perspective with an audience. The authorities would likely be the heroic figures, and Jesus would be a false messiah, an upstart rabble-rouser. When we return to Mark as composed, we can see how much the narrator leads the audience to approve of Jesus and to reject those who oppose him.

The narrator guides the hearers' evaluation of a character by the way the character is introduced and portrayed. For example, the narrator introduces Jesus in the first line as "the anointed one, the son of God," then repeatedly confirms it by means of John's prophecy, the spirit's descent, and the voice from heaven. By the time Jesus first speaks, the hearer accepts him as a reliable character and is ready to hear and trust what he says. As the story progresses, this portrayal of Jesus as a reliable character is reinforced by the narrator's inside views of Jesus, which show Jesus to be perceptive, compassionate, loving, angry at oppression, and anguished over his death.

By contrast, the narrator leads audiences to an unfavorable view of the authorities. The narrator introduces the legal experts as people who teach without authority and then portrays them in opposition to the reliable protagonist Jesus. Subsequent inside views into the minds of the authorities show them intending to trap Jesus by questions, being afraid of the crowds, and seeking to destroy Jesus out of envy. Similarly, the narrator portrays the disciples and other characters in such a way as to control the hearers' judgments of them. The narrator's depictions show how the hearers are led to trust what Jesus says and does, why they distrust the opponents, and why they are ambivalent toward the disciples.

The narrator's standards of judgment

There is a system of beliefs and values implicit in the point of view from which the narrator judges and evaluates the characters in the story.[7] These beliefs and values are the narrator's ideological point of view or standards of judgment.

We can construct the beliefs and values of the narrator from many clues in the story: asides, manner of describing characters and events, choice of words, order of episodes, storytelling techniques, quotations from "the writings," the narrator's asides, as well as from the words and actions of those characters that the narrator has established as reliable or unreliable. We can sort out the points of view of the different characters as the narrator presents them by attending to the dialogue and actions of the characters, their distinctive manner of speaking, their internal thoughts and feelings, as well as their place in the society depicted in the story. The ideological points of view of the various characters are encompassed within the consistent overall point of view of the narrator, who, as the storyteller, relates and assesses the point of view of each of the characters.

Based on such an analysis, we can see that the narrator of Mark has one ideological point of view, that God's terms (as the narrator understands them) are good and that human terms are bad; that is, "thinking in God's terms" is the reliable view, and "thinking in human terms" is the incorrect view. These two points of view mirror each other by contrast. A good grasp of the narrator's point of view about these matters will bear much fruit for interpreting Mark's story.

God's Terms	Human Terms
faith	lack of faith
courage	fear
losing one's life for the good news	saving one's life
being least among humans	being great among humans
serving people	lording over people
saving (restoring) others	harming others
loyalty to God for the world	loyalty to self or group
love neighbor	secure self or group
giving up possessions	acquiring the world
life of relinquishment for others	life of acquisition for self or group

These standards represent the moral and conceptual skeleton of Mark's narrative.[8] The consistency of the Markan narrative in this regard is impressive, for the narrator and each of the characters in Mark exemplify one point of view or the other. The narrator embraces the viewpoint of God and tells a story in which the protagonist Jesus and most minor characters exemplify thinking in "God's terms," while the opponents of Jesus exemplify thinking in "human terms," and the disciples vacillate between the two points of view. The narrator guides the audience to embrace the things of God and to reject the things of humans. If the story is successful, the hearers will adopt the point of view of the narrator and evaluate the characters as the narrator does.

The Narrator's Style and Tempo

The style of the Markan narrator is simple and direct, using ordinary language to tell this amazing story. The characters, too, speak in everyday language. This plain style keeps the focus on the story itself without drawing attention to the storytelling.

The narrator's style is also terse, using few words to suggest images and evoke pictures.[9] Words are concrete and literal rather than abstract and symbolic. Descriptions such as "wearing camel's hair" or "like a dove" or "among the wild animals" are pictorial and suggestive rather than detailed and exhaustive. Connections between events are usually not spelled out. A careful examination of almost any episode will reveal to us how few words are employed to depict so much. As such, the spare style is full of gaps in description and meaning, which the hearers are invited to fill through imagination.

The style keeps the narration moving along, with occasional overviews, like long-distance shots in a film. Instead of "telling about" the story in generalities and abstractions, the narrator "shows" the events by a straightforward recounting of actions and dialogue. Episodes are usually brief, scenes change often, and minor characters appear and quickly disappear. The style is characterized by the frequent repetition of the word "immediately," the recurrence of "and" as an introduction to almost every sentence, and an abundance of participles. These stylistic features, along with the vivid use of the present tense for past action, keep the narrative flowing at a fast pace, which draws the audience quickly into the story and maintains their attention.

The brevity of style and rapidity of motion give the narrative a tone of urgency, which reinforces the urgency of Jesus' central message: "The right time is fulfilled, and the rule of God has arrived." The rapid movement of action and dialogue is broken only twice, with two monologues of Jesus: first when he tells a series of riddles from a boat and later when he prophesies to four disciples on the Mountain of the Olives. Otherwise, there is little extended teaching. Mark is clearly a story of action and conflict.

Also the tempo or pace of narration varies.[10] "Tempo" here refers to the relation between the theoretical time it would take for an event to occur in the story world (event-time) and the time it takes to tell about it (narrating-time). On the one hand, sometimes the tempo is very fast, such as, "He went out everywhere, into the whole surrounding countryside of Galilee" or "As many as touched it [the fringe of his garment] were restored." On the other hand, tempo may be suspended for a brief descriptive pause, as when the narrator explains to the audience the traditions of the elders related to purifications.

The tempo also slows down. The narrator conveys scenes in which the narrating-time begins quickly as the characters are brought together, but then slows down in the middle of the episode so that the time it takes to tell this part of the episode is roughly the same as the time it would take for such an event to occur, and then speeds up again as the episode is brought to a conclusion. The narrator puts emphasis on these places where narrating-time corresponds to event-time.

There is a pattern to the tempo in the story as a whole. Early in the narrative, the action shifts rapidly from one location to another, while the end of the journey slows to a day-by-day description of what happens in the single location of Jerusalem and then to a sustained, almost hour-by-hour depiction of the crucifixion. Because the whole narrative moves toward Jerusalem and toward death and resurrection, the slowing of the tempo intensifies the events of the crucifixion for the audience. A performer of Mark would have reflected the textual dynamics of tempo in the telling.

The Narrator's Patterns of Repetition in Storytelling

While the style is simple and direct, the Markan narrative turns out to have complex patterns of storytelling. At first glance, Mark may appear to be a series of disparate episodes strung together that seem unconnected to each other. On closer look, however, these episodes are integrally related to each other by a variety of stylistic patterns and narrative connections. Stories that were meant to be heard, like the Gospel of Mark, were typically episodic and made connections not so much by linear progression as by various forms of repetition.[11] The Markan episodes are intertwined with each other by the repetition of words and phrases, the occurrence of foreshadowings and retrospections, similarities of scenes and situations, and the clustering of episodes in concentric or parallel patterns.

By design, these repetitions are not simple or exact. Rather, they reflect repetition with variation.[12] The repetitions are like motifs in a musical composition. The different patterns of repetition overlap and interweave in so many complex ways that it is really not possible to make a linear outline of Mark's story.[13] Awareness of these narrative patterns sensitizes the reader to the interconnections of various episodes that on the surface are only loosely related. The rich variety in repetition serves also to develop character, advance the plot, and amplify themes in Mark's narrative design.[14]

Verbal threads

The simplest form of repetition is that of certain key words and phrases.[15] These verbal threads may occur within episodes. For example, the narrator repeats "tax collectors and sinners" three times in one episode. Similar repetition occurs within virtually every episode: words in a question are repeated in the answer; words in commands and requests are repeated in their fulfillment; or the description of a situation is echoed in the reaction to it. Repetition of words alerts readers to key themes within an episode.

The repetition of words and phrases may also connect adjacent episodes. For example, Jesus' attack on the legal experts for devouring *widows'* houses is followed immediately by Jesus' praise for the poor *widow* who contributes her whole living. Key words may also be repeated in significant episodes throughout the story. For example, in the first lines of Mark's Gospel, "good news," "anointed one," "son of God," "desert," "proclaiming," "pardon," "ripped open," "tested," "handed over," "the right time," "the rule of God," "faith," and "follow," are all introduced. All these words and phrases are then repeated in new contexts throughout the story, where they echo for the hearers their earlier occurrences and at the same time accumulate meaning and associations that fill out the hearer's understanding. As the story progresses, the narrator introduces new motifs with the first occurrence of a new word, which also may signal a new development in the plot.

Verbal threads also invite readers and hearers to make connections between one part of the narrative and another. For example, the "ripping" of the temple curtain just before the centurion recognizes Jesus as "son of God" recalls by verbal association the "ripping" of the heavens just before God pronounces Jesus to be "my son." As verbal threads recur, they give the fabric of the story an intricate design and unity it would not otherwise have.

Foreshadowing and retrospection

Foreshadowing (which anticipates later events) and retrospection (which recalls earlier events) are major forms of repetition in Mark.[16]

Foreshadowing occurs in several ways. The narrator may make explicit references to events that are yet to occur in the story world—for example, that Judas will hand Jesus over. Or Jesus will say something that foreshadows later developments—for example, that the disciples will become fishers for people and that what is now hidden will be revealed. Or the narrator will narrate an event that anticipates a later similar event—for example, the death of John the baptizer at the hands of Herod foreshadows the death of Jesus at the hands of Pilate. The most obvious technique of foreshadowing in Mark may be that of prophecy—for example, Jesus three times prophesies his coming death and resurrection. Foreshadowings create suspense by leading the reader to experience in a partial and enigmatic way what will be fully understood only when what was foreshadowed happens.

Retrospection works in reverse. The narrator will recount an event that had occurred previously in the story world, will refer in the dialogue of the characters to events told earlier, or will allude to a prophecy in the description of its fulfillment. By means of retrospection, the narrator will often lead the audience to clarify and amplify their understanding of earlier events. For example, Jesus' riddle about the house of the strong one suggests that Jesus has already bound Satan. Hearers, therefore, recall Jesus' earlier confrontation with Satan in the desert and understand that event in a new way—as the binding of the strong one. There are other retrospections: Jesus' teaching to the disciples that John was Elijah leads hearers to see John in a new way; the disciples' frightened response to Jesus' walking on the sea in the second boat scene recalls the earlier failure of the disciples to understand his calming of the storm in the first boat scene; and so on.

Thus foreshadowing and retrospection are two ends of a thread or an earlier and later occurrence of a motif. They connect the narrative forward and backward: The foreshadowing anticipates an event that is coming; and when the event occurs, it recalls the earlier anticipation. This effect works for the audience just as it did for Rock in the story: By predicting his betrayal, Jesus anticipates for Rock that Rock will renounce him; and when Rock subsequently does renounce Jesus, Rock recalls in retrospect the earlier prophecy. For the audience, the eventual narrating of events that have been anticipated resolves the suspense created by the earlier foreshadowing.

Two-step progressions

The two-step progression is one of the most pervasive patterns of repetition in Mark's Gospel.[17] It occurs in phrases, clauses, pairs of sentences, and the structure of episodes. It is a key to understanding many lines and episodes. The examples given here can be multiplied from Mark's narrative many times over.

A simple example of a two-step progression is: "When it was evening, after the sun set. . . ." The time reference, "When it was evening," is repeated in "after the sun set." However, the second part adds precision to the first part. Together they constitute a two-step progressive description, in which the emphasis usually lies on the second part. In this example, the second step refers to the setting sun, which denoted precisely the end of the sabbath, when people were again permitted to travel and could therefore seek out Jesus for healing. Another example is "outside, in desert places." Again, this place description is repetitious, but the second part is more precise and identifies a setting important to the story. Other examples, referring to people, include the woman who was "Greek, a Syrophoenician by birth" and the widow who gave "everything she had, her whole living."

Two-step progressive repetition also occurs in the sequences of sentences and phrases. For example, these appear in questions, such as "What is this? A new teaching with authority?" and "Why are you such cowards? Don't you have faith yet?" or in commands, such as "Don't be afraid. Only have faith," and "Keep watch, and pray that you don't come to a testing." Two-step progressions appear in parallel statements, such as "The right time is fulfilled, and the rule of God has arrived," as well as in contrasting clauses, such as "The son of humanity came not to be served, but to serve and to give his life."

Two-step progressions also structure some episodes. The disciples ask Jesus two progressive questions: "Tell us, when will these things be? And what will the sign be when all these things are about to be brought to an end?" Jesus responds with a lengthy two-step answer addressing each question in turn. The authorities ask a two-step question: "Why don't your disciples walk according to the tradition of the elders, but instead eat bread with defiled hands?" Jesus answers the first part in direct response to the authorities and the second part in addressing the crowd.[18] Other episodes have a two-step progressive structure that moves from a general to a specific setting: Jesus goes to Capernaum, then to the synagogue; he goes into Jerusalem, then into the temple. In other episodes, the movement from a public to a private setting corresponds to a progression from Jesus' public teaching or action to his private explanation and clarification to the disciples.

The story of the blind man who is touched twice to be healed is a good analogy of how the two-step progressions affect hearers. Jesus touches him once and the blind man sees, but not clearly. Then Jesus touches him a second time, and he sees "everything clearly." Similarly, the two-step progressions guide hearers to take a second look, which clarifies and emphasizes.

The two-step repetitions create suspense by maintaining the audience's desire to see what is yet to come, because the recurrence of this pattern conditions them to wait for the second step, for further clarifications.

The overall Gospel may be viewed as a two-step progression. The first line of the Gospel refers to Jesus as "the anointed one, the son of God." At the end of the first half of the story, Rock acknowledges Jesus as "the anointed one." At the end of the second half of the story, the centurion identifies Jesus as "son of God." Although the characterization of Jesus is consistent in both parts, there appears, nevertheless, a progressive unveiling in the portrayal of Jesus from one half of the Gospel to the next. In the first step, he serves with power; in the second, his service results in persecution and death. The first half of the Gospel emphasizes the coming of God's rule in acts of power and mercy, and the second half emphasizes the persecution that results from living out God's rule in this age. The many smaller two-step progressions prepare hearers to be drawn more readily into seeing this larger second step of the overall narrative and accepting this clearer and more comprehensive view of Jesus.

Type-scenes

Similar episodes repeated with variation may be called "type-scenes." For example, Mark narrates similar episodes about people who come to Jesus for healing. These episodes have a common form: coming to Jesus, making a request, overcoming an obstacle to demonstrate faith, the touching or speaking Jesus does, the healing, and the reaction of the crowd. Audiences become familiar with this pattern and are better able to absorb any new variations introduced with each repetition of a healing story. Each additional repetition reinforces the basic pattern. There are also type-scenes of exorcisms, nature miracles, conflicts with the authorities, and misunderstandings by the disciples.

Markan type-scenes can be quite complex. For example, the scene with Jesus before Pilate repeats with variation the same complex dynamics as the scene with John before Herod: A person of authority has a choice to make about someone's fate at a public event and is viewed as being sympathetic toward the person; nevertheless, someone manipulates someone else to request the death of that person; and the authority figure executes the person against his own judgment out of deference to those present.

As expressions of repetition so crucial to effective oral storytelling, the type-scenes contribute to characterization, plot development, and thematic amplification.

Sandwich episodes

In this pattern of repetition, two similar episodes are placed in juxtaposition with each other. One episode is "sandwiched" (as an interruption) between the beginning and ending of another episode. For example, in film, a scene will change in the middle of the action, leaving the viewer in suspense, while the camera cuts to another scene. The camera will return to resolve the action begun in the initial scene, thus creating a frame around the middle story.

Such sandwiching of episodes occurs frequently in Mark's story.[19] For example, after Jairus asks Jesus to heal his dying daughter, audiences must wait, while the woman with the flow of blood touches Jesus to be healed, before finding out what happens to the daughter. When the family of Jesus comes out to seize him, hearers are in suspense about the result until after Jesus argues with the authorities. When Rock sits down "in the firelight" with soldiers in the courtyard of the high priest, hearers will experience Jesus' trial before learning what happened to Rock. Such suspense maintains audience interest, enticing hearers to stay alert through the second episode to find out how the first episode will end.

More important, the two paired episodes often repeat a common theme, one episode illuminating the theme by comparison or contrast with the other episode. Some paired episodes illuminate by comparison: Jesus' family saying he is out of his mind compares with the legal experts saying he is possessed; the faith of Jairus compares with the faith of the woman with the flow of blood; and Jesus' cursing of the fruitless fig tree parallels his attack on the temple authorities for failing to bear fruit for Israel. Other paired episodes comment on each other by contrast: Jesus sending disciples to heal (with no food) contrasts with Herod sending someone to execute John the baptizer (at a banquet); Judas betraying Jesus for money contrasts with the woman anointing Jesus with expensive ointment; and Rock's denial of Jesus contrasts with Jesus' courageous confession at his trial.

Framing episodes

In Mark, two similar episodes may frame a large section of the Gospel. In addition to delimiting what they frame, the two episodes can be experienced in relation to each other and in comparison or contrast with the material they frame.

For example, Jesus' journey to Jerusalem with his disciples begins with the story of the healing of the blind man at Bethsaida and concludes with the healing of the blind man at Jericho. The first healing of sight is difficult, done in two stages, indicating the difficult teaching to follow; the second healing of sight is instantaneous, indicating that the intervening episodes have clarified the teaching. Also, the prophecies and admonitions about the future that Jesus gives to four disciples on the Mountain of the Olives are framed, on the one side, by the episode of the poor widow who puts into the temple treasury out of her need and, on the other side, by the episode of the woman who anoints Jesus with costly ointment. In this example, the two framing episodes, connected by several verbal threads, depict acts of self-giving, and they also parallel the commitments that all the followers of Jesus will have to make if they are to remain faithful in the future.

Episodes in a concentric pattern

Mark occasionally arranges episodes in a concentric pattern, a common technique of ancient oral narration in which related episodes form rings around a central episode.

The five conflicts between Jesus and the authorities in Galilee show a concentric relationship of A, B, C, B', and A'. Paired episodes A and A' along with B and B' form an outer and an inner ring around the central episode, C.[20]

> A The healing of the paralytic
>> B Eating with toll collectors and sinners
>>> C Fasting
>> B' Eating by picking grain on the sabbath
> A' The healing of the man with the withered hand

Episode A (the healing of the paralytic) and episode A' (the healing of the man with the withered hand) reflect each other in structure, content, and theme: Both occur indoors, involve a healing, and include the same characters (Jesus, the authorities, and the person healed); both healings are delayed while the narrator reveals unspoken accusations against Jesus; and both accusations involve serious legal penalties. Furthermore, in both episodes Jesus responds to the unspoken accusations with rhetorical questions.

Episodes B (eating with the tax collectors and sinners) and B' (picking grain on the sabbath) are also related: both are concerned with eating, and both have to do with uncleanness (from tax collectors in B and from violation of the sabbath in B'). The form of both episodes includes an action, the authorities' objection, and Jesus' explanation of the action. Both involve the same characters (Jesus, the disciples, and the authorities). In both cases, Jesus answers with a proverb followed by a statement of his purpose and authority.

These four episodes (A, B, B', A') form an inner and an outer ring around episode C, in which Jesus teaches about fasting (in contrast to the eating theme of B and B'). By contrast with other episodes, the setting in episode C is indefinite and the questioners are not identified. Nor are the questioners hostile. As a result, this central episode focuses on Jesus' response rather than on conflicts or actions. Jesus' response in this central episode illuminates all five episodes of the concentric pattern. His reference to the bridegroom being "taken away" points to the possible consequences of opposition by the authorities in A and A'—the death penalty for blasphemy or for flagrant violation of the sabbath. His warning against putting new wine in old wineskins shows how the authorities use old categories of law and tradition (in all five episodes) to judge the newness that Jesus represents. And the result will be the destruction of both the wine and the wineskins.

Thematically, the whole series contrasts Jesus' authority with that of the Judean leaders. Jesus has authority to pardon sins (A), and he eats with sinners (B). He is special like a bridegroom (C). He has authority over the sabbath (B'), and he heals on the sabbath (A'). By contrast, the Judean leaders, as depicted in Mark, use their authority to accuse, and they fail to get an indictment.

These five conflict episodes create a circular progression as they are heard. One clash is followed by a second, then a third that clarifies the first two. With this clarification in mind, hearers experience another conflict that recalls the second episode and then a final clash that comes back around to recall the first episode. The five episodes also contain a linear progression. From the first to the fifth episodes, Jesus' anger with the authorities grows as he futilely tries to explain his actions, while the opposition of the authorities gradually escalates. For the hearers, this linear progression combines with the circular progression to form a climax in the final episode. At the end of the series, the entire conflict is propelled forward when the Pharisees go out to plot with the Herodians "how they might destroy him."

This is an elaborate example of concentric patterns that were common story-telling strategies in antiquity. We may discern other examples in Mark, such as the concentric relationships among the series of conflicts between Jesus and the authorities in Jerusalem. Such patterns help both the performer and the audience to remember the story.

Progressive episodes in series of three

Perhaps the most recognizable pattern of repetition in Mark is the progressive series of three episodes, identified by the similarity in narrative structure, the presence of verbal threads, common themes, the continuation of a conflict, the involvement of the same characters, and the repetition of a similar setting.[21]

In some cases, the three episodes occur in direct sequence: Jesus prays three times and each time returns to find the disciples sleeping; Rock renounces Jesus three times; Pilate asks the crowd three leading questions about releasing Jesus, each of which is rejected; the narrator recounts events of the crucifixion in three-hour intervals (nine o'clock, noon, and three o'clock); and the women at the grave appear in three successive scenes.

In other cases, the three episodes occur at intervals in the narrative. In a series of three episodes spread through the first third of the gospel, Jesus makes the disciples fishers of people: First, he calls four fishermen to follow him; second, he appoints the twelve on a mountain; and third, he sends out the twelve to proclaim and to heal. There are three separate scenes of growing conflict between Jesus and his disciples in a boat and three progressive episodes of conflict between Jesus and his disciples in which bread is the center of action and discussion. These two series are especially dramatic, because the third bread scene is also the third boat scene. During the journey to Jerusalem, Jesus prophesies his death three times. Each time, the response of the disciples shows that they do not understand, and each time Jesus then teaches them the values of the rule of God implicit in his predictions.

By conditioning hearers to expect series of three episodes, the narrative holds them in suspense as the series builds to a climax. When the series unfolds fully, hearers look back from the perspective of the third scene and understand more clearly the issues involved in the first and second scenes.

Other Literary Features

Other stylistic features of Mark's narrative also knit the narrative together and are significant for interpretation: questions, riddles, quotations from the writings, prophetic oracles, and irony.

Questions

Within this brief story, the characters pose an extraordinary number of questions. The questions occur in patterns and multiples, and often they distinguish the speech patterns of one character from another. Many of them are rhetorical—questions for which no answer is expected or only one answer is really possible. In Mark's story, questions heighten the drama by creating suspense and tension, intensify the conflicts, and reveal character. The few examples of each type given here should alert today's readers to their use throughout the story.

In dialogue with the disciples, Jesus often hurls double rhetorical questions, revealing his surprise and frustration at the disciples' failures: "Why are you such cowards? Don't you have faith yet?" "How long am I to be with you? How long am I to put up with you?" "Simon, are you sleeping? Weren't you strong enough to watch a single hour?" Because the questions are left unanswered, they emphasize the matter at issue and leave it temporarily unresolved.

In dialogue with the authorities, Jesus most commonly poses a single rhetorical question followed by an assertion in which he himself gives the obvious answer: "Can the attendants of the bridegroom fast while the bridegroom is with them? As long as they have the bridegroom with them, they can't fast." "Why does this generation seek a sign? Amen I tell you, surely a sign won't be given to this generation." "Aren't you greatly misled because of this? You don't know either the writings or the power of God." Jesus' rhetorical questions to the authorities enhance his authority as the one who really knows and who is able to resolve the conflict at hand.

The disciples also pose questions. Their dialogue is composed mostly of single questions asking Jesus to explain something. Often, they are rhetorical questions expressing the disciples' disbelief at what Jesus has said or done: "So who is this that even the wind and the sea obey him?" "Are we to go off and buy two hundred denarii worth of bread and give it to them to eat?" At other times, they genuinely seek an answer: "Why weren't *we* able to drive it out?" "Then who can be saved?" These questions tend to reveal the disciples' lack of faith and understanding. And insofar as the audience may be posing similar questions in response to events in the story, the questions encourage them to identify with the disciples.

The opponents pose mostly accusing questions: "Why is he eating with the tax collectors and sinners?" "Why are they [your disciples] doing what is illegal on the sabbath?" On two significant occasions, opponents offer two rhetorical questions in a small concentric pattern framing an accusation. The first time the authorities confront Jesus, they ask in their minds: "Why does this man talk like this? [A] He blasphemes! [B] Who can pardon sins except God alone? [A']" And at Jesus' trial, the last time they confront Jesus, the high priest asks: "What further need have we for witnesses? [A] You heard the blasphemy! [B] How does it appear to you? [A']" In both passages, the middle sentence emphasizes the charge of blasphemy leading to Jesus' conviction.

All the questions, but particularly the rhetorical ones, engage hearers by leading them to answer the questions for themselves or to want to know how they will be answered by the story.

Riddles

Often in a novel or a short story, a character will tell a brief story or recount a dream. The interpretation of the character's story or dream may not be immediately clear, but the brief story or dream told by the character is invariably meant to be important in the larger encompassing story told by the narrator. Mark's Gospel has many such "stories within a story," for the protagonist Jesus tells stories that illuminate the whole Gospel.

The stories that the Markan Jesus tells are commonly referred to as parables. However, because the word *parable* has become overloaded with many meanings and because the Markan parables are often cryptic and obscure, it is more appropriate to refer to them as "riddles." The narrator treats the riddles as cryptic, because characters in the story (and the hearers) must decipher them in order for their meaning to be disclosed. Most of the riddles in Mark are about the hidden presence of the rule of God in the story world; that is, they are cryptic stories about a hidden reality. Depending on who hears them, the riddles will either reveal more about the rule of God or they will obscure matters further.

Jesus' riddles in Mark are allegories—analogies with several points of correlation—that interpret events and people in the framework of the rule of God.[22] This interpretive function becomes apparent when we look at the riddles that Jesus explains to the disciples. For example, Jesus tells the riddle of the sower and then explains it allegorically in relation to the proclamation of the rule of God and the responses to it. The sower is the one who proclaims (above all, Jesus), the seed is the word, and the soils correlate with the responses of various characters in the Gospel as a whole. Jesus tells a riddle about defilement, then explains what it means: Unclean food will not defile people, but evil plans and actions will. He tells a riddle about a man who went away and told his doorkeeper to keep watch, then draws the allegorical parallels with his own impending absence and how the disciples (and others) are to stay alert for his return. Thus almost all of the Markan riddles are allegories about the dynamics of the rule of God in the larger story world.

We can use these riddles that Jesus explains as a basis to interpret other riddles that Jesus does not explain. For example, we can see that the riddle about the strong man is an allegory about Jesus' defeat of Satan. The two brief riddles about secrets being revealed affirm that the present hiddenness of God's rule will eventually come to light. The riddles of the seed growing secretly and of the mustard seed/weed allegorize the hidden and uncontrollable growth of the rule of God. The riddle of the vineyard interprets events in light of God's relation to Israel in the story, including the reason God sends a son, the causes and consequences of his death, and the fate of the vineyard within the future of this story world.

In Mark, Jesus' riddles have a dual purpose. On the one hand, he tells riddles as a call to understanding. He prefaces or concludes some riddles with commands to "Hear! Look!" "Look at what you hear," "If any have ears to hear, let them hear," and "Hear me everyone and understand." On the other hand, Jesus also tells riddles so that those who reject God's rule will not understand—"so that looking they look and don't see, and hearing they hear and don't understand. Otherwise they might turn and be pardoned!" At the point in the story when Jesus states this reason for telling riddles, the authorities have already rejected Jesus and committed a "sin to eternity" of claiming that he is possessed by an unclean spirit. They have shown themselves to be blind and deaf to the rule of God. The effect of the riddles for those who already do not perceive God's hidden rule in Jesus is to obscure matters further.[23]

Sometimes speaking in riddles enables Jesus to avoid arrest. By telling a riddle about binding the strong one rather than by making a direct statement, Jesus avoids a charge of blasphemy. By using a riddle about defiled food, Jesus cryptically announces a contravention of written laws. With the riddle about the vineyard, Jesus explains his authority as God's son in an indirect way that does not expose him to indictment.

What is the effect of a story with riddles? On the one hand, the hearers, who overhear these riddles, are in a better position to understand them than the characters are, because from the outset the hearers know Jesus' identity as the one anointed to usher in the rule of God. On the other hand, some riddles may be enigmatic and cryptic even to the audience, leading them to wonder whether they understand any better than the disciples do. This effect leads the hearers to be further involved in figuring out the story so they will be on the inside rather than on the outside of understanding.

Quotations from the writings

In J. D. Salinger's *Franny and Zooey*, the character Seymour lists quotations from various religious and philosophical writings on the back of his bedroom door. These quotations provide clues to unlocking the meaning of Salinger's story. Other literature yields similar examples—a character cites a passage from a familiar writing or quotes a well-known figure from the past. Such references are never incidental. They are pieces of the puzzle that today's reader puts together to interpret a story.[24]

In Mark's Gospel, there are twenty-two explicit quotations from "the writings," which include the Law (the first five books of the Hebrew Bible), the Psalms, and the Prophets—all held in common as sacred writings by the Judean characters in the story.[25] (In our translation, these quotations have been set off in parallel poetic lines or explicitly identified as quotations by the characters who cite them.[26])

The narrator cites the writings explicitly only once, in the opening prophecy from Isaiah (and Malachi) about John the baptist. The rest of the citations occur in dialogue between Jesus and other characters. In part, the quotations serve to reveal the characters who quote them. For example, the quotations in debates over legal matters show Jesus' superior knowledge and authority to interpret Scripture, and at the same time they show the ignorance and blindness of the authorities, who are supposed to be legal experts in the writings.

The quotations from the writings also serve to interpret the significance of characters and events, often allegorically, as the parables do. For example, Jesus quotes Scripture to explain to the disciples in a brief allegorical analogy of their impending flight: "I will strike the shepherd, and the sheep will be scattered." Other quotations from the writings explain the hypocrisy of the Pharisees, the purpose of the riddles, the stumbling of the disciples, and so on. Jesus cites the writings as explanations to other characters; but their presence in the story serves the same function for the audience, who overhears them.

In addition to explicit quotations, there are numerous allusions to the writings, especially in Jesus' words of warning to his disciples on the Mountain of the Olives and in the depiction of Jesus' death. For example, Mark weaves words and phrases from Isaiah, Zechariah, Daniel, and various psalms into the fabric of the passion narrative: "with the clouds of heaven," "one eating with me," "and he flogged Jesus," and "they divided his garments," among many others. These rich allusions open the story to numerous associations for the audience and show how Jesus' death was part of a larger cosmic design and purpose.

Prophecies

The narrator recounts many prophecies in the course of this story. Some are quotations from the writings, while others originate from characters in the story, first John and then Jesus. As we have shown above, a prophecy will foreshadow certain events, and the events in turn are subsequently described in words that remind the audience of the prophecy and confirm its fulfillment.[27] From the very first lines, the hearers are led to expect the prophecies to be fulfilled. Prophecies from the writings are fulfilled, new oracles given by John and Jesus are fulfilled, and Jesus gives prophecies that will be fulfilled in the future of the story world beyond the plotted events. Because the prophecies relate to the rule of God, the hearers come to see how the rule of God actually provides the impetus, the framework, and the goal of the events that constitute the story world.

The fulfillment of prophecies within the plotted events enables Mark's narrator to end the Gospel in a powerful and enigmatic way. Throughout the narrative by means of prophecies in oracles, riddles, and warnings, Jesus foreshadows the future of the story world after the plotted events will end. Because the audience has good reason to believe that Jesus' words about the future will come true—as indeed his word has come true so frequently within the narrative—the narrator is able to end the story abruptly and without closure, with the women saying nothing to anyone about the risen Jesus. As a result, the audience expects the not-yet-fulfilled prophecies to come true.

In Mark, prophecies are fulfilled in the narrative by the complex development of unfolding events and not in a way that treats the characters as puppets on a string. For example, Jesus knows that according to prophecy it is God's will for him to live for the rule of God even if it means that he will die; yet at the same time Jesus must choose to do what God wills and not what he himself wants. Also, Jesus quotes for the authorities an oracle about a stone that "the builders" reject; yet it is their anger with Jesus for citing the oracle against them that in part leads them to choose the very act that fulfills the oracle! Jesus quotes for the disciples an oracle that prophesies they will be scattered when the shepherd is struck; yet it is their false confidence that this will never happen to *them* that in part leads to the fulfilling of the prophecy! For the audience, these prophecies increase the pathos of the characters' struggle with their destiny.

Irony

Irony is a prominent feature of Mark's story.[28] *Verbal irony* occurs when a speaker intentionally says one thing but means the opposite. *Dramatic irony* occurs when there is a discrepancy between what a character blindly thinks to be the case and what the real situation is or between what a character expects to happen and what actually happens.

The most obvious examples of verbal irony in Mark are the ironic jeers of Jesus' opponents. The soldiers mock him by hailing him as "king of the Judeans." They mean the opposite: How ridiculous that this pathetic man should be considered a king! Others taunt him to prophesy or to get off the cross or to tear down the temple. Sarcastically, they mean the opposite: How helpless he is—hardly the anointed one of God!

In dramatic irony, the characters in the story are blind to the irony of the situation, while the audience hears the ironic contrast between what the speaker says and the way things really are. For example, the illustrations of verbal irony given above turn out to be part of a larger dramatic irony. When the opponents ridicule Jesus for claiming to be king of the Judeans, the audience understands that the statements they intend as verbal irony *really are true* in the larger drama of the story: Jesus can prophesy; in a different sense, he really is king of the Judeans; and he cannot save himself except by losing his life.

In a general way, dramatic irony is integral to the overall design of the Gospel, for the rule of God turns out to be different from what most characters in the story expect. For example, the authorities expect God to affirm their own authority and interpretation of the law, when the real situation, as the narrator depicts it, is that God has given that authority to Jesus the Nazarene. The authorities expect that those who have the greatest honor in human eyes will be greatest in the rule of God, but the values of the rule of God are the reverse of their expectations. The contrast between the opponents' expectations and the real situation comes to a climax at the trial: The opponents think they have rightly condemned this blasphemer to death, when in fact it is they who are under condemnation for rejecting God's agent.

Irony is also used in the portrayal of the disciples. Rock vehemently insists that he will die with Jesus rather than deny him. But the audience knows the real situation is otherwise, because Jesus has just prophesied that Rock will renounce him three times. Furthermore, the very name "Rock" is ironic. Simon tries to behave like a strong person, but he is really the opposite of the nickname Jesus gave him, for he falls asleep and later flees at the incriminating remarks of a servant girl of the high priest. The disciples in general hope to gain honor, wealth, and power from their association with this anointed agent of God's rule, but what they get is an invitation to serve everyone and the likelihood of persecution for following Jesus. They expect one thing; they encounter the opposite.

Irony draws the hearers into accepting the narrator's point of view. By showing the authorities ridiculing Jesus as "king of the Judeans," the narrator leads the hearers to sympathize with Jesus and to smile slyly, thinking, "There's more truth to that than they realize." And because the audience understands what the characters do not, the audience is led to be on the inside, perhaps even to feel superior to the characters. In a sense, irony creates a community between the audience and the narrator, who together share something that puts them on the inside.

The ironic ending of Mark, however, punctures any self-confident superiority the audience might have, for the ending turns irony back upon the audience. Now it is the audience who expects one thing but gets another. Throughout the story, Jesus commanded people to be quiet, but they talked anyway. At the end of the story, the young man commands the women to go tell, but, in an ironic reversal, the women are silent. The irony perpetrated on the audience thus becomes a challenge, a challenge to proclaim the good news courageously in the face of persecution rather than be silent as the women were.

Conclusion

One might summarize the work of the narrator as follows. On the one hand, the narrator tells a story full of gaps, rife with all forms of suspense, punctuated with puzzles and riddles to decipher—with characters who are amazed at developing events, with twists and turns, with paradoxes, and with great irony. The story is deliberately ambiguous, and the meaning is often hidden—if not to the audience, then certainly to the characters in the story. The story ends without closure. The meaning of life is hidden, because the rule of God is hidden except to those with ears to hear and eyes to see. It is not obvious to the world that those who follow Jesus are on God's side. For the narrator, life is paradoxical, ambiguous, ironic, open, uncertain.

On the other hand, the patterns in the narrative manifest a fabric of order and purpose underlying the uncertainty and the ambiguity. There are patterns of twos and threes and concentric circles, forecasts and echoes, frames and sandwiches, repetitions of type scenes, and verbal threads. The whole story is painted with strokes from the Judean writings, with the designs of prophecy and fulfillment. There is a pattern of purpose to what seems frightening and out of control. But this pattern of purpose must be seen with the eyes of faith. As when one looks at a puzzle, one may gaze at Mark for a long time in order finally to discern the fabric of God's rule in the way and in the places and in the people where Mark claims it to be present. In a sense, then, the narrator tells a story designed to lead the audience to experience all the joys and triumphs of the rule of God hidden in the present age amid the suffering and ambiguity of life—while awaiting Jesus' return in power and glory.

Mark is clearly designed for oral performance. Early followers of Jesus who performed Mark employed strategies of storytelling to express these oral arts that are still available to us embedded in the written texts, oral arts such as the various forms of repetition we have detailed here as well as other dynamics of narrative such as irony and the use of riddles. Patterns of repetition would have served also to help the performer keep the story in memory, and they would have assisted the audience in recalling the story.

The composer of Mark has brought considerable storytelling skills to the task of challenging ancient audiences and today's readers to think in a new way about life, to have faith, to embrace the new reality, to rethink the nature of power, and to gain the courage to live this new life despite fear. The Markan narrator tells this story in an engaging and a delightful way, often with playfulness, cleverness, and humor. At the same time, the narrator is telling a story that is both disturbing and challenging, a story about life and death, the fate of the world, and thus the fate of the hearers. As such, the prevailing tone of the narrator toward audiences is one of great seriousness.

The narrative patterns and oral features we have discussed in this chapter can be illustrated in virtually every episode of the Gospel. Because form is inseparable from content, storytelling inseparable from story, we will make use of these patterns and strategies as we analyze the settings, the plot, and the characters of this artful Gospel.

CHAPTER 3

The Settings

Settings provide the narrative with a "world" where events take place and characters act. Settings in a narrative include the cosmic depiction of space and time, the cultural ethos, and the political configurations of the story world, geographical locations, humanly constructed spaces, and so on.

In an unfolding story world, settings are not incidental backdrops to events. Rather, settings serve many functions: generating atmosphere, providing the occasion for a conflict, revealing traits of the characters as they interact with the settings, and evoking associations present in the culture of the audience. Settings may convey important themes and even provide the overall structure for a story. Together, settings provide the conditions—the possibilities and the limitations—within which the characters chart their destinies.[1]

To disregard setting is to miss a great deal about a story. Consider, for example, how the setting can determine the action of a story: the atmosphere of the sea in *Moby Dick* or the world of small country estates in Jane Austen's novels. The South provides the formative context for Alice Walker's *The Color Purple*. In *The Odyssey*, Dante's *Divine Comedy*, and Eudora Welty's short story "The Path," journeys give structure to the story and reinforce the quest of the characters. If the settings of these stories were altered, the stories themselves would be changed significantly.

Similarly, in Mark, the settings are related to the actions and the events of the story in a variety of ways.[2] The cosmic setting provides the divine-human stage for the events that drive the plot. The sociopolitical setting (Israel under the Romans) projects an atmosphere of oppression and threat. The journeys of Jesus and the disciples around Galilee and up to Jerusalem provide the structural framework for the narrative as a whole. On this journey, physical settings serve thematic development: private and public contexts, Israelite and Gentile territory, the desert, the sea, and others. Settings are crucial to specific episodes: the occasion for conflict (work on the sabbath), the cause of action (no food in a desert), and the force that drives an episode (a storm at sea). At minimum, settings in Mark set the mood and give commentary, sometimes ironic, on the action.

Settings in Mark are seldom neutral. Throughout Galilee and at his entrance to Jerusalem, Jesus receives an enthusiastic reception. Yet Jesus also moves in a hostile world and encounters antagonistic powers in highly charged situations. In Galilean towns and synagogues, he confronts violent demonic forces and antagonistic authorities. In Gentile territory, he meets a legion of demons and a crowd of angry residents. In the hostile atmosphere of Jerusalem, he faces overwhelming political opposition.

As a dimension of setting, the "time" is also highly charged. The sabbath day poses an occasion for the threat of indictment to Jesus. The Passover festival, a volatile celebration of national liberation from slavery in Egypt, intensifies the conflicts in Jerusalem and provides a highly meaningful context for Jesus' death.

When we consider settings in the context of ancient performance events, the challenge of a performer-as-narrator was to suggest settings of place and time by means of verbal emphasis, gesture, and movement in the performance space and, in so doing, to draw audiences by imagination into the world of the story so that they "see" the various settings and grasp the ways in which these settings figure in the meaning and impact of the story. A performer of Mark could assume that audiences would be familiar enough with the settings in the story for them to make sense. In this way, the narrator could take some things for granted with the audience and, at the same time, indicate *how* they would like the audience to think about those settings. What follows are depictions of the various kinds of settings as they are portrayed in the story world.

The Cosmic Setting

The larger setting of Mark's story is the "creation that God created." This creation is a closed and bounded cosmos, a flat earth with heavens extending from the earth up to where God dwells.[3] The heavens are encompassed by a canopy above the earth on which are hung the sun, the moon, the stars, and "the powers in the heavens." On mountains, the characters are closer to the heavens, while clouds bear the divine presence down from above. The "four winds" originate from the "ends of the earth." The nation of Israel is at the center of this cosmos, surrounded by the Gentile nations, all under the aegis of the Roman Empire. Jerusalem is the capital city of Israel, and it is dominated by the huge complex of the temple—the religious, political, and economic center of Israel.

This world is inhabited by God and angels, Satan and demons, unclean and clean animals, as well as by humans. In this creation, nature and human history are one: "Famines" and "earthquakes" accompany "wars" and "battles," while a "darkened sun" and "falling stars" announce the "coming of the son of humanity" in judgment. Furthermore, people understood this created order to include social boundaries meant to keep some people holy before God by separating Israelites from the impure Gentiles and by separating the leaders of Israel from Judeans considered to be defiled—lepers, tax collectors, a woman with a flow of blood, and people possessed of unclean spirits.

In Mark's story world, creation is awry. Humans were created to have dominion over the rest of creation, but the actual situation in the story is just the reverse: Humans are possessed by demons, wracked by illnesses, and threatened by storms at sea. Above all, they are oppressed by other human beings: The Roman armies occupy Israel; and the leaders of Israel, who are appointed by and accountable to Roman authorities, dominate the Judean people. The boundaries meant to guard holiness have become barriers that exclude those who need God's help the most. In Mark's portrayal, this is a bleak, "faithless generation," full of evil that is often perpetrated under the guise of serving God. The world as a whole is the house of the strong one, Satan's territory, an atmosphere hostile to human need and antagonistic to God's rule.

Yet the beginning of this story proclaims that the whole cosmic setting is changing. Into the midst of this bounded world gone awry, God opens the heavens and sends the spirit upon Jesus, who announces that "the rule of God has arrived." The arrival of God's rule changes cosmic space, because the power of God from above is now available on earth for healing and exorcism. The power of God's rule breaks out of local, national, and natural boundaries to make all space into God's space. After the execution and resurrection of Jesus, followers are to spread the holy power of the rule of God outward from Israel into the Gentile nations to the ends of the earth.

The arrival of the rule of God also changes cosmic time. For Mark, time is marked more by key moments and opportune times than by days and hours. And *now* is the opportune time, the long-awaited arrival of God's rule promised by the prophets. Jesus' inauguration of God's rule, bringing the blessings of God into the midst of this present evil age, will become fully present in power before "this generation passes away."[4]

The transformations that take place at the cosmic level with the arrival of the rule of God are foundational for the dynamics of the whole story. The arrival of the rule of God drives the plot of the story, gives new possibilities and threats to all the characters and character groups, leads to changes in the political order, and influences all the other settings that are encompassed within the cosmic renewal. As such, the arrival of the rule of God represents a renewal of the whole creation. Jesus proclaims the arrival of the rule of God at the outset of Mark's story and, in a sense, the rest of the story plays out the consequences and projects the fulfillment of that momentous announcement into the imminent future.

The Political-Cultural Setting

The immediate narrative stage for the establishment of God's rule is Israel under the military control of the Roman Empire. Herod Antipas is the Roman-appointed king in Galilee, and Pilate is the Roman procurator over Judea and Jerusalem.[5] The Judean authorities in Jerusalem include the high priest Caiaphas—appointed by Rome and accountable to Rome—along with the high priests, the elders, and the rest of the national "Sanhedrin" council. They govern Judea and Jerusalem and administer the temple—for as long as they keep order and provide tribute for their Roman overlords.

The society depicted in Mark's story is typical of the preindustrial agrarian societies of antiquity. The rulers, including the high priests, the elders, and other aristocratic landowners, constitute a very small elite group—people of status and wealth—who dominate the populace. In Mark's narrative world, the Pharisees and legal experts (scribes) are retainers of the elites. They interpret and apply the Judean laws and traditions given by God to Moses. These leaders of Israel—by neglect and by exploitation—have not produced "the fruits of the vineyard" on behalf of the populace, as God demands.

The rest of the characters in Mark's narrative world, including Jesus and the disciples, are people who live at or below a basic subsistence level, for there is no middle class. These include peasants who still hold land, day laborers, tenant farmers, tradesmen in the villages, and fishermen around the Sea of Galilee. They get their identity from their villages ("Joseph from Arimathea," "Mary the Magdalene") and their family ("James the son of Zebedee," "Mary the mother of James"). They also include the Markan crowds. Among them are characters below the subsistence level such as lepers, beggars, people who are blind or deaf, and those oppressed by illnesses, physical disabilities, and unclean spirits. Mark's Jesus brings the new social order of the rule of God into this sociopolitical setting of Israel, calling for radical change.

In Mark's story, the rest of the earth is comprised of the Gentile nations—the Roman Empire and the nations under its domination. Like the Judean leaders, the Gentile rulers "lord over" the people and their great ones "exert authority over" them. The disciples are to proclaim the rule of God to these nations, just as Jesus had proclaimed it to Israel.

The Journey

The journey of Jesus with the disciples provides a frame for the events described in the story. Furthermore, the journey structures the narrative as a whole. The first half of the story depicts travel throughout Galilee and the surrounding Gentile territory. The second half of the story focuses on Jerusalem in three stages: first the pilgrimage to Jerusalem, then Jesus' actions and teachings in Jerusalem, and finally the story of the crucifixion and empty grave. Of course, the journey is more than movement across a landscape. The "way of God" that Jesus travels represents Jesus' efforts to inaugurate the rule of God in Israel, efforts that end (temporarily) in his execution at Jerusalem. And the settings intensify this movement toward his death by creating a spatial funnel that narrows as he moves toward Jerusalem.[6] Then the story opens out again with the empty grave and the promise of the return to Galilee.

Patterns of movement on the journey

Jordan River. The story begins at the Jordan River, in the desert of Judea, the place of entry into Jerusalem. The opening prophecy twice calls for people to prepare the "way of the lord."

Galilee. After John's arrest, Jesus and the disciples travel throughout Galilee, first in Capernaum and surrounding villages and then throughout all Galilee, even making several forays into Gentile territory. Jesus moves quickly ("immediately") from place to place, changing settings more than forty times in these travels. The reason for this urgent movement is the spread of the rule of God. Jesus says, "Let's go elsewhere, to the next towns, so I might proclaim there too, for that's why I came out."

Galilee is the place where Jesus first brings God's rule and where its inbreaking is received enthusiastically. The settings in Galilee provide the context in which Jesus' increasing popularity becomes apparent. For example, Jesus' following becomes too large for houses. First, Jesus enters the house of Simon in Capernaum, and by evening the whole city is gathered at the door. When he returns to Capernaum, so many people gather that there are not even places at the door. Later, in another house, such a huge crowd gathers that Jesus and his disciples do not have a chance to eat. Subsequently, houses are no longer a setting of public activity for Jesus. This same problem occurs also in towns, and at one point the crowds are so large that Jesus is not able to enter a town openly.

The settings then move to open spaces, such as "beside the sea." When Jesus first passes by the Sea of Galilee, he is alone and he chooses four fishermen to follow him. When he returns to the sea, a crowd follows him. Later, he is followed to the sea by crowds "from Judea and from Jerusalem and from Idumea and across the Jordan and around Tyre and Sidon." He tells his disciples to "keep a little boat waiting for him because of the crowd, so they would not press him." When Jesus next travels by the sea, the crowd is so huge that he has to sit out in a boat to teach. A similar pattern in the open setting of the "desert" also displays this growing popular response to Jesus.

However, Galilee is also the place where Jesus first encounters complication and conflict in many settings. He is not always free to journey as he wants. Nor is the way of God that Jesus travels in Galilee an ordered journey. Thus, while the rapid movement among these different settings accentuates the urgency and success of Jesus' efforts to proclaim, to exorcise, and to heal, they also reveal his inability to control the obstacles and conflicts that he encounters at every turn.

Gentile territory. On several occasions, Jesus travels beyond Galilee to Gentile territory. First he goes to the region of the Ten Cities across the Sea of Galilee, where he exorcises the "legion" of demons. Then he goes to the territory around Tyre, encounters the Syrophoenician woman, passes through Sidon back to the Ten Cities, and feeds four thousand Gentiles in the desert. Later he travels to the areas around Caesarea Philippi. In Mark, there is a distinction between the holy land of Israel and unclean Gentile territory. Mark depicts Jesus bringing the rule of God even to Gentile territory, foreshadowing a time when the disciples will proclaim the good news to "all the Gentile nations."

The same patterns of response to Jesus in Galilee recur in Gentile territories: increasing popularity, intense opposition, withdrawal, and crowds in the desert. The recurrence of these patterns in Gentile territory shows that, in the story world, the Gentiles respond to Jesus in the same ways as the Judeans.

The journey to Jerusalem. The major turning point, which comes halfway through the story, is marked by a shift in setting. At Caesarea Philippi, a setting far removed from Jerusalem, Rock recognizes Jesus as the anointed one. At that point, Jesus begins a sustained journey to Jerusalem and to his execution.

The verbal motif of "the way" appears most often in this journey to Jerusalem. The word occurs eight times, providing markers for the journey and commentary on its import. This journey begins "on the way" to the villages around Caesarea Philippi. After this, the journey moves to Capernaum on the way through Galilee, then to Judea and beyond the Jordan to Jericho, then near to Jerusalem at Bethphage and Bethania, to the Mountain of the Olives, and culminating in the entrance to Jerusalem and the temple.

Because the "way of God" is a metaphor for following Jesus in the service of the rule of God, it becomes the setting where Jesus instructs his disciples on the expectations and the cost of following. The audience, also, is led to struggle with the disciples on this journey toward greater understanding.

Jerusalem. When Jesus reaches his destination, he enters Jerusalem to the acclaim of the crowds accompanying him.[7] In Jerusalem, the feast of the Passover—the celebration of liberation from domination in Egypt—evokes an atmosphere of expectation and tension.

Also in Jerusalem, the conflicts intensify as Jesus confronts the authorities with the rule of God in his actions and teaching in the temple. Yet because the daytime settings are public, the favorable crowds protect him from arrest. At night, Jesus withdraws to private settings outside the city. Only at the last does he enter the city, at night, where he has arranged secretly for the Passover meal.

After the meal, Jesus and his disciples go to the Mountain of the Olives. Earlier the private mountain settings were places of refuge. Now, while he prays, a hostile crowd from the authorities arrives with swords and clubs to arrest him. And here, at the end, the pattern we have seen in other settings is reversed; the opposition triumphs, the crowds no longer protect Jesus, and the authorities turn the crowds against him. Jerusalem, the capital of Israel, the place where God dwells in the temple, is the place where Jesus is rejected and killed.

New beginning in Galilee. The final scene points back to Galilee, back to the beginning of the story, back to the place where the rule of God had been so welcomed. The young man's message to the women at the grave with instructions for the disciples to go to Galilee suggests a fresh start for the disciples and for anyone in the future of the story world who chooses to follow Jesus. Furthermore, Galilee points toward the Gentile nations, where Jesus had said "the good news is to be proclaimed."

In the journeys projected into the future of the story world, the disciples will encounter the same opposition from authorities in Judean settings and authorities in Gentile settings, for Jesus prophesied that they "will be handed over to [Judean] sanhedrins and beaten in synagogues" and that they "will stand [trial] before [Gentile] governors and kings." Just as it had led Jesus, the "way of God" will lead followers to settings of confrontation and rejection.

Settings recalling Israel's past

On the journey, some settings recall events in Israel's history.[8] By evoking these memories in the life of Israel, the Markan settings connect for hearers events in this story about Jesus with events of deliverance in Israel's history.

Jordan River. After the exodus of Israelites from Egypt, the crossing of the Jordan River signaled the entrance to "the promised land." In the first century, Jewish prophets led followers to reenact the crossing of the Jordan River in hopes of precipitating Israel's liberation from the Roman Empire. John's baptism at the Jordan recalls the river as a threshold experience in Israel's history. There Judeans and Jerusalemites come to John to "turn around" in anticipation of the inbreaking of the rule of God.

The desert. The desert is outside human habitation, a dangerous and threatening place with wild animals and a lack of food. This is the place where God had prepared the Israelites to enter the land of Israel. Later, God led the Israelites again across the desert from exile in Babylonia to restore the nation. In Mark, the opening prophecy from Isaiah recalls these events by announcing a voice in the desert summoning people to "prepare the way of the lord."

In Mark, the desert is also a place of testing. The Israelites were tested during their forty years of wandering in the desert. By contrast, in Mark, Jesus success-fully endures there forty days of testing by Satan; he is even among wild animals, and the angels serve him. Later, Jesus returns alone to deserted places to pray, times that recall his earlier temptation. The desert also tests the disciples, twice revealing their lack of faith to feed people there with bread.

The sea. In Israelite understanding, the sea was a place of chaos and destruction, as it is in Israelite creation stories and in the story of the flood. Similarly in Mark's story, Jesus refers to the sea as a place to throw someone "with a millstone tied around the neck" or a place to have a mountain removed in order to destroy it. The herd of two thousand pigs is destroyed in the sea. A dramatic storm on the Sea of Galilee threatens to destroy Jesus and the disciples.

Despite the destructiveness of the sea, divine authority brought order out of the chaos at creation and parted the Reed (Red) Sea on the journey out of Egypt. So, too, Jesus in Mark demonstrates that he has been given authority over nature: he stops the wind, calms the sea, and later walks on the sea. By so doing, Jesus shows his access to God's power over the threats of nature, and Jesus expects the disciples to exercise the same authority through their faith in God's power.

Mountains. Mountains were places for epiphanies and revelations, because mountains reach up into the lower heavens and bring people closer to God. God revealed the law to Moses on a mountain. On a mountain, God was made mani-fest to Moses and later to Elijah. From a mountain, Moses saw the promised land. Similarly, in Mark, divine glory is manifested in Jesus on a mountain, and a voice from heaven reveals to the three disciples with him that Jesus is God's only son. Also, Jesus appoints the twelve on a mountain, and he is on the Mountain of the Olives when he reveals to four disciples the future of God's rule in prophecies and warnings.

The mountain was often a place of refuge and safety for figures in Israel's past. Likewise, in Mark's story, Jesus warns that, at the threat of war, people in Judea should "flee to the mountains." Jesus himself retreats to a mountain several times—to pray, after feeding a crowd in the desert, and later at Gethsemane.

Public and private settings

Throughout the narrative, there is a rhythm back and forth between public settings and private settings. Public and private settings mark the two main plotlines of the story: Jesus' interactions with the authorities and Jesus' interactions with the disciples.

On the public side, villages, synagogues, houses, deserted spaces between villages, by the sea, Jerusalem, and the temple constitute the public settings in which Jesus exorcises demons and carries out most healings and acts of power over nature. Here he teaches the crowds.

Here also his public actions trigger opposition from the authorities. These conflicts between Jesus and the authorities occur in public settings, such as synagogues, where they are openly pitted against each other for all to see and where public honor is won and lost. As the story progresses, Jesus stops going to synagogues, and he teaches elsewhere. The authorities then confront him in open spaces by the sea and across the Jordan. In Jerusalem, he publicly confronts all the authority groups of Israel in the temple. Ironically, Jesus is somewhat protected in the temple, because of the favorable crowds. Subsequently, a trial before Pilate and a Roman crucifixion provide the ultimate public settings for the shaming of Jesus.

On the private side, Jesus often retreats with the disciples to private settings. He takes them aside into a house, explains the riddles privately in a boat, goes off to a mountain with three disciples, teaches four of them on the Mountain of the Olives, takes them aside on the journey to Jerusalem, and eats the Passover meal with them privately in the upper room. These settings provide the context for Jesus' private teaching to his disciples. As such, private settings contribute to the secrecy motif of the story, because those characters who are present, the insiders (as well as the audience), have access to what goes on there, while the other characters, the outsiders, do not.

Private settings all through the Gospel reinforce for hearers the solidarity and intimacy between Jesus and the disciples, because there Jesus confides so many things to the disciples, such as the explanations of the riddles, prophecies about his death, and warnings about the future. In the privacy of the Passover meal in an upper room, he seals a covenant with the disciples in relation to his impending death. At Gethsemane, he seeks their support in his anguished prayers.

The conflicts between Jesus and the disciples occur in these private settings. Jesus has very few conflicts with the disciples in public, for in public the disciples are aligned with Jesus in his conflicts with the authorities. In private settings, the conflicts between Jesus and the disciples bring no threat to public honor, either for Jesus or for the disciples—even though the disciples compete privately among themselves for honor. Therefore, for the audience, it is clear that the disciples are "with" Jesus even when they are in opposition to him.

The journey as the way of God

Thus the journey is the "way of God," a metaphor for following Jesus in the service of the rule of God. This is confirmed by the verbal threads that depict "going ahead" and "following" on the journey. John is sent "ahead" of Jesus, and Jesus goes "ahead" of the disciples. Jesus comes "after" John, and the disciples "follow after" Jesus. These words are not only spatial descriptors; they reflect the pattern of life that is "the way of God." John goes ahead of Jesus by anticipating the pattern of Jesus' life: he was "sent" by God, "proclaimed," was "handed over," and was "put to death." In turn, Jesus was sent by God, proclaimed, was handed over, and was put to death. Likewise, the disciples are to follow: they are sent in order to proclaim, they will be handed over, and they are to take up their cross and lose their lives. Thus "the way of God" anticipated by John and traveled by Jesus is to be followed by the disciples. Even after his crucifixion, at the very end of the story, Jesus will continue to "go ahead of you to Galilee"—the place of the original inbreaking of the rule of God.

The structural setting of the way leads hearers also to join the journey of "the way of God." In the constant shifting of the settings in Galilee, the hearers are seldom left to linger but are quickly caught up in the action at the next location. The subsequent pilgrimage to Jerusalem leads them to struggle along with the disciples and stirs up their desire to see just what will happen at the end. Thus the settings point the audience toward Jerusalem, where the conflicts come to a head and the characters are fully revealed. In so doing, the story draws the audience into the journey and the destiny of Jesus. And, at the end, the story leads them to continue the journey in their own real world.

Conclusion

We began by saying that settings provide a world for the narrative. Settings present audiences with a world to consider in their imagination. The role of an actual performer of Mark in the ancient world was to draw audiences into the world of the story so that they might encounter in their real-life world the changes in the structures and possibilities of the cosmos that have taken place as a result of the arrival of the rule of God. A similar dynamic may be true also for modern readers. As with film, a story like Mark draws audiences today into another time and place, into the possibilities and limitations of another way of viewing the world. Ancient hearers and modern readers emerge from the experience of Mark with some new ways of seeing their own world and a different sense of belonging in the world. In particular, Mark's story invites today's readers to see the possibilities of the rule of God and to join the journey with Jesus. Thus setting is more than just a location and more than just an atmosphere. In the end, it represents the way people imagine the world and think of their place in it.

CHAPTER 4

The Plot

Plot has to do with events: how they are arranged, how they are connected, and what they reveal. Events are actions or happenings that bring about change. Events, of course, are inseparable from settings and characters: settings provide the conditions for events, and characters are the agents who cause and react to events. But to focus on plot enables us to see the design of events that gives a narrative its meaning and direction.[1]

Approaches to the Plot

In this chapter, we will look at Mark's plot briefly from several different angles and then offer an extended analysis of the conflicts that constitute the plot.

The unity of Mark's plot

Mark's story is unified around one overall theme: God is establishing God's rulership over the "creation that God created" and bringing it to fulfillment within the generation. We want to emphasize the cosmic nature of the Markan drama so that we do not limit the nature and scope of God's rule to individual salvation or to cultural and political transformation. While this cosmic dimension of the story often lies in the background of events on stage, the audience does not forget that the watershed event in the story is the announcement at the beginning: "The rule of God has arrived." This is what unifies Mark's story: the inauguration of God's rule over all creation, over all people, over all of nature, over Israel, over all the nations, and over the Roman Empire. The events that follow in the story—exorcisms, healings, nature miracles, human transformations, conflicts with authorities, prophecies, persecution, death, resurrection, proclamation, and the projected cosmic upheavals—are all consequences of the active presence and power of God now made present in Jesus and those around him. The entire plot of Mark is unified around this theme.

Jesus is center stage. He is the human agent commissioned to initiate this goal of bringing God's rule over creation. In this endeavor, Jesus struggles to establish the rule of God in the face of obstacles and opposition. Within this overall movement, there are three plotlines, each represented by Jesus' interactions with a set of characters: nonhuman forces, the authorities, and the disciples. These plotlines all serve the overall goal of the narrative, without digressions or unrelated subplots. Most issues raised by the story are resolved, although some issues are strategically left unresolved.

Events contribute to the unifed development of the plot in several ways. We can explore the functions of an event in the plot by asking how it relates to other events in the story and what difference it would make if the event were omitted. Some episodes are key events: initiating events that propel the story forward, events that are turning points, or events that climax a series of episodes.[2] For example, the anointing of Jesus with the holy spirit is an initiating event that propels forward the inauguration of the rule of God; Rock's recognition of Jesus as the anointed one is a turning point between Jesus' travels around Galilee and his journey toward Jerusalem; and the condemnation of Jesus by the Sanhedrin is the climax to a long series of efforts on the part of the opponents to indict Jesus.

Other events serve the plot in less significant ways. Some events follow from the key events in the plot. For example, exorcisms come as a consequence of Jesus' successful confrontation with Satan in the desert. Other events lead up to key events. For example, miracles pile up until they eventually lead to Rock's recognition of Jesus as the anointed one, and Jesus' conflicts with the authorities accumulate until the Roman authorities put Jesus to death. Similar events may develop themes in the plot. In Mark, it is not unusual for events to serve the plot in several ways at once.

Beginning, middle, and end

One way to look at plot is to see the ways in which options narrow or expand as the plot develops. The plot of Mark fits well Aristotle's definition of a story having a beginning, a middle, and an end: at the beginning, many things are possible; in the middle, the possibilities narrow; and at the end, everything seems necessary and inevitable.[3]

We can trace Mark's plot to see how possible outcomes narrow and expand. At the beginning of the story, the rule of God arrives and people of Israel are called to turn around. Perhaps all will follow Jesus, and the rule of God will arrive effortlessly. The initial responses of the disciples and the populace are encouraging. Almost immediately, however, the authorities harden against Jesus, and the disciples begin to have trouble understanding him. By the middle of the story, after Rock finally realizes that Jesus is the anointed one, possibilities narrow significantly, as Jesus begins a journey to Jerusalem on a collision course with the authorities leading to confrontation in Jerusalem. Thus, at the end of the story, when we get to the events in Jerusalem, everything seems necessary and inevitable: Jesus' actions seal his fate, the disciples flee, and the authorities condemn him to death and execute him.

At the very end of the narrative, possibilities open up again and expand into the future. The resurrection begins to reverse the outcome in Jerusalem and prefigures the return of Jesus in glory and power. The secret of Jesus' identity may now "be brought into the open." The disciples and other followers are now challenged to take up Jesus' earlier mandate to proclaim the good news to all the nations.

Connections in Mark's plot

Plot can also be discerned in connections between one event and the next. Mark, as is typical of ancient narrative, presents his story as a series of episodes that are only loosely connected, so that the relationship between them is frequently not obvious. Within episodes, there are often explicit causal or explanatory or consequential connections, such as "for," "because," "but," "therefore," and "with the result that." However, between episodes, the connection is usually a simple "and," suggesting a minimal temporal connection (and then this happened after that).[4] Occasionally, there is an explicit causal connection with the next episode: Jesus eludes the efforts of the high priest to trap him, *so* they send others to catch him in his words. Causal connections between one episode and the next are sometimes implied: the authorities conspire to destroy Jesus, and (so) Jesus withdraws to the sea.

Sometimes the implied causal connection between one event and the next is "ironic"—the outcome of the action being different from what the character intended. Jesus commands people to be quiet, but they proclaim anyhow, and a subsequent episode will recount the results of their proclaiming. Jesus tells people to "hear" the riddles for greater understanding, but in the next episode the disciples' minds are hardened. The authorities hope to eliminate the threat of Jesus and secure their position; yet in the next episode, Jesus rises from the dead.

Sometimes events are connected rhetorically, such as those episodes that occur in a concentric pattern or in a sandwiching relationship or in a series of three. These serve to advance the plot but not necessarily in a cause-effect relationship. Even events for which the audience is unprepared can be related thematically. For example, the young man who flees naked at Gethsemane seems to appear out of nowhere. However, his nakedness graphically portrays the shame of the disciples' flight recounted in the preceding episode; and his momentary arrest and escape reinforce the threat of arrest for Rock in the courtyard scene depicted in the following episode. Such thematic connections enhance the plot but are not crucial to it.

The key effect of the loose connections between episodic events in Mark's plot is that it does not narrow down the causes of and relationships among events. The simple "and" introducing so many lines and episodes leaves open possible connections to many previous episodes and events. For example, the betrayal of Jesus by Judas is at once brought about by the will of God, the actions of other characters, and the nature of the character himself. Each of these elements, then, represents a cause that brings about this subsequent event. Looking back through the narrative to determine the many factors that lead to a particular event reveals the complexity of Mark's plot.

The fulfillment or nonfulfillment of expectations

Plots are often organized around problems and possibilities that are raised in the plot and then dealt with by the events that follow. People are sick. A storm threatens life. The authorities oppose Jesus. The disciples resist his teaching. How will these problems be dealt with?

Mark's plot also raises possibilities by means of prophecies, announcements, mandates, and commissions. Prophecies are made, and then the audience follows along to see how they will be fulfilled. Announcements are given, such as "You are my beloved son" and "The rule of God has arrived," and then the audience follows to see how these expectations will be met. Mandates and commissions are offered, such as "Turn around and put faith in the good news" and "Follow me" and "If any want to follow after me, let them renounce themselves and take up their cross and follow me," and the audience then watches to see how these mandates are heeded by the characters as the story develops.[5]

Striking features of Mark's narrative are the many twists and turns resulting from the expectations raised by the plot. Expectations may be revised or overturned. Expectations may be fulfilled ironically. Some expectations are raised in the story and then dashed: the promising start for the disciples leads to failure at Jerusalem. Other expectations are left without certainty of fulfillment: in the future of the narrative world, will the disciples see Jesus in Galilee? Thus Mark's story fulfills some expectations and leaves others open-ended, without closure.

The outcome of Mark's plot

Does Mark's plot end in tragedy or triumph? The plot begins with Jesus' astounding rescue of many people from the tragic situations of their lives. Yet the plot of Mark bends inexorably toward Jesus' tragic death. Mark's Gospel is a plot in which the human situation of Jesus and the disciples changes for the worse.[6] This happens due not to some fatal flaw or miscalculation on Jesus' part, as in many Greek tragedies. Rather, his fate is inherent in the nature of his mission and the resistance of the world to that mission. Jesus succeeds in being faithful to God, but the powers that be do not accept his message, and he is executed. Yet there is a twist; what looked like a tragedy turns out to be triumph. Jesus is resurrected, and his projected return in power and glory will vindicate him.

However, while Jesus will triumph in the end, the plot is certainly tragic for some of the characters. By their efforts to save themselves and their positions of power, the authorities undo their role as the tenants of the vineyard and face future judgment. In regard to the disciples, the end of the story leaves their ultimate fate in question. Even for faithful followers of Jesus, the resurrection of Jesus does not easily obliterate the tragedy of his death. And if the disciples do succeed in proclaiming God's rule, they will face their own personal tragedies in the persecution that will result. In a similar way, the tragic or triumphant fate of the hearers, facing the decision whether to follow Jesus faithfully, hangs in the balance.

The plot involves conflict

Conflict is the struggle of forces vying to prevail.[7] Conflict is at the heart of most stories. Without conflict, stories would be only a sequence of events strung together without tension or suspense or struggle on the part of the characters. Conflict reveals the core values and beliefs of a narrative. Of the many approaches to plot we have outlined, we have chosen the analysis of the conflicts as the most helpful way to do a detailed analysis of Mark's overall plot.

Conflict analysis names the overall goal in the narrative and then identifies the forces that help or hinder that goal. The driving goal in Mark's narrative is for God to establish rulership over the world. From this perspective, we can see how different characters further or oppose that goal, and we can see the unexpected ways the goal is met in spite of obstacles and opposition. God's pursuit of this goal through Jesus sets people and groups in conflict with each other. These conflicts serve to reveal the true character of those who oppose the rule of God, those who are faithful to it, and those who fail in their efforts to follow. Also, the opposition and misunderstanding involved in the conflicts provide an opportunity for the protagonist to explain to other characters (and to the audience) the nature and values of the rule of God.

Stories can present several kinds of conflict: conflict with supernatural forces, as in Isabel Allende's *The House of the Spirits*; conflict with nature, as with the old man in Ernest Hemingway's *The Old Man and the Sea*; conflict with society, as in *Beloved* by Toni Morrison; conflict with other individuals, as are the characters in Bernard Malamud's *The Assistant*; or a character may be in conflict with herself as in *The Bell Jar* by Sylvia Plath. It is helpful to sort out the different conflicts of a story, to trace each line of conflict, and to see how the conflicts interrelate.

In Mark's Gospel, the protagonist Jesus is engaged in each of the kinds of conflict listed above: he battles the unclean spirits; he overcomes threatening forces of nature; he confronts the Judean and Gentile authorities; he struggles with the disciples; and he agonizes within himself about his death. These are the primary conflicts. There are also minor conflicts with which we will not deal: John the baptist confronts Herod; Jesus is at odds with his family; and Jesus has brief conflicts with some minor characters, such as the Syrophoenician woman.

We have focused our conflict analysis on three main plotlines: (1) Jesus in conflict with demons, illness, and nature; (2) Jesus in conflict with the authorities; and (3) Jesus in conflict with the disciples.[8] These conflicts are about power—kinds of power, the misuse of power, the limits of power, and the use of power to serve. The three lines of conflict interweave and overlap at significant points, yet each conflict has its own direction, content, ambience, and resolution. Our analysis of each conflict includes a consideration of the origin, escalation, resolution, and consequences of the conflict, how the conflict can be characterized, what the conflicting points of view are, and what is at stake.

Ancient performers of Mark had ways to display effectively the nature of these conflicts and their increasing intensity through the expression of emotions, the portrayal of the characters, the use of the voice in inflection, volume, and pace, as well as the employment of facial expressions and body posture. The impact of the drama on audiences would have been quite powerful.

The Rule of God Initiates the Conflicts

Before we begin the analysis of conflicts, we want to stress that the precipitant of all the conflicts in Mark is the arrival of the rule of God. In Mark's story, God is the active "character" or force who drives the whole plot, for God takes action to bring the "creation that God created" to fulfillment: God prophesied powerful words through Isaiah; God sent John; God ripped apart the heavens and sent the holy spirit upon Jesus; God anointed Jesus to usher in God's rule; and God empowered Jesus and the disciples to do acts of power. It is God who initiates rulership and God who brings forth the fruit of it. And it is God who will establish the divine rulership in power when Jesus returns within a generation.[9]

We can glean God's role from a variety of elements in the narrative: God's words and actions in the story, citations from the writings, the riddles of Jesus, the values promoted by the story, and so on. On the basis of these clues, God's overall role in the story goes like this: God created the world, established a law for the people in the writings, and revealed a plan for the future through the prophets. In the words of the riddle, a vineyard owner (God) established a vineyard (Israel), leased it out to farmers (the Judean authorities), and sent slaves (prophets) to reap the fruit from the vineyard. But the farmers used violence against the slaves to control the vineyard for themselves.

Mark's narrative opens with the lord of the vineyard (God) sending the son (Jesus) to the vineyard, not only to bring forth the fruits of the vineyard for Israel but also to call Israel to its historic role among the Gentile nations. The time is ripe for God to restore creation. What is at stake is not just the fate of Israel but also the fate of all the nations in the imminent culmination of God's rulership over the whole world.

It is God's activity, then, that triggers the action to follow in the narrative. Through the words and actions of God's agent Jesus, God's rule over creation challenges every cosmic power and every human claim to power—both within Israel and from "the Gentile nations," including imperial Rome. There are several key reasons that the rule of God evokes such opposition.

First, the rule of God generates conflict because it initiates a transformation of the cosmic and social orders. As we saw in our analysis of setting, creation is awry: demons dominate people, illnesses make them less than whole, nature threatens to destroy, and humans oppress other humans. The arrival of God's rule means that there is now access to power to restore creation by restoring humans to their proper role in the *natural* order. In addition, God's rule calls for a new *social* order free from the kind of human oppression that characterizes Judean and Roman rulers. So Jesus condemns the authorities for being negligent, destructive, and oppressive. The result is that he has major conflicts with the powers that be.

Also, God's rule initiates conflict because it invades the territory of uncleanness as configured in the culture of Mark's story.[10] In Mark's story, society has created boundaries to guard against contact with those who are unclean. The authorities believe people attain holiness by separation from the people and things that render them unclean—lepers, women's blood, corpses, people with unclean spirits, impure food, and so on. The arrival of God's rule shatters this orientation, because, instead of withdrawing from defilement, God is now actively spreading holiness and wholeness through the power of the holy spirit. Hence, Jesus comes into direct confrontation with the leaders who are guarding the very boundaries that the rule of God seeks to overcome.

In addition, God's rule engenders conflict because God is acting outside the traditional channels of power. From the point of view of the Judean authorities in Mark's story, God works from the established center in Jerusalem. By contrast, for Mark, God's rule begins from the periphery, from the edges. The pardon of sins that took place in the temple now appears in Galilee. The interpretation of the law that emanated from Jerusalem now occurs in the village of Capernaum. The authority of the high priest and the Sanhedrin council is now assumed by a woodworker from Nazareth. The rule of God begins among people of no social consequence—not among the rulers but among the peasants, not with the so-called righteous but with the "sinners." As a result, Jesus comes into conflict with authorities.

In all of this, the rule of God generates conflict because it ruptures the conventional conception of God and creates a new understanding of God. Instead of guarding boundaries, God now crosses boundaries. Instead of remaining in the temple, God breaks out to become available everywhere (signified by the tearing of the curtain). Instead of withdrawing from defilement, God spreads holiness. Instead of working from the center, God works from the margins. God sends an anointed one who does not dominate but who undergoes persecution and death in the service of others. In all of these matters, the authorities are trapped inside the old wineskins of their conventional legal and cultural views, unable to see the new wine in their midst. By judging the new wine by the categories of old wineskins, they destroy the wine—and they also end up destroying the wineskins as well.

Stage 1: The inauguration of the rule of God

In the story world, God's rule comes in two stages. The first stage opens with Jesus proclaiming and enacting the rule of God, and it continues after Jesus' execution and resurrection into the imaginative future of the story world until the second stage arrives, the final establishment of God's rule in power.

In the first stage, Jesus inaugurates in and around Galilee the rule of God with its abundant blessings and joys. Jesus gathers disciples and establishes family-like relationships among all who respond—regardless of status, gender, state of purity, and even nationality.[11] Jesus heals people of their ailments, exorcises unclean spirits, welcomes tax collectors and sinners, and feeds people even in the desert. For the common people of Mark's story, whose subsistence is marginal and often threatened, provisions of heath and food are good news indeed!

This first stage proclaims and demonstrates the rule of God so that people have the opportunity to respond to God's rule before it is finally established. Jesus and his followers sow the seeds of God's rule, and people reveal by their responses whether they belong to the rule of God. During this period, the joys and blessings of God's rule are abundantly real for those who turn and show solidarity with God's rule. But, given the opposition depicted in Mark's story, it is also clear that the rule of God has not yet come in full power and glory. Two features stand out: the rule of God comes in hidden ways, and it comes with limited power.

First, the rule of God is hidden.[12] It does not come with unambiguous signs from heaven, but in unexpected places and outside traditional channels. Jesus preserves the hiddenness of God's rule by talking in riddles and refusing to give signs on demand. Characters must discern the rule of God for themselves. Some are blind. Others, to whom the mystery of the rule of God has been given, perceive that the exorcisms and the healings disclose that God is already beginning to rule over the world.

Also contributing to the hiddenness of God's rule is that Jesus does not announce his identity, nor does he allow others to announce it. When the demons blurt it out, he orders them to keep quiet. When the disciples realize he is the anointed one, he orders them to tell no one. When he finally reveals his identity at the trial before the high priest, the hiddenness of God's rule remains, for the truth of Jesus' claim is still hidden to those who do not have eyes to see.[13] Furthermore, Jesus invites followers to live a life whose meaning and greatness will be hidden to the world until the end comes. For it is not apparent to most people in Mark's story world that Jesus and his followers, who are persecuted and put to death, are the agents of God's rule.

Second, in this first stage of God's rule, power is limited. To be sure, Jesus and his followers have access to God's power over all nonhuman forces—demons, nature, and illness. In these conflicts, God's agents are clearly victors. However, the power of God's rule is limited, because God does not grant Jesus and his followers the authority to force God's rule on other humans. God's rule is such that people are to use power to serve others, not to dominate or oppress them.

This situation of limited power and authority places the agents of the rule of God in jeopardy. Because God's rule challenges all other claims to authority, conflicts ensue between those who choose to accept it as good news and those who oppose it, especially the Judean and Roman authorities. And while Jesus and his followers have authority to denounce human oppression, they do not have authority to stop the oppressors by force. Otherwise, God's agents would themselves be guilty of lording over others. Thus, by confronting and denouncing oppressors and by doing so in commonality with the vulnerable and oppressed, God's agents invite reprisals on themselves and become victims of the very oppression they oppose. In this conflict, Jesus and his followers appear to be the losers.

In the future of the story world, the first stage of God's rule lasts beyond Jesus' execution and resurrection as the disciples and others carry on the work of proclaiming to Israel and the nations.

Stage 2: The culmination of the rule of God

About halfway through the story, Jesus begins to tell about the final establishment of the rule of God. From this point on in the narrative, the imminence of this second stage of the rule of God casts a shadow over subsequent events. In the future of the story world, the complete establishment of God's rule is to take place before Jesus' generation passes away (before all those living have died). Then there will no longer be an opportunity to turn around, for judgment will come.

At its culmination, the rule of God will no longer be hidden. It will be revealed "in glory." Everyone will behold the son of humanity coming on clouds to gather the chosen ones. Also, the rule of God will no longer be limited in power. It will now come in power also over humans and all creation. God will openly and finally resolve all conflicts, for God will establish God's rule "in power."

The final resolution of God's rule will involve a surprising reversal. Those who were great in the eyes of the world, who lorded over others, the wealthy and the powerful authorities in Israel and in Rome, will be the least and condemned. By contrast, those who gave their lives as servants to others for Jesus and God's rule will be greatest. In Mark's projection of the future, God's agent to rule will be Jesus. In the imaginative future of the story world, this reversal will be foreshadowed during the generation between Jesus' death and the end: Jesus will be raised, the temple will be destroyed, and the vineyard will be given to others.

In summary, God's rule over demons, angels, nature, and people comes first in hiddenness and limited power. This rule demands ultimate allegiance and generates conflicts with those who resist or oppose. The imminent establishment of the second stage of God's rule in power within a generation gives urgency and intensity to these conflicts during the first stage, because at that future point, God will resolve all conflicts by judgment and salvation. The story world will not last beyond the conclusion of that generation before this end occurs. It is within this larger framework of God's rule that we can now examine the three lines of conflict at center stage.

Jesus in Conflict with Cosmic Forces

As agent of God, Jesus has power over nonhuman forces that threaten and oppress people—Satan, demons, illness, and nature.

Immediately after Jesus becomes God's son, the spirit drives him out to the desert to undergo testing by Satan. The depiction of Jesus enduring the forty days, being with angels, and emerging to proclaim the rule of God suggests that Jesus is the victor in this direct encounter with Satan, a conclusion supported by Jesus' subsequent authority over unclean spirits.

We do not limit the significance of the victory over Satan to Jesus' authority over demons. Satan is the "lord of the house," and his influence extends across the creation. Demons possess people and try to destroy them and seek to gain power over Jesus. Mark uses some of the language of exorcism when he depicts Jesus cleansing a leper and calming a storm. Satan comes and takes away the seeds of the good news that fall on those beside the way. Characters can act—even unaware—as agents of Satan. The authorities behave like Satan when they test Jesus and seek to destroy him. Jesus calls Peter "Satan" when he seeks to block Jesus' path to rejection and execution. The confrontation between God's agent and Satan in the desert lies in the background of all events. Knowing that this larger cosmic struggle has been won by God's agent, who overcame the power of Satan and who successfully resisted the tests of Satan, assures the audience that God will ultimately prevail in establishing rulership over all creation. And each time Jesus and the disciples exorcise demons, the audience is reminded of this assurance.

The victory over Satan is directly connected to Jesus' exorcisms. In the desert with Satan, as Jesus later explains in a riddle, he "binds the strong one," and then he can "plunder Satan's goods" by exorcising demons. Thus the resolution of the conflict with Satan occurs in the testing at the beginning of the story. While there are escalations within specific episodes of exorcism, there is no developing conflict with demons across the story. Subsequent exorcisms are simply a consequence of the initial resolution, a mopping-up operation. Thus in Mark's depiction, Satan is not the last enemy to be defeated but the first. By binding Satan in the desert, Jesus breaks the stranglehold of Satan over the world. By liberating a demoniac who is possessed by a "Legion" of demons, Jesus foreshadows the outcome of the conflict with Roman authorities who "occupy" Israel and the Gentile nations. Jesus also grants authority over demons to those who follow him. By quelling demons, Jesus demonstrates that God's rule over the world "has arrived" and that it will prevail.

Jesus convincingly demonstrates his power over demons—the demoniac in the synagogue at Capernaum, the man possessed of "Legion," the daughter of the Syrophoenician woman, the boy with the deaf and mute spirit, along with others recounted in summary statements. The conflicts between Jesus and the demons are hostile, filled with anger and fear. It is a confrontation of naked power—the "holy" spirit within Jesus is in conflict with the "unclean" spirits that are possessing the demoniacs. The goal of Satan and the unclean spirits is to survive by dominating and destroying people. Having bound Satan, Jesus' goal is to destroy the unclean spirits in order to liberate people.

This conflict with unclean spirits involves displays of power that are dramatic and violent, loud and emotionally wrenching. The demons are powerful forces that seek to destroy those whom they possess. The demons throw down those they possess, convulse them, cause foaming at the mouth, cast them into fire and water, or lead them to scream and slash themselves with stones. The demons seek also to get power over Jesus by naming him as "the holy one of God" and "son of the most high God." The demons embody in an extreme way the nature of evil controlling Mark's human characters—afraid, dominating others, trying to save themselves, and willing to be destructive in order to survive.

The contest is clearly one-sided. As "the stronger one" empowered by the holy spirit, Jesus is far more powerful than the demons. The demons recognize who Jesus is, and they are terrified of him. The unclean spirit in Capernaum screams at Jesus, "Did you come to destroy us?" Later, the "Legion" pleads with Jesus, "Don't torment me." Jesus rebukes the demons, driving them out with commands that they immediately obey. Jesus must sometimes elicit information about the unclean spirit in order to effect the exorcism, but there is no question what the outcome will be.

Jesus has similar power over illnesses and disabilities—other nonhuman forces that oppress and diminish people. In the culture, such illnesses and disabilities were generally understood to be the consequence of sin, one's own or one's ancestors. In Mark's narrative, it is God's will that these be overcome. So Jesus removes leprosy, heals illnesses, cures afflictions, reverses paralysis, and restores sight, hearing, and a withered hand. As with the exorcisms, Jesus gives commands to or touches the ill person, and the response is immediate. In one case, Jesus pardons the sins that caused the paralysis. In another case, Jesus makes the maladies "go away from" the supplicant, much as he dispels demons. And Jesus authorizes his disciples to heal.

Also, as another aspect of restoring creation, Jesus has authority over nature as a nonhuman force that can destroy or deprive people. Jesus commands the wind and calms the storm, walks on the sea, twice multiplies bread and fish for hungry people in the desert, and causes a fig tree to wither to the roots. In each case, Jesus is responding to a threat from nature or a failure of nature to provide the resources to meet human needs. Jesus expects his disciples to exercise the same authority over nature.

The exorcisms, healings, and works of power over nature occur mostly during Jesus' activity in Galilee. As Jesus moves to Jerusalem, these acts of power become rare, and they function mainly as commentary on the action. On the journey to Jerusalem, Jesus does only two healings (of blind men), events that serve in the story as foils for the disciples' failure to "see" what Jesus is teaching them. On the journey, he does only one exorcism, which illustrates the disciples' lack of faith. In Jerusalem, Jesus performs no works of power except for cursing the fruitless fig tree, which parallels his attack on the temple for the failure of Israel's leaders to produce fruit in God's vineyard. In the first half of Mark, conflicts with nonhuman forces predominate; in the second half, conflicts with people predominate.

Thus the Markan Jesus clearly has authority over nature, demons, and illness. By contrast, difficulties arise in the conflicts with people, for Jesus has no authority to control people. He cannot exorcise or heal when that act depends on someone's faith in God's power and no such faith is present. When people at Nazareth do not have faith, Jesus is not able to heal many. And he is powerless to make people have faith. Jesus has no authority to "lord over" people; he cannot make someone do what he wants them to do. He can order people to be quiet, but he cannot make them obey (as he can the demons). Thus, because of the limitations on his power, Jesus' conflicts with people are more difficult and more evenly matched than those waged directly with demonic forces and with nature.

Jesus in Conflict with the Authorities

The conflicts between Jesus and the authorities are dramatic and hostile, characterized by deception and clever repartee. Jesus initiates the conflict by his actions and words, and the authorities oppose him, whereupon he defends and counterattacks. In Mark's story, this is a conflict between living on God's terms and living on human terms.

What is at stake is the establishment of God's rule in Israel and ultimately the world. On the one side is Jesus' calling for a radical renewal of Israel at the national as well as the individual level in submission to the rule of God—in ways that the authorities consider illegal. On the other side are the Judean leaders of the nation and the guardians of tradition who have authority and legal power both in Jerusalem and in the countryside. They are dedicated to protecting God's laws, guarding holiness, and maintaining their positions in society and with the Romans. Behind them stands the power of the Roman agents, Herod in Galilee and the procurator Pilate in Judea—with the authority to carry out executions. And behind them stands the imperial powers of Rome, who authorize Herod and Pilate, who require tribute, who keep a military presence of soldiers to carry out executions and to quell riots, and who "rule over the Gentile nations." The conflicts between Jesus and the authorities are public, and the authorities act to defend their honor before the people.

This conflict is life-threatening, because the fate of Jesus—and the fate of the authorities—is in the balance. Jesus is superior in debate and cleverly evades their efforts to indict him, and through most of the story he has the populace on his side. As Jesus escalates the conflict by going to Jerusalem and attacking the temple, so also the opposition broadens and their strategies escalate. Jesus is at a disadvantage because he has no authority to dominate people, while the opposition will use force in order to prevail. The suspense builds as to when and how the authorities will destroy Jesus and what it will mean. And the resolution, when it comes, is ironic.

The development of the conflict in the plot

With a mandate to usher in the new order of the rule of God, Jesus initiates a movement with the people, seen as a threat by the political authorities. He establishes an alternative center of authority by choosing twelve disciples—"twelve" representing metaphorically the whole of Israel (the twelve tribes). He assumes authority to interpret laws, abolish traditions, pardon sins, cross purity boundaries, and declare how the temple should be run. Here we trace the plot through the geography of Jesus' journey.

Galilee. Tension and suspense are especially clear in the opening five clashes between Jesus and the authorities in Galilee—the episodes told in a concentric pattern. In the conflicts, the fundamental issue is: Who has authority to speak and act on behalf of God? The leaders are the traditional authorities in Israel with the responsibility to interpret the law, guard the traditions, and deal with the nation's sins through the temple system. By contrast, as agent of God's rule, Jesus assumes God wants the people healed and freed from demons. Jesus tells the authorities that they should judge the new reality of God's rule (fresh wine) by new standards (new wineskins), but instead the authorities question and accuse him.

In these five conflicts in Galilee, the opposition against Jesus widens. One by one, a new group is introduced into association with an already established group of opponents: first the local legal experts, then the legal experts of the Pharisees, then the Pharisees, then the Pharisees with the Herodians. Also, their efforts to get Jesus intensify: First the opponents accuse Jesus in thought only; then they question the disciples about Jesus' actions; next they query Jesus directly about an offense against a custom; after that they ask Jesus about the illegal behavior of the disciples; then they watch Jesus in order to get charges against him for illegal behavior; and finally they go off and plot to destroy him. By the end of the five conflict episodes, when the authorities begin plotting against Jesus, the sides are clearly established.

During the remainder of Jesus' activity in Galilee, the polarization of the two sides solidifies, and the opposition expands to include legal experts from Jerusalem, Herod, and Pharisees from Jerusalem. The authorities from Jerusalem slander Jesus by claiming that he acts by authority of the ruler of demons. In turn, Jesus counters that they have committed an unpardonable sin in judging the holy spirit to be an unclean spirit. Later, the authorities accuse him of not following the tradition of the elders and seek to discredit him as a prophet by asking him for a sign of his authority. In turn, Jesus calls the Pharisees "hypocrites" and rails against the harm their teaching does to people. The execution of John by Herod and the threat to Jesus (Herod thinks Jesus is John resurrected) only increase the suspense.

The journey to Jerusalem. During this stage, there is little direct conflict between Jesus and the authorities. Nevertheless, Jesus anticipates the impending clash with authorities in Jerusalem, prophesying that he will be condemned and executed by the high priests, the legal experts, the elders, and the Gentiles—all the Jerusalem opponents who will be arrayed against him. Only once on the journey do authorities actually figure in the action: when Jesus returns to John's former territory around the Jordan, the Pharisees try to maneuver him into making the same statement about divorce and re-marriage that resulted in John's death by Herod.

Jerusalem. The climactic confrontation in Jerusalem comes quickly. Jesus attacks and briefly occupies the temple, violently upending the tables and chairs used for buying and selling, driving the merchants out, and citing the writings in defense of his action. As a reaction to this, the national authorities are determined to get him. First they want to destroy him; next they look for a way to seize him; and then they plan a deception. At this point, the issue is: How will they finally get him?

Meanwhile, Jesus and the authorities engage in debate. The high priests, legal experts, and elders try to trick him into a (for them blasphemous) claim that he is acting on God's authority. When that ploy fails, they send Pharisees and

Herodians to catch him in his words. Then come the Sadducees. Nevertheless, Jesus prevails in debate with the authorities, humiliates them before the crowds, and exposes their hypocrisy. In these debates, Jesus cites scriptural authority for his actions, tells riddles against them, quotes Scripture to condemn them, outdoes them with his knowledge and interpretation of the law, verbally attacks the scribes who exploit widows, and prophesies judgment on them.

In these debates, Jesus publicly challenges the honor of the authorities. He even suggests that they do not know the writings of Scripture, saying, "Haven't you read in the scroll from Moses . . . ?" The authorities in turn try to trap him. They accuse and threaten Jesus in order to humiliate him in public. Each time, his successful riposte further challenges their honor. Frustrated by Jesus' cleverness and the crowd's support of him, the authorities give up on public debate and turn to clandestine efforts to seize him.

So they arrest him at night, and marshal evidence at a trial. At Jesus' trial, the authorities organize false witnesses to convict Jesus of pronouncements against the temple. When the authorities cannot get credible evidence against him, the high priest tries to elicit a confession, whereupon Jesus acknowledges that he is the anointed one. They then sentence him to death.

After that, the conflict is over, and consequences follow quickly: the Judean leaders ridicule Jesus and hand him over to Pilate for execution. When Pilate wavers, the high priests stir up the crowd to call for Jesus' execution. Pilate caves in to the crowd and hands Jesus over for mocking by the soldiers and execution. In turn, the Judean authorities continue to ridicule him, as the Gentile authorities carry out the sentence of death.

From near the beginning, the authorities sought to have Jesus put to death. The first accusation against Jesus, which is articulated only in the mind of the opponents, is the charge of blasphemy—the very charge upon which the authorities finally condemn him to death! His adroit avoidance of such serious charges throughout the story contributes significantly to the suspense. Thus, although Jesus is under constant threat throughout the story, he nevertheless succeeds in evading incriminating charges until he has completed his work. At the trial, in response to a question addressed to him by the high priest, Jesus himself volunteers the evidence they need. Thus, in a sense, Jesus is in control, even determining when his opponents get their indictment.

While the conflict with Judean authorities is center stage, as we have seen, the imperial authorities also come to the forefront. It is the Roman authorities alone in Judea who have the authorization to carry out executions. As such, the imperial representatives are present and active—Pilate and the Roman soldiers. Pilate sarcastically asks Jesus if he is "king of the Judeans." When Jesus responds with the words, "You say so," there is an ironic way in which a Roman is acknowledging the truth, because Jesus' words imply that Pilate has said Jesus really is "king of the Judeans." Subsequently, the Roman representatives reveal their oppressive nature. Pilate acquiesces to the chants of the crowd to have Jesus crucified. Then Pilate has Jesus flogged and turns him over to the soldiers for execution. The soldiers hit, spit on, and mock him as "king of the Judeans." This irony is reinforced when Pilate puts the title "king of the Judeans" above the cross. Little do they know that he really is the king of the Judeans. And, more than that, he is God's agent to sit on God's right hand over the nations in the final establishment of God's rule.

The authorities' side of the conflict: Defending God's law

We can assess the point of view of the authorities in Mark's story only if we keep in mind that the authorities do not know that Jesus is the son of God. They have had no access to the private vision at his baptism, his confrontation with Satan, or his private teachings. We can base our evaluation of the authorities in the story only on what they observe of Jesus or apparently hear about him. In this light, the Markan authorities can be viewed sympathetically in terms of the culture of the time.

From their point of view, Jesus is an impious lawbreaker who dares to claim his actions are God's will. The authorities see Jesus assuming God's prerogative when he pardons sins. Such a violation of divine prerogative is blasphemy, a charge punishable by death. Similarly, the authorities view his disciples' plucking of grain and Jesus' healing on the sabbath as work, which is forbidden on the sabbath in Israelite law. As guardians of purity, the authorities also disapprove of Jesus' eating with "tax collectors and sinners," as well as other violations of purity. Not surprisingly, from their perspective, Jesus' behavior and claim to authority appear to be demonic.

For the authorities in Jerusalem, Jesus' attack on the temple is especially flagrant. The buying and selling in the temple were services for pilgrims, providing unblemished animals for sacrifice and exchanging unclean coinage for sacred temple money. Further, they fear that Jesus' action will cause a "riot among the people"—and by implication bring on Roman reprisals. From their point of view, they have more than enough reason to arrest him for his dangerous behavior. At the trial, Jesus adds insult to injury: he responds to the high priest's question about whether he is the anointed one, the son of the Blessed One, with the words "I am," a claim to divine prerogative. He further claims that, as son of humanity, he will sit at God's right hand and that the authorities will be judged. From the perspective of the Sanhedrin council, this is indeed shocking blasphemy deserving of death. That *this* person, who has said and done these things, should claim to be the anointed one of God, is from the authorities' point of view extremely offensive.

The authorities have official law and tradition on their side. Nevertheless, the narrator has guided the readers to side with Jesus against the prevailing norms of the culture depicted in the story and to view the authorities as living on human terms—seeking greatness, saving themselves, and lording over others.

Jesus' side of the conflict: Message and evasion

The dilemma for Jesus is this: how can he inaugurate God's rule—which involves violations of prevailing legal interpretations and contraventions of prevailing cultural standards—while at the same time evading the efforts of the authorities to trap him? With no authority from God to force his proclamation on anyone, either by ordinary or extraordinary means, he must use his wits to usher in the rule of God, challenge the authorities for failing to live on God's terms, and—at the same time—avoid their efforts to indict and condemn him.

Jesus avoids indictment by several means. For example, rather than repeat the "blasphemous" words of pardon to the paralytic, Jesus asks the authorities if it is easier to forgive or to heal, and he proceeds implicitly to forgive the paralytic with words of healing that are not open to the charge of blasphemy. Later, when the authorities watch him in order to charge him with doing healing work on the sabbath, he proceeds to heal simply by commanding the man to stretch out his hand—not by touching the man, which would be considered work! Sometimes he makes it difficult for the authorities to trap him in his speech, by referring to himself indirectly as the son of humanity rather than directly claiming authority over sin and the sabbath.

Furthermore, he talks in riddles, for example, telling a parable of the lord of a vineyard who sent his son, which everyone recognized was told against the authorities but which the authorities could not use against him. At other times, he gives an ambiguous answer or throws a question back at the authorities to prevent them from "catching him in his words." Also, he quotes the Scriptures to justify his actions, for example, by referring to David eating bread from the temple or by quoting a prophet regarding the purpose of the temple, thus making it harder for the authorities to hold him accountable.

Thus, in spite of the efforts of the authorities to get Jesus, he eludes them until he is ready to answer the question of the high priest. Despite the threats, Jesus proclaims and carries out the activities of the rule of God. In fact, the conflicts actually become opportunities for Jesus to explain how he differs from the authorities, to counterattack, and to condemn them for their failure to live on God's terms and for their opposition to God's rule.

The resolution of the conflict

Within the narrated events of Mark's story, the narrator resolves the conflict between Jesus and the authorities when the Judean authorities condemn Jesus to death and Pilate executes him. The immediate consequences are that the Judean and Roman authorities have removed the threat to the social order posed by Jesus and his followers and have secured their positions of authority and honor by their public shaming of Jesus.

However, this immediate resolution is ironic. The authorities think they have eliminated Jesus, but the opposite situation prevails. In Mark's narrative world, they have revealed themselves to be false authorities—envious, destructive, and blind to the way in which God rules in the world. It is they who have been on trial and are here condemned. By condemning and executing God's son, the real authority in Israel, they have rejected God, who sent him, and thereby sealed their own doom.

This irony is, of course, hidden from the authorities, but it is not hidden from the audience. Discerning hearers can see that the apparent resolution will soon be reversed. The subsequent resurrection establishes the reversal, and Jesus' impending coming on the clouds of heaven will confirm it for all to see. This final reversal will occur in the imminent future of the story world, within a generation: Jesus will be established in power and will receive honor from God, while the authorities—Judean and Roman alike—will be shamed and condemned.

Jesus in Conflict with the Disciples

Jesus' conflict with the disciples is of a very different kind from that with the authorities. One is a conflict with the powers that be, the other a conflict with his followers. There Jesus is in conflict with outsiders who want to destroy him; here Jesus is in conflict with insiders who struggle to be faithful to him. The authorities defend their honor in public, while the disciples compete among themselves for honor in private. The conflict with the authorities is defined by winning or losing, while the conflict with the disciples is characterized by their alternating success and failure. However, both conflicts deal with the choice of whether to live on God's terms or human terms.

Jesus creates the circumstances for the conflict with the disciples by calling them to follow him. Jesus' goal is to make disciples who will imitate him in helping to inaugurate the rule of God in Israel and then among "all the Gentile nations." The disciples' goal is to fulfill Jesus' mandates for them *and* to gain glory and power from following Jesus. Thus this is also a conflict within the disciples themselves—whether they will follow Jesus all the way or embrace the safe, self-serving, face-saving values of the culture. At stake in this conflict are these questions: Will they become faithful disciples and proclaim the rule of God after Jesus' death and resurrection? And what will be their fate in the rule of God?

Jesus' conflict with the disciples is not a conflict of unrelieved opposition, like the conflict between Jesus and the authorities, for the disciples are sometimes faithful and sometimes not. Furthermore, while the narrator leads the audience to align both with Jesus and with the disciples, this alignment is complex. On the one hand, the hearers align with Jesus and the values of the rule of God and therefore judge the disciples for their failures. On the other hand, the hearers identify with the disciples and their very human struggle to follow Jesus, for the situation of the audience is similar to that of the disciples. Finally, there is a partial resolution of this conflict, even though much is left unresolved.

The development of the conflict in the plot

There is suspense in the conflict with the disciples, for the audience does not know whether the disciples will succeed. Nevertheless, there are developments to this conflict, because the disciples do make several breakthroughs—and then they fail again in similar or different ways. The progressive stages of this conflict between Jesus and the disciples are usually marked by a series of three similar episodes.

Galilee. In the first part of the story, the disciples seem to succeed effortlessly. In a series of three episodes, Jesus makes them fishers for people: First he calls four fishermen; later he appoints twelve to be with him; and still later, he sends them out to proclaim and to heal.[14] This first stage establishes the disciples as on Jesus' side, as belonging to the rule of God. Nonetheless, there soon are indications that the disciples have trouble following Jesus. They do not understand his riddle about sowing seed in the rule of God. Even after Jesus explains the riddles privately for the disciples, their subsequent behavior and later misunderstandings suggest they have not understood.

In the series of three boat scenes and three bread scenes, the disciples show that they have neither faith nor understanding. In the boat, Jesus expects them to have faith during the storm at sea. When they do not, he calms the storm himself. And they learn nothing from his action, for when they have a chance to deal later with the wind on their own, they only struggle at the oars. Jesus expects them to have faith to feed a crowd in the desert, and he even shows them by having them distribute the food. Later he gives them another chance to supply food for a crowd in the desert, but they are incredulous at the idea, as if they had not witnessed the first feeding. Both the lack of faith and the failure in understanding come to a head in a scene that is a climax both to the boat series and to the bread series. In this scene, the disciples worry about having only one loaf; and Jesus realizes their blindness. He becomes impatient and asks them a series of questions about the two earlier feedings. The disciples' minds are hardened, and they are dangerously close to being like the authorities. They do not trust God's power in this age. And they do not recognize "the mystery about the rule of God" being established throughout creation.

The journey to Jerusalem. Halfway through the story, the disciples have a breakthrough and recognize that Jesus is the anointed one. This resolution leads immediately, however, to further conflict at a different level when Jesus predicts his execution and resurrection. Rock rejects Jesus' statement, for the death of the anointed one is intolerable to him. Jesus then calls him "Satan" and tells him that he is not thinking in God's terms. At this point, Jesus announces a new standard for discipleship: those who want to follow him are to renounce self, take up their cross, and risk losing their lives for the good news.

On the journey, this conflict between Jesus and the disciples is expressed through a series of three prophecies Jesus makes about his death and resurrection. After each prophecy, the disciples react in such a way as to show that they are still thinking in human terms—Rock rebukes Jesus, the disciples argue about who is the greatest disciple, and James and John ask for positions of power in the age to come. The disciples are still seeking power rather than coming to understand that being least—and perhaps even facing death—is the lot of those who live out the values of God's rule in this age.

On the way to Jerusalem, the disciples mirror the oppressive behavior of the authorities: they exclude someone exorcising in Jesus' name; they rebuke children; they are shocked that a wealthy man who has kept the commandments might not inherit eternal life; and they compete for positions of honor and power. In turn, Jesus warns the disciples to cut off limbs if necessary to avoid offending little ones who have faith; he gets angry; he suggests that they might not enter the rule of God; and he warns that in the coming age they might be least.

This stage of the conflict involves a clash between the values of the rule of God and thinking in human terms. The disciples embrace some of the values of the society. But Jesus turns those values upside down with paradoxical statements: if they truly want to save their lives, they will risk their lives in service to the good news; and if they want to be most important, they will be servants of all and lord over no one—even at the cost of persecution by the authorities of this age.

The issue is: Will the disciples understand what it means to live on God's terms and come to accept the consequences, both for Jesus and for themselves? By the end of the journey, this issue is resolved, for James and John indicate that they are willing to undergo persecution, and in Jerusalem the disciples speak of their determination to die with Jesus.

Jerusalem. On the Mountain of the Olives, Jesus gives a lengthy prophecy to four disciples, forewarning them of conflicts and persecutions that lie ahead. He announces his impending absence, warns them not to be led astray, and admonishes them to stay alert.

However, after the Passover supper, Jesus tells the disciples that they will not remain faithful: "You will all stumble, because it is written, 'I will strike the shepherd, and the sheep will be scattered.'" They protest to the contrary, but their subsequent actions betray them. Again, their failure is expressed in two separate series of three episodes. Three times the disciples fall asleep and fail to keep watch. Three times Jesus returns from prayer to find them sleeping. Then Judas, one of the twelve, leads a crowd to arrest Jesus, and the disciples all flee. Rock renounces Jesus three times, and then Rock too flees, sobbing. This is the last time the disciples appear in the story.

The disciples' side of the conflict: Overwhelmed by the rule of God

From the beginning, the Markan disciples do not know that Jesus is the anointed one—and Jesus does not tell them! Nor do they have the advantage of knowing anything about Jesus' baptism, the voice from heaven, or Jesus' confrontation with Satan in the desert. Nevertheless, when Jesus calls them, they leave everything and follow him. Later, without any provisions, they go out to heal and exorcise and to call people to turn around. Despite obstacles, they stay with Jesus. Even so, the unbelievable power and possibilities of the rule of God exceed their comprehension. What the rule of God presents to them is far beyond and far different from what they expected.

For example, Jesus expects the disciples to understand the riddles, calm a storm, and provide food in the desert. Yet the riddles about the rule of God confuse them, and they do not understand. Naturally, they think the fierce storm on the Sea of Galilee might destroy them, and they do not believe they can feed huge crowds with only a few loaves and fish. The disciples' responses to Jesus' expectations reveal their understandable incredulity at Jesus' power: "So who is this that even the wind and the sea obey him?" "You're looking at the crowd pressing you, and you say, 'Who touched me?'" "Are we to go off and buy two hundred denarii worth of bread and give it to them to eat?" "How will anyone be able to satisfy these people with bread here in a desert?"

Gradually, the disciples do come to grasp that Jesus is the anointed one. Sharing cultural expectations of the time, the Markan disciples expect the anointed one to come in power and glory to restore all things in Israel. As characters in the story, the disciples naturally assume they will benefit from their association with Jesus. Having left everything for the rule of God and now being in Jesus' inner circle, they expect prosperity, importance, and positions of power as Jesus establishes God's rule in Israel. Now, however, Jesus tells them—for the first time—that he will be rejected, killed, and rise, and that they too must renounce themselves and risk persecution. Unsurprisingly, the disciples resist these new and unforeseen expectations with rebukes, arguments, silence, and expressions of shock.

Nevertheless, in spite of these difficulties, the disciples continue to follow. And when Rock reminds Jesus how they have left everything to follow him, they are finally told—for the first time—of a reward. In this age, they are to receive a hundred times as many family members (but no fathers) and many houses and fields (most likely referring to the many families and houses they share from hospitality on their travels from village to village)—along with "persecutions." In the coming age, they are to receive "life eternal."

The disciples come to accept the idea of facing persecution and death, and they follow Jesus to Jerusalem. When Jesus prophesies to them on the Mountain of the Olives about the persecutions that will happen to them after his execution, they become even more committed to following him faithfully. So on the way to Gethsemane when Jesus says they will all fall away, they refuse to believe it. Rock says, "Even if it's necessary for me to die with you, I'll definitely not renounce you." And the narrator adds, "And they were all saying the same thing." By means of a change in the typical Markan pattern of dialogue between Jesus and the disciples, the disciples have the last word in this episode rather than Jesus. This last word of commitment emphasizes the disciples' determination to face execution with Jesus.

Yet when they are put to the test, they are overcome by fear—from the crowd sent by the high priests, the swords and clubs, and the arrest of Jesus. So, to save themselves, they flee. Even so, Rock follows from a distance and then bravely sits with the soldiers in the firelight. However, when he is directly accused by bystanders, he denies any knowledge of Jesus, and he too escapes. Rock's weeping shows how much he (and all the disciples) wanted to follow, whatever the cost, but when face-to-face with the real possibility of crucifixion, they did not follow through.

In the conflict with Jesus, the disciples go through a revolution in their lives—leaving family and possessions, giving up their own hopes for glory and power, and relinquishing the cultural values to become least and servant. Yet the events swirling around Jesus are overwhelming, and, although they stay with him to Gethsemane, the threat of arrest and execution is just too much, and they flee.

Jesus' side of the conflict: Making faithful disciples

Jesus successfully calls disciples to follow him, and he sends them out in pairs to assist him in his work of proclaiming and healing. But just as he has no power over the responses of the authorities, so also Jesus has no power to make the disciples understand or have faith.

Because they have left all to follow him, Jesus expects that the disciples have the secret about the rule of God and that they will therefore understand. He is surprised and disappointed by their failures. His impatience is expressed in double rhetorical questions: "You don't understand this riddle? And how will you get the other riddles?" Because they have seen his works of power, Jesus expects that the disciples will have faith in the power of God's rule available to them in the present. Again he is disappointed and responds with questions: "Why are you such cowards? Don't you have faith yet?" "Why are you discussing that you don't have bread? Don't you understand or comprehend yet? Are your minds hardened?"

Once the disciples grasp that he is the anointed one, Jesus has to prepare them for persecution. He struggles to get them to see that he is on a mission to serve and to oppose domination in the quest to usher in God's rule. Unless they understand what God wants—not seeking glory but being least, not lording over but serving, and not seeking security for oneself or maintaining one's privileges but being willing to lose one's life in confrontation with those who dominate—they will not understand Jesus or the rule of God. And he challenges them to do these things not as ways to get honor and power in the future but simply because this is the nature of God's rule.

Further, he has to get them to see that if they are to be faithful to the mission of the rule of God, they too will have to be prepared for rejections and persecution. Given the way the world is, persecution will be the lot of those who follow God's rule in this age. So, to remain faithful, they must be prepared for death. As John the baptizer was handed over, as Jesus is to be handed over, so also will the disciples be handed over. In the face of their resistance, Jesus gets angry and impatient. When the disciples cannot exorcise a demon, he says in exasperation: "O faithless generation! How long am I to be with you? How long am I to put up with you?"

Jesus continues to prepare the disciples for what lies ahead. In Jerusalem, he gives a lengthy prophecy to them about what will happen after his crucifixion and resurrection. He warns them about opposition, hatred, persecutions, and temptations that will come to them in the course of proclaiming the rule of God to all the Gentile nations. Before Gethsemane, Jesus warns them that they will scatter at his arrest. At Gethsemane, he is dismayed by their failure to stay awake. He asks: "Simon, are you sleeping? Weren't you strong enough to watch a single hour?" His last words to them are a futile admonition for them to go with him to face the betrayer and the crowd that comes to arrest him.

The resolution of the conflict

Within the plotted events of the narrative, the resolution of this conflict is negative. The disciples are not prepared to lose their lives. In the face of persecution and death, they flee and renounce. At the same time, the conflict within the disciples is also resolved negatively. They want to be loyal to Jesus, but they are unable to do so. When loyalty to Jesus brings them face-to-face with the possibility of execution, their instincts to save themselves are too strong. Yet Rock's remorse is shown sympathetically in his weeping.

The question remains: Will the disciples learn from this failure and follow Jesus faithfully in the period after the resurrection and before his return in glory? This issue is not resolved within the plotted narrative; the narrator leaves the fate of the disciples in the future of the story world undetermined.

The possibility of restoration is there. Jesus has told the disciples that he will go ahead of them to Galilee. And the young man at the grave says to the women:

"Go tell his disciples, even Rock, 'He's going ahead of you to Galilee. There you will behold him just as he told you.'" Everything about this statement suggests the possibility of restoration. Simon is again called Rock, his discipleship name (Jesus addressed him as Simon at Gethsemane!). Jesus is still "going ahead," and they are to follow.

Then the women at the grave in their turn flee in fear and say nothing to anyone at all. Like the disciples earlier in the narrative, they are unable to grasp and trust the power of God, now the power shown in the resurrection of Jesus.

Thus the narrator leaves open whether or not the disciples are restored. The pattern of fulfillment of prophecy throughout the narrative suggests that the prophecy of a reunion of Jesus and the disciples in Galilee will be fulfilled. Also, some earlier prophecies suggest that the disciples will be restored and become faithful followers in the future. For example, Jesus prophesies that James and John will drink the cup that he drinks, and he gives lengthy instructions for the disciples to follow in facing opposition after his death. However, other statements suggest that the disciples may not succeed, such as Jesus' saying, "For all who are ashamed of me and my words in this adulterous and sinful generation, also the son of humanity will be ashamed of them when he comes in the glory of his Father with the holy angels" and "whoever endures to the end will be saved"—with the implication that some may not endure.

On hearing the story a second time, the audience will find many suggestions that the disciples might be restored and at the same time many suggestions that they might not finally make it into the rule of God or that they will be in the rule of God but among the least. The ultimate fate of the disciples is to be decided in the unplotted future of the story world.

In any case, the narrator does make it clear that soon all would come to light. In the future of the story world, the son of humanity will return within the generation, at which time the fate of all in the rule of God, including the disciples, will be decided. That is, all conflicts in the story are projected to be resolved finally when the rule of God is established in power and the new age has fully arrived.

Conclusion

What do the conflicts reveal about the world of this story? The plot shows that the rule of God has arrived and opened up incredible new possibilities for human existence. The plot also demonstrates that the rule of God is difficult to discern and even harder to follow. God's rule subverts prevailing legal interpretations, cultural norms, and political realities. Some characters, like the authorities, will not see the rule of God at all. Others, like the disciples, will catch a glimpse and struggle to come to full insight.

Perhaps the audience will see that things are not what they seem to be: the religious leaders do not enter the rule of God; what the world considers great is not true greatness; those who have the most power will not prevail at the end; those who serve and refuse to lord over others are God's people. The crucifixion and resurrection of Jesus bring these insights to those who have eyes to see. In Mark's view, the end of history will bring them to light for all to see.

The plot also raises questions about the kind of power people exercise and the consequences of exercising power. The plot shows that there are two kinds of power. One power comes from God and serves people by bringing life and wholeness. The other power—dominating or patriarchal power—is humanly self-serving and is destructive in its efforts to preserve and secure the power holder. In the end, all the conflicts are about the clash between the values of the rule of God and human self-serving values. The conflicts show how difficult it is to let go of one's security, one's honor, one's power, in order to enter into the sphere of God's rule. The more power one has, the more difficult it may be to let go. Nevertheless, in Mark's view, true greatness is in the capacity to risk loss in the exercise of servant power for the good of others.

This story was composed for oral performance as a gripping narrative that would have engaged audiences and led them to see the stark choices that lay before them in their own lives. Ancient performers of this story would have been profoundly committed to the life they were depicting and proclaiming in this Gospel. Such performers would have brought out the passion and the pathos, the suspense and the intensity, the promise and the tragedy of these conflicts, so that hearers would be led to place themselves squarely on the side of the God who was establishing lordship over all creation, over all nations, and over all people. And, as we shall see, the unresolved nature of the plot leaves audiences to make that decision for themselves.

CHAPTER 5

The Characters I: Jesus

A n analysis of the characters in Mark's story overlaps the analysis of the conflicts, because characters are integrally related to plot. At one level, characters are agents in a plot—a character aspires to a goal, a character is the object
of an action, other characters help to further goals or become obstacles to them,
and so on. Yet the reverse is also true: the actions of the plot are expressions of
the characters, and they reveal the characters for who they are. In this sense, characters can be memorable in their own right; after all, we recall Hamlet or Juliet
as we recall real people. Thus we can analyze not only what characters "do" but
also who they "are," treating them as autonomous figures in the plot and assessing
them as we assess real people.[1]

In Mark's story, there are four human characters or character groups. First,
Jesus is the protagonist. Second, both the Judean and the Roman authorities are
the antagonists. The authorities can be treated together, because the different
groups that oppose Jesus share similar traits and carry an ongoing role in the plot.
Third, the disciples also can be treated together as a character group. They relate
to Jesus as "the disciples" or as "the twelve." Even when Rock, James, and John
have particular roles, they typify the disciples as a whole. Fourth, there are the
minor characters. While not a character group as such, those who relate to Jesus—
the people in general, and particularly the suppliants—can nevertheless be treated
together because, with few exceptions, they have similar traits. Also, the crowds
function as a minor character.[2] These are the characters and character groups we
will treat in this chapter and the next.[3]

All we know of a given character is what we know from the story. We cannot
go beyond what the Markan narrator has told us or implied in order to specu-
late about the character's actions or motives—either on the basis of the treatment
of that character in other Gospels or through efforts to reconstruct the historical
character. We are treating these figures only in terms of their characterization in

Mark—even when we are using helpful background information from the culture to understand the portrayal of the character better.

Approaches to Characterization

Characterization refers to the way a narrator brings characters to life in a narrative. A narrator may "tell" the audience directly what characters are like. Or the narrator may "show" the characters to the audience by having them speak and act and by having other characters talk about them and interact with them. The narrator of Mark's Gospel primarily "shows" the characters through action and dialogue.

Mark creates characters who are consistent. Their portrayal coheres within scenes and, if they are ongoing characters in the plot, their portrayal coheres from one scene to the next. Mark does not develop full-blown characters as we find in modern literature. Rather, Mark presents rich characterizations by being minimally suggestive. The narrator reveals these characters in a gradual process, guiding what the audience knows and when they know it. The hearers see how the character is introduced, has initial impressions confirmed or amplified or adjusted or overturned, observes how the character exits the narrative, and considers what the implied future is for the character.

Also, the audience makes inferences about characters. The audience notes who they are, listens to what they say, watches what they do, sees how they interact with others, and considers what others say about them. Characters are also revealed by their point of view, the settings they inhabit, their names or anonymity, how they respond to the arrival of the rule of God, their capacity for change, and so on. In some narratives, we might also consider what characters look like. However, apart from a description of the clothes of John the baptizer and the transformation of Jesus' appearance on the mountain, Mark's narrator gives no description of any character's appearance. Mark presents characters primarily as agents—what they say and do is most important.

Other considerations to look for in analyzing characters include what drives and motivates the characters, what they seek and work for, what they fear and avoid, how they measure up to the values and beliefs that make up the standards of judgment in the story, what their traits are, and how they are illuminated by comparison or contrast with other characters. The composer of Mark uses many methods in characterization and, for an ancient narrative, offers some surprisingly complex characters.

Finally, the Markan narrator also reveals characters in terms of their place in the society in which the story is set—whether they are male or female, who their kin are, if they have a position of authority, if they are considered by the society to be clean or unclean, whether they are from Jerusalem or a peasant village, and so on. The place in society shapes the characterizations, influences the way characters interact with other characters, and determines the power dynamics that take place between them. Consider, for example, the importance of social place in John Steinbeck's *The Grapes of Wrath* or Margaret Mitchell's *Gone with the Wind*.

Characters as types

Ancient characterization in Greco-Roman literature tended to portray stylized characters who were unchanging and predictable. Characters were not developed psychologically and showed little inclination to introspection. Hence the narrator's inside views were limited. The outward actions and words of a person reflected what was inside a person's mind or heart. This approach to character was a reflection of the way people viewed each other in the culture of the time.[4] There was little individualism, and people got their identity from the social group to which they belonged. Conformity to the group was more important than individual development. Therefore, the narrator can portray characters as a group, and an individual within a group (such as Rock) can behave in ways that typify and, indeed, represent the group as a whole.

An example of character types in Mark may be seen in the riddle of the sower. Each seed/soil combination portrays a different type of character. The seeds sown beside the way typify the authorities, who hear the word, but immediately Satan comes and takes away the word. The seeds falling on rocky ground are like the disciples who hear with joy but stumble when trouble comes. The seeds sown among thorns are like the rich man who hears the word but because of the desires of the world is fruitless. Those sown on good soil typify the disciples and the suppliants who proclaim and reap results. Likewise, the characters themselves in Mark's story represent typical responses to the rule of God.[5]

Mark deals with the limitation of characters types in part by providing individual exceptions to the stereotypical members of a group: exceptions to the negative portrayal of the authorities include Jairus the synagogue leader, Joseph the council member, and the good scribe; the woman who anoints Jesus is an exception to the negative portrayal of the wealthy; and Herodias and the high priest's maid are exceptions to the positive portrayal of women.[6]

Ancient characters tend not to change a great deal. In modern novels, characters are often dynamic, changing and developing, with a consonant transformation of personal traits. In Mark's story, most characters show little or no change or development. Rather, events and conflicts bring out the traits and nature of the characters. As the plot moves to a climax, the characters are shown fully for who they are in the face of death.

However, there is need for caution here. Mark was influenced by the narratives of the Hebrew Bible, where the characters are less stylized and more open to change. Mark's characters are often rich in suggestive detail and even, at times, surprising. In fact, Mark's story assumes that people will be able to turn around and put faith in the good news—indeed, to undergo a reorientation in life. The arrival of the rule of God offers new possibilities and confronts people with a crisis of decision. Jesus challenges people to follow him in the way of service even at the cost of life—to break with the values of family and village to become part of the new order of the rule of God. We see such changes most clearly in the struggles of the disciples to follow Jesus.

Standards of judgment

Another way to understand Mark's characters is to consider how they measure up to the overall norms of the story. As we saw in chapter 2, "The Narrator," the standards of judgment are those values and beliefs embedded in a narrative by which the hearers are led to judge the characters and their actions. The norms of judgment represent the moral fabric of a narrative—the positive values that the narrative promotes and the negative behavior that the narrative condemns. In Mark, the positive norms of judgment are equivalent to the values of the rule of God—God's will for people.

Mark has woven the narrative tightly in this regard, for, as we have seen, the whole Gospel reflects a moral dualism. The positive way is a matter of living "on God's terms"—having faith and courage, undergoing persecution for the good news, being least and servant in a life for others, and not lording over others. By contrast, the negative way is living a destructive life "on human terms"—being without faith and fearful, saving one's self, acquiring the world, being great, and using power over others. The Markan characters consistently embody one or the other of these two ways. Jesus as well as the minor characters (for the most part) embody what God wants for people. The authorities embody what people want for themselves. The disciples vacillate between the two ways.

Again, observing the way characters typify these standards does not exhaust Mark's characterizations. Mark's characters are not simply moral exemplars of one standard or another, as in Aesop's fables. Jesus is a complex figure who is more than the sum of the standards of judgment. The authorities show resourcefulness in their strategies for opposing Jesus. The disciples are in conflict within themselves over their struggle to follow Jesus, and they exemplify both positive and negative standards. The minor characters reveal such rich characterization as to elude treatment as simply stock characters. Often the minor characters meet some standards and not others. And, as we have said, there is the possibility for characters to turn around or to fall away.

Comparison and contrast

Mark's narrator also reveals characters by comparison and contrast with other characters in the story. For example, the authorities are illuminated by being a mirror opposite of Jesus and of the minor characters. Also, the minor characters often serve as foils for the disciples because they do what the disciples fail to do.

We can see these comparisons and contrasts most clearly within individual episodes and between episodes that are juxtaposed or sandwiched. For example, Jesus restores the man with the withered hand, while the authorities try to destroy Jesus. The disciples do not understand the riddles, but the Gentile woman in Tyre does. The poor widow giving "her whole living" parallels Jesus giving his whole life. At the same time, this widow who gives away her living contrasts with the authorities, who "eat up the houses of the widows."

Traits of the characters

The hearer participates actively in the process of creating the characters in imagination. An important part of the hearer's imaginative construction of characters involves assigning traits or attributes to a character.[7] A trait is defined as a personal quality that typifies a character, usually by persisting throughout that character's appearance in the story. The hearer will find some traits used explicitly in the narrative to describe the character and will infer other traits from the words and actions of the character. For example, Jesus appears as "authoritative," "clever," and "enigmatic," while the authorities are "hostile," "self-serving," and "afraid," and Rock is "impetuous."

Based on the whole characterization, the audience builds up a broader picture of each character. Interpreters may assess whether a character is complex (with many traits) or simple (having few traits), open to change or fixed, difficult to figure out or transparent, consistent or inconsistent.[8] Based on these features, interpreters may note that a character has changing and conflicting traits, is complex and unpredictable, and is intriguing and mysterious. By contrast, other characters may be less complex, have fewer traits, and act in predictable ways. Or a character may function in the plot with only one or two key traits.[9]

These features are helpful in identifying differences among the characterizations in Mark. Jesus has many traits and acts in new and surprising ways. He adapts to obstacles and opposition. The disciples are in conflict within themselves about the rule of God, and they change and develop as they face challenges and crises. The authorities are characters with fewer, less-conflicting traits. They do not change except to increase their opposition to Jesus and are generally predictable in their behavior. Because of their cameo appearances, the minor characters often manifest few traits and are often transparent and predictable, even though their characterization may be made complex with suggestive details.

Identification with characters

In all of this, the narrator guides the audience's distance from or identification with characters in the story.[10] The narrator can lead the audience to relate to characters in a variety of ways: approve of or align with a character in that character's efforts to prevail; feel sympathy for a character; identify with a character by seeing oneself in the character; or emulate a character by wanting to be (like) that character. Conversely, the narrator may lead the audience to disapprove of and to oppose certain characters, to be repelled by characters and to reject them.

Summary

Character analysis is really what we do all the time when we make judgments about people we meet or characters we encounter in a story or a film. In our study, we are only making explicit what tends to happen as we encounter other people and make decisions about them. We have simply tried to clarify some ways we look at characters before turning to the analysis of the characters themselves.

Jesus

In the opening words, the narrator establishes Jesus as the central figure of this story by announcing that Jesus is "the anointed one, the son of God." These epithets immediately place Jesus as the one chosen by God to lead Israel and also as a figure to rival the Roman emperor, who is also called "son of God." However, these epithets do not tell what task Jesus is anointed for or what it means for him to be God's son. These meanings unfold in the narrative in terms of all the aspects of Jesus' characterization. Only at the end of the story is the audience able to see more fully who Jesus is.[11]

What follows immediately after the narrator's opening announcement confirms for the audience the importance of this character: an oracle from God announces his coming, John prepares his way, Jesus is baptized, the heavens are opened, the spirit comes on him, and God's voice declares him as son. By the time Jesus first speaks to announce that the rule of God has arrived, the audience is prepared to trust whatever he says and does.

The unfolding story shows that Jesus is the Judean anointed by God to inaugurate God's rule. He has the power of the holy spirit, a profound grasp of the Scriptures, and a determined sense of mission. He is a peasant woodworker from the village of Nazareth in Galilee. His father is never mentioned; his mother's name is Mary. He has four named brothers and some sisters. He has no position of power or status in the life of the nation, but he gathers a group of twelve others around him and goes about the countryside healing, exorcising, eating with sinners, and calling people to enter God's rule. He assumes his authority is directly from God, and he works outside the official channels.

In Mark, Jesus is the son of God, but not by virtue of a special birth or a divine nature. He becomes God's son at his baptism, when God anoints him with the holy spirit. In Mark, Jesus is neither God nor a divine being, but a human, a son of humanity, who has been given great authority by God. Jesus is the commissioned agent of God, sent as an ambassador to act on God's behalf and to inaugurate God's rule in Israel, a rule that will soon enough encompass all nations and, indeed, all creation. He is God's son because God has given him the authority of a son and because he is in turn obedient to God. He is also son because he is the human heir who will sit on God's right hand when God's rule comes fully in power. For all these reasons, he is God's "beloved son" or "only son."

Characterization

Jesus is a character with many and varied traits. What Jesus "does" reveals primarily the extent and nature of his authority from God. What Jesus "says" discloses his understanding of himself as agent of God and his purposes. Both what Jesus does and what he says express his values and show his integrity in living up to those values.

What others say about Jesus and how others react to him reveal the unusual and controversial aspects of this character. Reactions to Jesus include fear, offense, amazement, fierce loyalty, and determined opposition. Although God knows him as son and the demons recognize him to be God's son, no one else recognizes him to be such: His family thinks he is out of his mind; the authorities say he is a blasphemer, a criminal, and possessed by an unclean spirit; the crowds see him as John the baptizer raised or Elijah or a prophet; and the disciples do not recognize him as the anointed one until halfway through the story. The centurion is the only human character who calls Jesus "son of God"; yet, given that character's limited role and perspective, it is likely that he does not grasp the full implications of what he is saying.

The narrator shows Jesus developing as he struggles with the people being healed, his popularity with the crowds, the rigidity of the authorities, and the hardheadedness of the disciples. As a result of his encounter with the Syrophoenician woman, Jesus learns that his mission extends beyond Israel to the Gentiles. And after Rock identifies him as the anointed one, he makes a deliberate turn toward Jerusalem.

The narrator consistently maintains a favorable point of view toward Jesus, leading the audience to align with Jesus and his norms. Yet the awesome, mysterious, and demanding aspects of Jesus' character keep the audience somewhat at a distance, and the difficulty of following Jesus leads hearers to identify with the diverse reactions to Jesus by other characters.

Agent of the rule of God

Jesus is the agent given authority by God to inaugurate a rule that will eventually encompass all nations and involve the restoration of all creation. He invites all to enter into God's rule, both those who welcome it and those who are uncomprehending and hostile. The narrator portrays Jesus as a person of word and deed. He is empowered by God to heal and to confront oppressive forces wherever he goes. He is God's agent, offering a new teaching with authority, speaking in riddle-like stories and paradoxical sayings.

Jesus expresses an individuality rare for the ancient world, acting and speaking in unconventional ways. However, like the prophets of Israel, he is not acting on his own but as agent of God. Because his authority comes from God, he is strong-willed and independent. Neither traditions nor laws nor public pressure nor fear of indictment prevent him from truthfully acting and teaching "God's way." He will act alone if he must, even facing execution as one abandoned by all. Nonetheless, Jesus is not a loner. He calls others into a family-like relationship with himself and with each other. He inaugurates a movement, a loose network of people, that will culminate in the fullness of the rule of God.

God's rule is rooted in values that are unconventional in the society as depicted in the story. The rule of God represents a new reality. It bursts old wineskins and, in so doing, risks the destruction of those who embrace it. As such, if Jesus is to be faithful, he must resist pressures from "this adulterous and sinful generation" to turn aside from his commitment to the rule of God. Immediately after his baptism, he is tested by Satan. He is tested by the authorities, who seek a sign from heaven and who repeatedly try to trip him up. He is also tested by the disciples, who object to his commitment to face rejection and execution in Jerusalem. And, of course, he struggles to submit his will to God's will at Gethsemane. Nevertheless, his fierce commitment to carry out his task as agent of God's rule enables him to endure in faithfulness.

The authority of Jesus

As noted, Jesus has authority from God and is empowered by the spirit. Everything he does and says stems from a conviction that "the rule of God has arrived." He assumes awesome powers for himself—pardoning sins, interpreting laws, appointing twelve to share the authority, exorcising demons, healing, commanding nature, prophesying, entering Jerusalem royally, and occupying the temple.

Empowered by the *holy* spirit, Jesus exercises power over what is *unclean*. He exorcises unclean spirits. He touches a leper, but instead of being defiled himself, the leper is made clean. He heals the woman with a flow of blood, exorcises a legion of demons on Gentile territory from a man who lives among graves and near pigs, raises a dead girl, and eats with a Gentile crowd in the desert, all involving contact with people considered to be unclean. Contrary to written laws of the Scriptures, Jesus asserts that contact with unclean people or things or food does not render one unclean.

Jesus' authority includes prophetic wisdom and insight. He refers to himself as a prophet, and the crowds associate his activity with the ancient prophets. His actions manifest God's present rule and foreshadow God's future complete rule. Jesus sometimes prophesies the future in minor matters such as where to obtain a donkey or where to find lodging, but also in important matters such as the circumstances of his death and the events to take place after his death in the final establishment of God's rule. Sometimes he has insight into the minds of other characters, although generally the narrator does not depict him as knowing what other characters are thinking. Also, Jesus pronounces judgments against those who blaspheme the holy spirit, who cause stumbling, and who eat up the houses of widows.

Jesus has authority from God to challenge national political institutions. Jesus knows God's will in legal matters, establishing the priority of some laws over others, nullifying certain written laws, condemning oral traditions, and disregarding some ritual practices. At every point, he interprets the law so as to serve people, as an expression of God's command "to love the neighbor as oneself." He attacks the temple, driving out those serving the sacrificial cult and declaring God's will for it to be a house of prayer for "all the Gentile nations."

In the story world, the anointed one is given far more authority than the characters expect him to have, particularly in regard to his power over demons, illness, and nature, far more authority than Elijah, John the baptizer, one of the prophets, and David. There are, however, definite limits to his authority, which Jesus himself acknowledges. He is not God, for "God is the only Lord" and "No one is good except God alone." He does not have authority to determine who will sit on his right or left in glory, nor does he know the exact day or hour when the end will come. Jesus must submit to God, for he cannot save himself except through entrusting his life to God.

As a low-status person with no worldly position or power, Jesus must be clever in order to evade the efforts of the authorities to silence him. Because he has no power from God to lord over others, his confrontations with the authorities show him to be vulnerable and contingent. The point is not that he *could* exert authority if he wanted to. In Mark's depiction, Jesus does not have power from God to exert authority over others. He *can*not make people be quiet or heal someone when no faith is present or make the disciples fearless or the authorities turn around. Furthermore, even as Jesus acts on God's behalf, he is not protected from harm. The saying "whoever receives me receives not me but the one who sent me" by implication also means that "whoever rejects me rejects the one who sent me." In such a position of vulnerability, Jesus is persecuted and put to death.

However, while the story depicts Jesus' vulnerability in this age, it also portrays Jesus as the one whom God will establish in power in the future. At the final establishment of the rule of God over all nations, within a generation of his crucifixion, Jesus will come in glory on the right hand of the Powerful One. Jesus' brief transformation on the mountain foreshadows the time when the son of humanity will come in the "glory of the Father."

Faith

In the story, Jesus has extraordinary trust in God. He leaves his work and his family, depending on others to provide food and houses as he travels about. Jesus is the prime example in the story of how everything becomes possible for one who has faith, because he remains dependent on God, for whom all is possible. Healing, for example, requires trust that the healing is possible—not only on the part of the person being healed but also on the part of the healer. For Mark, faith as trust is access to the power of God. In this regard, Jesus' prayers are related to his faith, for Jesus teaches that when a prayer or request is made to God in faith it will be granted, and he tells the disciples that their inability to perform a difficult exorcism was due to their failure to pray. The portrayal of Jesus at prayer reinforces the depiction of him as a person of faith.

The narrator portrays Jesus' faith as submission to God's rule not only in terms of trust but also in terms of obedience. At Gethsemane, Jesus reminds "my Father" that "everything is possible for you" and asks that God remove the cup. Jesus asks for what he himself wants, but in the end he asks to do what God wants, even if it means his being faithful in the face of death. In this complete dependence on God, Jesus renounces himself, chooses to be least, and loses his life in the service of God's rule. This relationship, whereby God gives authority to Jesus and Jesus in turn relies so completely upon God, is what characterizes Jesus as "the son of God."

Serving and not lording over others

While faith is at the heart of Jesus' relation with God, serving defines his way of relating to other people. Jesus teaches the disciples to be everyone's servant—that is, not to use their power like one who is in a position to lord over others and be served by them but to use their power like house servants or slaves, to serve without regard for status or reward, and to use their power on behalf of others with less power than themselves—not because it is a personal sacrifice but because it helps and empowers others.

Jesus himself serves others with his power from a position of strength, not weakness. That is, his authority comes from God, not the pressures or desires of other people. Thus Jesus' idea of service does not become a matter of doing what others want him to do, except insofar as that is consonant with the values of the rule of God. For example, he will heal those who request it, like Bartimaeus, but he will not grant the Pharisees a sign. His first allegiance is to God; then he loves the neighbor as self.

Jesus uses his power to serve people by liberating them from demons, illnesses, sin, uncleanness, the threats and deprivations of nature, and oppressive laws and traditions. Jesus does not do these works of power in order to demonstrate that he is the anointed one. Rather, his works are the expression of his compassion to bring the wholeness of the rule of God to those who are "like sheep without a shepherd."

Jesus serves the minor characters who come for healing.[12] In response to people's faith that God will heal, he heals readily. He sees faith in people's persistent efforts to seek him out for healing, and where faith is weak, he encourages it. Jesus forces healing on no one. He does not seek people out but heals those who come to him. He initiates a healing only when he is taking responsibility for a healing on the sabbath, as he does, for example, for the man with the withered hand.

Jesus heals freely, with no strings attached for those being healed. He does not demand that they believe he is the anointed one (and no one does) or even that they believe in the God of the Judeans (the Syrophoenician woman does not). He does not require a person to be morally good, and he interprets the desire for healing as an indication of turning to God. Jesus does not expect to gain personally from healing; he does not broker his healing for worldly status or power. In fact, in Mark, Jesus never asks anyone he heals to follow him. Usually he orders them, sometimes harshly, to keep quiet and to go home. They proclaim or follow on their own, but Jesus does not consider either action a condition or expectation for healing.

Jesus serves the disciples by teaching them without controlling their responses. He is loyal to the disciples, even when he is angry or impatient in his urgent efforts to teach them. He respects their freedom to choose, using general conditional statements to affirm what is to be done or avoided: "If any want to follow after me, let them renounce themselves," and, "Whoever wants to be great among you will be your servant." Also, Jesus leads the disciples primarily by example—in the way he helps those with less power than he, in the way he challenges the authorities who have more power than he, and in the way he faces persecution rather than abandon his mission. In the end, the narrator depicts Jesus as not clinging to the disciples or trying to force their loyalty, for he dies without knowing their future behavior or their ultimate fate. He dies as a result of his obedience to God and entrusts the rest to God—and to the choices of the disciples.

While Jesus serves others, he also allows others to serve him. He benefits from the hospitality of others throughout his journey. The disciples take care of his needs at key points. The women who came up with him to Jerusalem were serving him when he was in Galilee. Especially in Jerusalem, Jesus freely receives spontaneous acts of service from others: a woman anoints him, and the disciples prepare the Passover meal. After his death, Joseph of Arimathea buries him, and women come to anoint his body.

At the same time, Jesus confronts the authorities with the nature of God's rule and with their failure to serve. He does not soften his words to please or appease the authorities but names and condemns their failures. He calls the Pharisees hypocrites and the high priests bandits. He cites the writings and tells riddles against them. Yet he also gives them the same freedom that he gives to the disciples. After each confrontation, he moves on, leaving the authorities to choose their response. Even the one time he does use force, violently overturning tables and chairs in the temple, he symbolically occupies the temple only briefly and then withdraws, leaving the high priests to respond to his action.

Jesus uses analogies to explain how he serves people without lording over them. For example, in the riddle of the sower, he depicts his relationships with people as noncontrolling: the sower sows the word then "sleeps and rises," trusting God to bring a harvest. (After Jesus finishes "sowing" the words of this riddle, he "sleeps" in the boat during the storm!)

Thus Jesus will not rule over others. He is not a military messiah who uses a sword; nor is he a demagogue who manipulates crowds. Like the son in the riddle of the vineyard, Jesus has come to receive the produce of the harvest from the vineyard, but he uses no force to obtain it from the farmers. He does not even fight to defend himself, but he endures the consequences of his opponents' scorn. In Mark, Jesus is not "the son of David," for it is not the "rule of our father David" that Jesus inaugurates but "the rule of God"—in which people in family-like relationships are to serve each other and those outside and not to lord over anyone. These relationships are nonpatriarchal—that is, they are without "fathers."

Renouncing self, being least, and losing life for others

The narrator portrays Jesus as obedient to the authority given him under God's rule and renouncing all personal claims to wealth, power, status, and even his own life. Jesus never uses his power and authority to his own advantage. Jesus does not make personal claims for himself. Until the very end, he avoids saying that he is the anointed one and the son of God. This silence not only enables Jesus to avoid indictment but also suggests that it is not up to Jesus to make these claims for himself. He acknowledges his identity only when confronted directly with the recognition of him by Rock and the specific questions of the high priest. As agent of God, he uses the provocative "I am"—words associated with God's self-designation in the writings—yet he uses it only in contexts where it could also mean simply "It is I" or "I am the one."

In Mark, Jesus usually refers to himself in the third person with the epithet "the son of humanity." This self-designation unites many aspects of Jesus' role: his authority to pardon sins, his authority over the sabbath, his rejection and execution by the authorities, his rising, and his future role in gathering the chosen ones and judging all. Thus Jesus' use of "son of humanity" affirms that from beginning to end he is a "human" and a representative of humanity who depends on God for his authority.

Jesus' ultimate renunciation of himself occurs when he relinquishes his own safety and undergoes execution for the sake of the larger purposes of God's rule. In a sense, Jesus meets all the standards of his own teaching in his death. His willingness to die expresses his total faith in God for salvation. His crucifixion is the ultimate consequence of a life of service and of his refusal to oppress others to save himself. And in this tragic execution—misunderstood, falsely accused, abandoned—he is least of all.

Jesus faces death

In the story, the portrayal of Jesus moves from that of the powerful one who relieves human suffering through healings and feedings to the vulnerable one who is rejected and executed.[13] The characterization of Jesus is basically the same at the end of the story as at the beginning. The difference between the first and second half of the story is the nature of the opposition and the kind of authority Jesus is given to deal with each. In the first half, the narrator stresses the good news of the inbreaking of God's rule, and Jesus is shown overcoming demons, illness, and forces of nature. In the second half, the narrator stresses how the authorities of this age persecute and destroy those who follow the rule of God, and Jesus is shown to be faithful in the face of this persecution as he prepares his disciples for his execution and their coming persecution.

Jesus knows the inevitability of his death and moves inexorably toward it. He is a village teacher from Galilee coming into the heart of the nation's power in Jerusalem and challenging them on their own turf. Jesus invites the hostility of the authorities by entering Jerusalem with a crowd of supporters and by attacking the temple. Yet Jesus' coming execution is not portrayed as his own desire. Far from passively accepting death, he protests and condemns the attitudes and actions of the authorities, particularly in his riddle to them about the farmers in the vineyard. Nevertheless, he does accept that his execution will be the unavoidable consequence of giving a faithful witness to the rule of God. Jesus fears crucifixion, and his admonition to the disciples at Gethsemane suggests that he knows the weakness of his own flesh in the face of such a death. In prayer, he wrestles with his fear. The narrator depicts him as alarmed and anguished, "sad to death," as he prays that he might not have to die; yet he also prays to submit to God's will for him to be faithful.

Finally, having subordinated his will to God's, he faces his approaching execution without fighting his captors or lashing out at subsequent abuse and mockery. He gives truthful evidence for his death sentence to the Judean authorities, and he does not compromise that faithful witness before Pilate. He endures ridicule silently. Beyond this, he experiences the full pain of crucifixion without relief from drugs or wine.

Although the audience has heard Jesus prophesy his execution, the audience is led, time and again, to wonder if Jesus might escape his fate: the high priests cannot get witnesses whose testimonies agree; Jesus is silent; Pilate favors Jesus; the crowd gets a chance to ask for Jesus' release; and perhaps Elijah will come to take him down. But each time, the raised hope is quickly dashed by some development in the plot. The impending execution moves swiftly to a conclusion: "And Jesus, letting out a loud cry, died." There is to be no reversal, no deliverance from this execution. God does not rescue Jesus from his death.

The execution

As we have noted, Jesus begins as a man who powerfully impinges on the world around him, but at the end of the story the focus shifts to what befalls him. The depiction of his death therefore maintains both a poignancy and a powerfulness.

Jesus faces death alone, for his relationships fall away at the end. The women alone remain, and they watch from a distance. This isolation of Jesus increases the pathos of the story. First, Jesus is betrayed by a disciple close to him. Then, at Gethsemane, his closest companions fall asleep and cannot keep watch. When he is arrested, the disciples all flee, and Rock renounces him. Without support from his followers, he is subjected to a trial by the Judean leaders that is characterized by false testimony and mockery. The subsequent trial before Pilate leads to his abandonment by the crowd. The phrase "handed over" conveys how vulnerable and helpless he is. He is handed over to hostile Judean authorities, who in turn hand him over to the Roman authority to be crucified by Roman soldiers. Finally, Jesus' cry to God attests to his sense of being abandoned by God at his death. Jesus dies alone, and a stranger buries him.

Add to this the portrayal of physical anguish. A crowd with swords and clubs seizes him and leads him away. Some of those convicting him spit on him, then cover his head and strike him. The guards beat him. He is bound and handed over to Pilate, who has him flogged. Then the soldiers, too, spit on him and beat him over the head with a reed pole. After these beatings, Jesus is so weak that they have to conscript someone to carry his cross. The crucifixion lasts six hours.

In the midst of abandonment and pain, Jesus faces humiliation and shame as one scorned and mocked. Jesus' crucifixion as "king of the Judeans" was an obvious occasion for ridicule, a source of taunting for the soldiers, the bystanders, as well as the high priests and legal experts. Even those crucified with him join the ridicule.

Until Jesus' cry of despair from the cross, the narrator has portrayed Jesus as a man who is confident in his understanding of God. On the cross, however (with a line from Psalm 22, a psalm of a righteous sufferer), Jesus cries out in isolation and despair: "My God! My God! Why did you abandon me?" The narrator could have chosen to end Jesus' life on a note of triumph but instead suggests that even though Jesus chooses to die in obedience to God, he experiences abandonment in death. Mark's narrative portrays Jesus undergoing the full impact of his death.

Thus the narrator does not depict Jesus' dying a heroic death of "noble" proportions, for Jesus dreads execution, as one who is alarmed and anguished, sad to death. Nor does the Markan Jesus die stoically as a martyr, for his only words in death are an anguished cry from the cross asking God why he has been abandoned to this fate. The only triumph Mark depicts in Jesus' death is his human faithfulness to God—with his own fear and torment and sadness, and despite the pain and humiliation and abandonment brought on by others.

The meaning of Jesus' crucifixion

The significance of Jesus' death became a central concern of later Christian theology. The theological significance of the death is not, however, Mark's primary concern. Although the Gospel does suggest some meanings for Jesus' death, as we shall see below, what is central for Mark is that Jesus was executed—and raised! The execution was the tragic consequence of Jesus' faithfulness to the rule of God. That is, for Mark, as long as "this faithless generation" prevails, those who follow the rule of God will be persecuted, even executed, as John the baptizer was and as Jesus prophesies in regard to the disciples. Preeminently, Jesus, the agent who inaugurates the rule of God, is crucified by the powers of this age. But this is not the end, for this age does not have the last word. Jesus is risen, and God's rule is coming shortly in power and glory. Thus, for Mark, it is the fact of Jesus' execution and resurrection—as part of a life of faithfulness—that is central, rather than any particular theological meaning of them.

Therefore the modern reader needs to be cautious not to read into Mark theological meanings that later came to be associated with Jesus' death.[14] To begin with, Mark does not portray Jesus' death as a sacrifice for sin. Mark portrays Jesus already pardoning sin during his life and authorizing others to do the same. His death is not needed to make forgiveness possible. Furthermore, Mark does not emphasize Jesus' suffering as such. Clearly, Mark portrays crucifixion as the painful death that it was. However, most crucifixions took a full day or more, whereas, in Mark, Jesus died after only six hours on the cross. Nor does Mark consider that there is merit in enduring persecution or execution for its own sake. Jesus does not want to suffer, and he even tells his disciples to pray that they not come to such a testing. Rather, for Mark, suffering due to persecution was the tragic consequence of faithfulness to God's rule in an "evil and adulterous generation." It is the commitment to be faithful, in spite of such a cost, that Mark honors.

The narrative of Mark is concerned to establish two causes for Jesus' execution: first, it is brought about by human actions; that is, the authorities initiate and carry out the death penalty against him. Second, it was according to the will of God, and clearly, in Mark, Jesus goes to his death believing that it is God's will for him to be faithful even to death. Most first-century people believed *both* in human responsibility *and* in divine causation. As moderns, we tend to think that either God or humans should be considered responsible, but not both. For the ancients, it was both, and the narrator is very careful to portray it as both.

The narrator also portrays Jesus as believing that his execution has meaning. Twice the Markan Jesus suggests an interpretation. First, Jesus suggests it is an act of service that is "a ransom for many." The word "ransom" was not part of the language of sacrifice but a term that depicted the release of a slave or a hostage. That is, in Mark, Jesus sees his *whole life*, including his execution, as a means by which people are ransomed or liberated for a life of service in the rule of God. As so often in the narrative, no further elaboration is offered. However, the context of the whole narrative and its rhetoric suggest that the narrator understands Jesus' death as such a powerful expression of faithfulness that it freed others from their own fear of rejection, persecution, and execution—so that they too would have the courage to spread the good news of the rule of God to the ends of the earth.

Second, at the final Passover meal, Jesus portrays his execution as sealing a covenant. Here Jesus speaks of his "body" and his "blood," terms that when used together would suggest to first-century audiences the idea of political executions of people who stood in opposition to the government.[15] Jesus adds to this meaning when he speaks of "my blood of the covenant poured out for many." This is not a reference to sacrifice for sin but to a covenant sacrifice. Covenants in antiquity were ratified by pouring blood from a sacrifice on both parties to the covenant. Thus the narrator presents Jesus asking, if you will, that his execution seal the covenant of the rule of God with "the many," the new community of Judeans and Gentiles alike who follow Jesus in the way of service and who are also willing, if need be, to stand in the face of all opposition and risk the consequences.

Given Jesus' mission and the nature of this "sinful generation," Jesus, like John, was bound to be crushed by the powers that be. His faithfulness in death clarifies, on the one hand, the unjust and oppressive nature of those powers and, on the other hand, the nature of human greatness on God's terms—the commitment to live for the rule of God even when such a commitment leads to a shameful execution. And the crucifixion also reveals the nature of those who witness it—whether they condone the violent rule that crushes Jesus or embrace the rule of God that serves and brings life even in the face of death.

The narrator recounts events at the crucifixion that show the outcome of Jesus' death. God rips the temple curtain, sealing the destruction of the temple as a result of God's absence there and assuring the subsequent access to God everywhere. Embodying the start of the new ordering of God's people are a Gentile (the centurion) and a Judean (Joseph of Arimathea) who respond favorably to Jesus' death. The key to this reordering of God's people is that they "see" the rule of God in Jesus. While the authorities are blind to this, the centurion sees how Jesus dies and says, "this man was son of God."

Similarly, the narrator wants the audience to see that this humiliated man is really God's king. The narrator uses irony to draw the audience into this insight and at the same time to reveal Jesus' character. Everything the opponents say is mockery, but the narrator intends the audience to understand the opposite: what they say in derision is true. Jesus is enthroned with one on his right and one on his left. The charge reads: "The King of the Judeans." He wears a crown woven from thorns, and those who jeer him call him king. The mockery is ironic testimony to the true kingship of Jesus as agent of God's rule. However, God's rule in this age is hidden in this scene, except to those who think "in God's terms."

The narrator leads the audience to see in the crucifixion the ultimate paradox of God's rule, that the anointed one is king precisely because he was willing to live for others even when it meant this humiliating outcome. Only when Jesus has "died like this" does the narrator allow a human character in the story to acknowledge Jesus as "son of God."

The empty grave

In Mark, Jesus' death is not the end. Jesus is raised.[16] The grave is empty. "He's not here! Look, the place where they put him!" While there are no resurrection appearances in Mark, the fate of Jesus is clear. He has been raised to God's right hand, and he will return within a generation in glory and power. The absence of a resurrection appearance puts the emphasis on the life Jesus lived. The empty grave is the seal of God's approval. Jesus the Nazarene, who served others, who confronted oppression, and who was executed in the service of the rule of God, *this* is the kind of person God will welcome into the rule of God in the age to come. Jesus modeled the nature of the new social order, and he anticipated the life of nations in the cosmic transformation that would take place in the age to come. Thus the resurrection puts a seal of approval not only on Jesus but also on all who would follow in this way. And the absence of Jesus until he returns emphasizes that the role of proclaiming the rule of God—of bringing "the good news to all the Gentile nations"—has now been entrusted to those who would go and do likewise.

CHAPTER 6

The Characters II:
The Authorities, the Disciples,
and the Minor Characters

In this chapter, we turn our attention from Jesus the protagonist to the characters with whom Jesus interacts: the authorities with whom Jesus is in conflict from the beginning, because they reject Jesus and the rule of God he proclaims; the disciples, who struggle to follow Jesus and enter the rule of God; and finally the minor characters with whom Jesus interacts briefly but who nevertheless help to illuminate the rule of God.

The Authorities

In Mark, the Judean and Roman authorities in Israel hold positions of power, share the same basic traits, and are united by their common opposition to Jesus and the rule of God. In cultures such as the ancient Mediterranean, where religion, economics, and state were inseparable, both Judean and Roman authorities wielded political, economic, and religious power. Individuals such as Herod, Pilate, and the high priest act as representatives, while the high priests and high-status retainers such as the Pharisees and the legal experts oppose Jesus as groups. The Judean leaders are center stage. The Roman Empire is ever present as the force that gives authorization to their position and power.

The narrator presents each group acting on its own and in collaboration with other groups: Pharisees and legal experts in Galilee confront Jesus over crucial legal issues and purity regulations; the high priests, elders, and legal experts in Jerusalem guard the temple and keep social order in Israel on behalf of the Romans; the Judean and Roman authorities each regard it as their right from God to rule, and they protect their God-given right; they do what is politically necessary for them to maintain power and control. At the same time, these various groups cooperate with each other in their efforts to destroy Jesus by forming various alliances. Therefore, with few exceptions, the authorities can be treated as a character group.[1]

Characterization

From the first mention of legal experts as ones who teach without authority, the narrator paints the authorities in a consistently negative light. The narrator builds their characterization through their opposition to Jesus and their efforts to thwart the new order of the rule of God. What the authorities *say* involves questions that imply accusations or aim at trapping Jesus. What they *do* shows their efforts to plot the destruction of Jesus. The narrator's inside views of their thoughts and emotions distance the audience from the authorities, showing them as unreliable characters. The authorities are characters with consistent and predictable traits that are in direct contrast to the values of the rule of God. They are the opposite of Jesus, and they illuminate his character through contrast.

In relation to the rule of God, the authorities are the hardened ground beside the way; the seed that falls on this ground does not penetrate, for "immediately, Satan comes and takes away the word sown in them." As a result, they will not "turn and be pardoned."

No authority from God

The Judean leaders assume they have God's authorization to rule. At the same time, they are dependent upon and accountable to their Roman overlords. In order to stay in favor with the Romans, they must keep the people under control. Therefore, they fear the people. Because the Judean authorities fear "a riot of the populace" they will do what they need to do to appease or to control the crowds: they give a noncommittal response to Jesus' questions of them, and they arrest him by deception. Herod executes John, and Pilate executes Jesus—in order to maintain their honor and thereby preserve their power over the people.

In Mark's portrayal, the authorities are prime exemplars of the "faithless" generation. As those who "think in human terms," the Judean leaders replicate Gentile (Roman) rulers who "lord over" people. Rather than trust in God, they use their own power to secure themselves. Because they have misunderstood God's power in terms of domination rather than service, they have become leaders of an "adulterous and sinful generation." By the end of the story, they have so abused their power that their authorization to be leaders will be taken away, for the lord of the vineyard will "destroy those farmers and give the vineyard to others."

No love for God or neighbor

The authorities do not love God with their whole "minds."[2] At the end of the controversies in Galilee, Jesus is angry and grieved by the rigid "hardening of their minds" against him. Later, Jesus says that the Pharisees worship God with their lips, but "their minds are far away from" God. Further on, Jesus claims that it is because of their "calloused minds" that the Pharisees allow a man to dismiss his wife. And the debates in Jerusalem make it clear that the leaders consider "*whole* burnt offerings" to be more important than loving God with the "*whole* mind."

Nor do the authorities love their neighbors as themselves. They do not interpret the laws and traditions to meet the needs of the people. They think that people were made for laws rather than laws for people. They will fulfill outward rituals and traditions—fasting, washing hands, and whole burnt offerings. But what is in the minds of the authorities is not love for neighbor but such things as "murder, adulteries, expressions of greed, malicious acts, deceit, amorality, envious eye, blasphemy, arrogance, reckless folly."

Blind and deaf

In Mark's depiction, the authorities are blind and deaf to the rule of God in Jesus. They do not see or hear what is before them. They see a paralyzed man walk and a man's withered hand restored, but they do not perceive God at work in these events. The Pharisees are leaders of a generation that seeks incontestable "signs" because they do not have the eyes of faith to discern the signs that Jesus does give. At the crucifixion, the Jerusalem authorities will see and have faith only if Jesus miraculously gets down off the cross.

The authorities' blindness to the rule of God stems in part from the way they interpret Scripture. They believe it is central to honor God by keeping the laws, regardless of whether the laws benefit the people. The Sadducees do not interpret the writings so as to affirm God's power to raise (and judge) the dead. The authorities in Jerusalem cannot see that the stone that the builders rejected will become the cornerstone. They are blind to the possibility that the writings could prophesy against them.

Their expectations about God's activity prevent the authorities from seeing that the rule of God might come outside traditional channels or in unexpected ways. Hence their expectations do not allow for an anointed one like Jesus—a Galilean peasant who challenges them, claims the authority to pardon sin, disregards certain traditions, and attacks the temple. They refuse to accept new wine, because they want to maintain old wineskins.

Finally, the authorities are blind to their own hypocrisy. They condemn Jesus for healing on the sabbath, yet on the very same sabbath day they plot with the Herodians to destroy him. They honor "the traditions of the elders" and, in so doing, they nullify the "word of God." They "eat up the houses of the widows," and "for appearance offer long prayers." They think of themselves as God's agents when they are really serving themselves.

Willful blindness

One of the many complexities of Mark's story—and one aspect that is difficult for modern readers—is why the authorities are blind to the rule of God in Jesus.[3] Are they responsible for their actions, or has God foreordained their actions? As noted in regard to Jesus, ancient people tended to see causes as both/and: *both* God is responsible *and,* at the same time, humans are responsible and accountable for their own actions. This is perhaps most explicit in Mark in Jesus' saying about Judas: "The son of humanity goes just as it is written about him, but how awful for that human by whom the son of humanity is handed over. Better for *him* if he had not been born."

This view of divine and human causes applies also to Mark's portrayal of the authorities. The narrator presents several reasons for their blindness: they have not been given the secret of the rule of God; Jesus speaks to them in riddles; Satan takes away the word sown in them; they do not interpret Scripture or Jesus' exorcisms aright; and their minds are hardened. In Mark's narrative world, not only God but also they themselves are responsible for their own blindness. The authorities are not puppets on a string.

In some instances, the authorities clearly choose to disregard God's rule. Herod knows John to be just, but nevertheless he has him executed so that, as the king, he does not lose honor in front of his dinner guests. Pilate considers Jesus innocent but chooses to satisfy the crowd by handing him over for execution. In the riddle of the vineyard, the farmers (the Judean leaders) know that the last agent of the owner (God) is the son (Jesus), yet they kill him anyway to get the vineyard for themselves. At other times, their expectations prevent the authorities from seeing that God is active in Jesus. The Pharisees acknowledge that Jesus does exorcisms, but they believe he is acting on the authority of Satan. At the crucifixion, the Jerusalem leaders acknowledge that he "restored others," but they do not believe that he is the anointed one because he "can't save himself."

Thus the authorities do not somehow crassly believe that Jesus really is the son of God and consciously oppose him anyway. Rather, in Mark's characterization, they are blind to God acting through Jesus. The narrator shows this most clearly by providing three exceptions, three members of the authority groups, who do see what Jesus is about: Jairus the synagogue leader who seeks healing for his daughter; the good legal expert who affirms Jesus and to whom Jesus in turn says, "You are not far from the rule of God"; and the centurion at the cross who says, "Truthfully, this man was son of God." These exceptions, standing out from the otherwise consistently negative portrayal of the authorities, show that the authorities as a whole have chosen not to understand.

The authorities have stopped their ears and closed their eyes. We see this most clearly, for example, in the story of the healing of the man with the withered hand. In that episode, the Judean authorities silently refuse to engage in debate with Jesus, because they are determined to get charges against him. The choice not to listen becomes a hardening that prevents sight. They *will* not understand Jesus, and therefore they *can*not understand. This hardening of their minds quickly turns into an active and hostile determination to destroy Jesus. And when Jesus' popularity really does become a threat to the public order—through his popular entrance to Jerusalem and his attack on the temple—they fear "a riot of the populace." Then they turn to deception and suborning witnesses as means to arrest and condemn him.

In opposing Jesus, the authorities also oppose God. In the ancient world, actions against an agent were considered actions against the one who sent the agent. Jesus says, "All who receive me receive not me but the One who sent me." This statement also implies the converse: all who reject Jesus reject not Jesus but the One who sent him. The authorities' rejection of God becomes evident early in the story. By mistaking an unclean spirit for the holy spirit as the source of Jesus' power to exorcise, they repudiate God so fundamentally that Jesus calls their blasphemy against the holy spirit a sin to eternity and affirms by prophetic oath that it will never be pardoned. At the trial, their condemnation of Jesus for blasphemy ironically renders the authorities themselves guilty of blasphemy. In their inability to see, the authorities have repudiated God and the rule of God breaking in through Jesus.

The authorities save themselves

In Mark's characterization, the authorities do not want to change; the present order serves them well. If they were to put people before laws, reach out to the unclean, relinquish the purity traditions, give up the traditions of the elders, sell their possessions and give to the poor, and put a priority on the love command over against the temple offerings, they would undermine their own power.

Mark makes their self-serving traits quite evident: the legal experts are enamored of formal greetings in the markets; they want the most important places at the banquets and in the synagogues; they increase their wealth by devouring the houses of widows; they seek Jesus' death to keep the vineyard for themselves; and they hand Jesus over out of envy. In Mark's characterization, the authorities do these things in order to secure themselves—their own honor and places of power—rather than trusting God for salvation.

Fear is at the root of their actions

For Mark, what lies at the root of the authorities' quest to secure themselves is fear—fear of losing their positions with their Judean and/or Roman patrons, and thus losing face before their peers, as well as losing their power and losing their wealth. In order to keep their positions, they must control the crowds, and therefore they fear the crowds. Five times in the Jerusalem episodes, the narrator emphasizes that the Judean authorities are afraid to speak or act because of the crowds. Because they hold power at the expense of others, they possess little security and need to maintain control over them.

This same fear is characteristic also of the Roman authorities, Herod and Pilate. Although Herod wants to protect John, he has John beheaded for fear of losing face—"because of the oaths and those reclining to eat" with him. Although Pilate is amazed by Jesus and knows that the high priests handed him over out of envy, he has him executed so that he can "do the satisfactory thing for the crowd."

In Mark's world, fear is the opposite of faith. Faith in God gives courage to risk for others, but the authorities do not risk for others. Ironically, in their efforts to save themselves, they sow the seeds of their own destruction.[4]

The authorities lord over people

At one point, Jesus warns the disciples that "those considered to be rulers over the Gentile nations lord over them and their great ones exert authority over them, but it is not to be like this among you." With these words, Jesus condemns the Roman emperor as well as the local agents of the Gentile nations under him, including the Judean leaders who act in the same manner as their imperial overlords. Instead of serving others, they use violence to secure and aggrandize themselves.

In serving themselves, the Judean authorities in Mark's story become destructive. They not only fail to meet needs but also harm people by lording over them. In the end, the Judean authorities go beyond the law in using false witnesses and stirring up the crowd to request the release of a murderer rather than Jesus. They also manipulate others—Judas and the crowds—to get Jesus executed. Pilate, who has the legal power to release or to execute people, agrees to execute Jesus in order to satisfy the crowd. Mark's depiction of Jesus' execution portrays the Roman authorities and their Judean collaborators as brutal in crushing any challenge to their rule.

The attitude of the authorities toward power is fully revealed at the crucifixion. They will do what they have to do to maintain their power and control. At the crucifixion, the authorities—Judean and Gentile alike—mock Jesus for his weakness and his vulnerability. Four times they ridicule Jesus: after he is convicted, when the soldiers mock him, when he is on the cross, and after he cries out.[5] In their blindness, they cannot imagine an anointed one who could not or would not choose to save himself. They cannot conceive of an agent of God who uses no force and refuses to lord over people. Losing one's life for others, renouncing oneself or one's status to become a slave or servant, and refusing to use the power you have to save yourself are all alien to the authorities' way of thinking. To them

Jesus is simply powerless and weak, not faithful and courageous. His crucifixion confirms for them that they are right.

The authorities will not stop with Jesus but will continue to persecute his followers. However, in Mark's world, they will soon learn the disastrous consequences of their behavior. At the return of Jesus, they will be judged, and they will learn that God's power is to be used for the benefit of others.

The audience and the authorities

Jesus and the authorities each claim to be acting as agents of God. The narrator has guided the audience to accept Jesus' claim and reject the authorities' claim—by aligning the narrator's point of view with the point of view of Jesus about the rule of God. In this regard, the central conflict in Mark is not between Jesus and his followers, on the one hand, and "the Judeans," on the other hand, as though Jesus and his followers were not themselves thoroughly Judean. Rather, the conflict is between the Judean Jesus and his followers as agents of God's rule, and the Judean and Roman authorities. As such, the conflict is about status, wealth, and use of the power and authority.

In the authorities, Mark has produced entirely negative figures who embody standards opposite to the rule of God. They have views contrary to Jesus and the rule of God around issues of wealth (they want to gain the whole world), status (they seek honor from others), and power (they lord over others). As we have noted, these figures are characters in a story and are not to be confused with the actual Judean or Roman authorities. Nevertheless, Mark's portrayals of authority accurately characterize the nature of power. It is not difficult for audiences to put themselves in the place of the authorities and to see the self-serving reasons that they behave as they do. Some hearers may well have identified with them. In the end, however, the audience is guided by the narrator to disassociate completely from the mentality and behavior of the authorities.

More than this, the hearers are themselves to proclaim the rule of God before the Judean and Roman authorities. They are called to risk being beaten in synagogues and being brought before governors and kings as testimony to them—to give them an opportunity to turn around and enter the rule of God before it is too late.

The Disciples

In Mark's story, the term *disciples* comes to refer to the twelve men Jesus chooses to follow him. At first two pairs of brothers are called, then Levi (who does not become one of the twelve), and then Jesus creates the twelve as a group, each of whom is identified by name. From then on, the term "disciples" basically refers to these twelve. Simon (Rock), along with James and John (sons of thunder), whom Jesus gives nicknames, form an inner circle of disciples.

There are also others who "follow" Jesus: Levi the tax collector; the disciples who eat with the tax collectors; "those around Jesus with the twelve" when he explains the riddles; the man who exorcises in Jesus' name; Bartimaeus who follows him after being healed; the bystander who draws the sword at Gethsemane; and especially the women at the crucifixion, who "had been serving him and following him when he was in Galilee." We might also include the minor characters who perform discipleship functions of proclaiming and serving, and even the crowds who "follow" Jesus around. Jesus invites the whole crowd to "take up their cross and follow after me," and he admonishes everyone to "keep watch."[6] Clearly, following Jesus and doing the work of discipleship are open to everyone.

Jesus appoints the twelve disciples to "be with him" and to be sent out "to proclaim and to have authority over the demons." They are called to extend the work of Jesus and to understand and embrace the vision of the rule of God over Israel, the Gentile nations, and all creation. No reason is given for Jesus' choice. They are not chosen for their moral character or their intelligence or their piety. Mark's twelve disciples—fishermen, tax collectors—are from among the common folk of the village of Capernaum and the surrounding area. They have limited honor and no social power, and they are not connected to any authority group.

Characterization

The characterization of the disciples shows a struggle between living on God's terms and living on human terms. The disciples strive to live on God's terms, leaving all to follow Jesus, clearly able to take risks. At the same time, they live "on human terms," preoccupied with their own security, status, and power.

Thus the characterization of the disciples is complex. What the disciples *do* reveals their loyalty to Jesus as followers and helpers. Yet what they *do* as well as what they *say* exposes their difficulties in following. The narrator's inside views of the disciples' thoughts and emotions are almost entirely negative, and the protagonist Jesus regularly corrects and warns them. Thus the narrator portrays them as disciples who are on Jesus' side but who fail to meet fully the expectations set by their teacher. They are complex characters in so far as they have conflicting traits.

Much of the characterization of the disciples is built on their lack of understanding, their fear, and their lack of faith. Understanding is crucial for the followers of Jesus in this story. Jesus calls for people to love God "with your whole understanding." Furthermore, the call to "turn around" means "to change your understanding" of God, the anointed one, yourself, and your values. Jesus seeks to get the disciples to understand and to grasp, to see and to hear. Unlike the authorities who refuse to understand, the disciples for the most part want to understand but are limited by their faulty expectations and their fears. Their fear is sometimes a matter of being overawed by the power of God in Jesus and sometimes a matter of anxiety about their well-being. Neither of these fears is an adequate response to the presence and demands of the rule of God. Fear is the opposite of faith.

The traits of the disciples unfold in response to changing developments in the narrative. After their initial acceptance of Jesus' call, the disciples move from a lack of understanding to misunderstanding and finally to understanding but with an inability to follow through in action. Thus the disciples start out as reliable but end up being examples of how not to follow Jesus!

The narrator also develops the disciples' characterization by contrast and comparison. The disciples are a contrast to Jesus in their failure to respond appropriately to the rule of God. Such teaching by negative example is common in ancient narratives. In Mark, the failures of the disciples constitute the primary device by which the narrator reveals Jesus' standards for discipleship, for much of Jesus' teaching comes in the course of correcting their behavior and attitudes. The narrator also develops a comparison between the disciples and the authorities, for the disciples often reflect the same mentality as Jesus' opponents. Finally, the narrator contrasts the disciples negatively in relation to the positive depiction of many minor characters.

Faith, loyalty, and authority

From the start, the disciples attach themselves to Jesus as disciples to a teacher. Having "left everything" to follow him, they stay "with him" and now get their identity from their family-like relationship with him.[7] Their successes and failures are always presented within the context of their relationship with him as insiders.

Mark's story portrays the disciples as devoted to Jesus. They become fishers for people—leaving work and family to follow, going to him on the mountain, then proclaiming, exorcising, and healing when he authorizes them to do so. They serve Jesus by following his instructions to take him in the boat, to find a donkey for him, and to prepare the Passover meal. They go with him anywhere he permits them, staying with him despite storms, trips to the desert, corrections, warnings, and little or no praise or assurance of reward. Even after he has told them to expect persecution and no special rewards, they proclaim their allegiance to him until death; they are loyal, even faithful, to Jesus—at least until his arrest.

Thus the disciples serve Jesus, and they serve other people by proclaiming, healing, and exorcising. In this sense, they fulfill their calling as disciples.

Lack of understanding, fear, and lack of faith

It becomes clear early in the story that the disciples have difficulty because of their lack of understanding and their fear. They do not get the riddles Jesus tells. They do not see the full possibilities of the rule of God—in a storm at sea or in a desert without food. At the same time, they are afraid—frightened by the storm, frightened by the power of Jesus to calm the storm, frightened by seeing Jesus walk on water, anxious about the lack of bread. They do not trust God's power over nature active in Jesus in the present. In short, "They were frightened with great fear."

Their fear and lack of understanding are interrelated. Their fear prevents them from understanding, and their inability to understand leaves them frightened. Thus the issue is not a lack of intelligence. Mark is showing something more profound. Fear inhibits understanding, and misunderstanding generates fear. The disciples are vulnerable to both fear and a lack of understanding because the rule of God is both awesome and contrary to customary patterns of thinking. The disciples are thinking in human terms and have not grasped the mind-set of faith in the rule of God.

Both fear and lack of understanding are rooted in the lack of trust in the rule of God. At one point, Jesus says to the disciples: "Why are you such cowards? Don't you have faith yet?" The works of power the disciples witness with their own eyes should awaken trust in God's rule. But "because they had not understood about the loaves," their minds were hardened. The episode of the father and his possessed son shows that people can ask for help even out of their lack of faith. Yet the disciples are not shown praying for such help.

In their fear and lack of understanding, the disciples are similar to the authorities. Like the authorities, they think in false expectations and limited categories. And like the authorities, they are afraid.

Seeking glory and resisting death on the journey

At midpoint in the story, when Rock identifies Jesus as the anointed one, the issue shifts from a lack of understanding to misunderstanding. The disciples now understand who Jesus is, but they misunderstand in thinking that the anointed one will march into Jerusalem triumphantly and will reward followers with positions of honor and power. On first hearing it, the disciples reject the idea that persecution and death may be a consequence of service in the rule of God. Once again, they have a human mindset.

As before, the disciples are afraid, not, at this point, from awe at God's power but from fear of persecution and crucifixion, both for Jesus and for themselves. As we have seen, crucifixion was a horrible and shameful death, and it was reserved for political criminals and for slaves. Naturally, the disciples fear it. They are afraid to ask Jesus what he means by the predictions of his death and resurrection, and they are afraid on the way up to Jerusalem. As the narrator says, "Those who followed were afraid."

Again, fear and misunderstanding are interrelated. Their misunderstanding leads the disciples to be frightened by Jesus' predictions of his death, and in turn their fear keeps them from understanding. As the narrator says, "They did not understand what he said, and they were afraid to ask him." And the fear and misunderstanding correlate with the lack of faith to act courageously in the face of loss and threat.

The disciples' way of coping with Jesus' talk about death is to cling to their personal hopes and values. Their desire for honor and power is so great that James and John are even willing to die with Jesus—*if* Jesus will give them "places to sit one on his right and one on his left" in his glory. But for the Markan Jesus, there is no reward for undergoing persecution. Serving and being least are just the way the rule of God is. It is not a way to gain favor or to be rewarded.[8]

As earlier, the disciples are somewhat like the authorities. The difference is that the authorities already have honor, power, and wealth, and they want to keep them and use them to dominate others, while the disciples do not have these things but want to acquire them. In the Markan story world, the desire for control and domination to secure one's self and one's group is tenacious. The lure of cultural values—or, in Mark's terms, "human" values—is great.

Hence the disciples have a strong desire to serve themselves. In contrast to self-serving values that will lead only to a life of competition and domination, Jesus is showing them relationships of mutual serving. But the disciples see honor as worth, power as privilege, wealth as blessing, and security as salvation. For that culture, serving was not noble or honorable but the work of slaves and women. So, rather than serve those below them, they want to secure their own privilege and honor. When James and John ask for positions of power beside Jesus, they understand that the rule of God will end in glory, but they do not grasp its nature as service. The key is that the mistaken values of the disciples keep them from carrying out the mission Jesus has given to them: to meet the needs of the people, to welcome children, to confront oppressors, and to be faithful even in the face of persecution and death.

In their quest to have faith in the rule of God, the disciples have left all to follow Jesus, but they have not yet renounced themselves and the human values that put a premium on saving and serving themselves. They do not fully grasp the vision of sharing wealth, being least, and serving as a vision for nations and all creation. Yet, by virtue of their experiences on the journey, the disciples do change. They come to see more clearly, paralleling the stories of the blind men, who also come to see. The disciples have now learned that following God's way entails persecution. They "see" clearly enough to "follow Jesus" to Jerusalem.

Fear and flight in Jerusalem

As they enter Jerusalem, it appears that the disciples may succeed in following Jesus. Their verbal opposition to Jesus' death as well as to their own persecution disappears. They also cease talking about their hope for power and glory from a martyr's death, and they accept his predictions of their fate in the future. They seem willing to follow Jesus on his (and God's) terms, for they have come to Jerusalem determined to be loyal to him to death.

On the Mountain of the Olives, Jesus warns four of his diciples of all that may befall them—being handed over to (Judean) councils, beaten in synagogues and standing before (Roman) governors and kings, being hated by everyone, brought to trial, all in an oppression the likes of which had not happened "from the beginning of creation until now." For the sake of the chosen ones, God even "cut short the days." Through all of it, Jesus admonishes them that "whoever endures to the end will be saved." These warnings enable the disciples to size up the full measure of what it means to follow Jesus.

In Jerusalem, the disciples have the opportunity to show their loyalty. But they have overestimated their capacity to be faithful. Their fear here is rooted in their failure to grasp their own human frailty in the face of death. On the way to Jerusalem, James and John boasted that they were able to undergo a baptism of persecution and death. Then at the meal in the upper room, all the disciples seem incredulous at the idea that one of them might hand Jesus over, and they ask, "Surely not I?" Back out on the Mountain of the Olives, when Jesus predicts that they will all stumble, Rock protests vehemently: "Even if it's necessary for me to die with you, I'll definitely not renounce you!" And all the others were "saying the same thing." The disciples falsely think they have the courage to face execution faithfully. As a result, they sleep and fail to "keep watch." Jesus depicts their character precisely when he says that "the spirit is eager, but the flesh is weak."

Sure enough, when the hour of testing comes, fear takes over and the disciples flee. Rock follows from a distance, but in response to questions by a servant girl, he folds. He renounces Jesus three times and, in the end, swears that he does not even know Jesus.[9] Rock, who earlier spoke on behalf of all the disciples when he acknowledged Jesus as the anointed one, now represents the disciples' realization of their failure. Rock remembers Jesus' prediction and breaks down sobbing. When all other considerations are stripped away, the disciples' fearful need to "save their lives" prevails. They are unable to face the consequences of association with and acknowledgment of Jesus, and in Rock's weeping they acknowledge their failure and their grief over it. This acknowledgment—in contrast to the authorities—makes it possible for the disciples to "turn around" and follow. Nevertheless, at this point of fear and failure, the disciples disappear from the narrative.

The failure of the disciples

Unlike the opponents, the disciples (apart from Judas) do not destroy Jesus to save their lives. They are not against Jesus. Rather, they fail at being for him. And those closest to Jesus fail the most. Rock, James, and John are privy to many things throughout the narrative—the resurrection of a twelve-year-old girl, the transfiguration of Jesus, the private teachings about the future. Yet they let Jesus down more than the others, because he asked them to keep watch for him and they did not do it. This depiction is especially biting when Jesus reverts to calling Rock "Simon" at the first instance of failure in Gethsemane: "And Jesus said to Rock, 'Simon, are you sleeping?'"

The failure of the disciples parallels the seeds that fall on rocky ground. The epithet leads the audience to expect strength and courage from "Rock," but the interpretation of the seed falling on "rocky" ground suggests a different and ironic meaning of that name. As we have seen, the disciples have hardness of mind and do not easily understand. As the riddle says: "And they don't have root in themselves but are short-lived. Then when oppression or persecution comes because of the word, immediately they stumble."

After the resurrection

The final episode of the empty grave evokes the same ambivalent responses. The women—Mary the Magdalene, Mary the mother of James the younger and Joses, and Salome—carry on the character role of the disciples in the plot, as they witness the crucifixion, burial, and empty grave. The audience wants them to succeed in following, to deliver the young man's joyful message to the disciples, including Rock. However, like the disciples, the women fail—in their fear of the power of God evident in the empty grave.

The message of the young man offers restoration for the disciples. Yet because the women say nothing, that restoration will have to depend on the disciples' recollection of Jesus' early words to them and on their willingness to return to Galilee. The fate of the disciples—like that of the audience—is still open. At the end, everything is possible again for the disciples, and yet in the new situation, in which their teacher is an executed criminal, the terrible fear remains.

The audience and the disciples

The narrator's characterization of the disciples leads the audience to develop ambivalent feelings toward them. The audience is led to identify with the disciples more than other characters and wants them to succeed. Hearers can easily put themselves in the situation of the disciples: the privilege of being called by Jesus, being surprised by his acts of power, being frightened by the prospect of death by crucifixion, and eager to flee rather than be arrested. The positive and readily understandable characteristics of the disciples maintain the audience's interest in the hope that, despite their failures, the disciples will succeed in becoming faithful followers of Jesus. Some inside views even evoke sympathy for the disciples, for example, when the disciples are awed by Jesus' authority over the storm, when their eyes are so heavy at Gethsemane, and above all when Rock lurches off "sobbing" after his denials of Jesus.

At the same time, the hearers also evaluate and judge the disciples by the values of the rule of God, the very values that Jesus has taught. In addition, the negative inside views often lead hearers to distance themselves from the disciples. Thus the narrator leads hearers to face squarely the harsh failures of the disciples and, at the same time, to care about them and about how they will fare in the future of the story world.

The narrator has depicted the disciples as afraid, with little faith or under-standing, concerned to save their own lives, and preoccupied with their own importance, but nonetheless leaving all and persevering in following Jesus. In the end, however, they fail to prepare adequately for death by persecution. Yet the audience is to learn from the failure of the disciples. If the disciples can fail again and again and Jesus still promises to go ahead of them, the hearers can also fail. The thrust of this portrayal poses questions to the audience: Can you choose to follow Jesus? What will you do when faced with death for Jesus and the good news? Can you remain faithful? And can you, if you fail, begin again?

And such proclaiming of the news about God's rule will not be easy for the hearers, as they have learned from both Jesus and the disciples.

The Minor Characters

The minor characters and the crowds are crucial in Mark's story. They are the broad peasant populace from whom Jesus and the disciples come. They are the least, who are to be served and whom the authorities fail to serve. Ironically, it is the minor characters themselves who demonstrate the service of the rule of God when the authorities and then the disciples do not.

Minor characters do not play ongoing roles in the story. They make brief appearances and then disappear. They are not a group character, because indi-vidually they are not connected to each other. Yet the similarities between many of them are so striking as to lead us to consider them together. The brevity of their appearances and, in most cases, their anonymity in no way diminish their impor-tance. The role of each is often quite memorable and, taken collectively, their impact on the reader is unmistakable and profound.[10]

Apart from Herodias and her daughter, the high priest's slave, and the soldiers who mock Jesus, the minor characters relate favorably to the rule of God: some emerge from the crowds for healing; others are lifted up by Jesus as examples; still others serve Jesus. Usually, they are marginal people with no power—children, women, a beggar, a foreigner, a poor widow. Many are excluded from common life because of their afflictions. Some are considered unclean—demoniacs, the leper, the woman with the flow of blood, and the Syrophoenician woman. Yet these minor characters constitute the fertile soil for the good news of the rule of God. And they are the mothers, sisters, brothers, daughters, and sons who make up the new family of the rule of God.

While most minor characters emerge from the crowds of common people, a few do not. As we have noted, there are minor characters from among the authorities who favor Jesus: Jairus the synagogue ruler; a wealthy woman who anoints Jesus; the legal expert who is not far from the rule of God; Joseph of Arimathea, "a reputable member of the council"; and the centurion who calls Jesus "son of God." These exceptions make it clear, in Mark's portrayals, that no group is fixed in its response and that a positive response from any character is welcomed.

Characterization

The minor characters have several typifying traits: an openness to Jesus, a persistent faith, humility, a disregard for personal status and power, and a capacity for service. Many are changed or have their situation changed by coming to Jesus. In the words of Jesus, they are the "little ones who have faith." Yet their portrayal is sometimes mixed: many do not obey Jesus' command to be quiet; the father of the demoniac boy needs more faith; and the legal expert is near but not in the rule of God.

For the most part, the minor characters are not interchangeable with one another in the flow of the story. An episode in which a minor character appears is commonly interwoven with those episodes around it by structural patterns and verbal threads. In addition, the narrator often juxtaposes a specific minor character to other characters in adjacent episodes for comparison or contrast. Also, the stories of minor characters sometimes provide important transitions or signal developments in the plot: the demoniac is freed from a demon just after Jesus has bound Satan in the desert; the Syrophoenician woman is the bridge to a Gentile mission; Bartimaeus's cry to Jesus as son of David sets up the entrance to Jerusalem.

Faith

The faith of the minor characters is important, because the work of the rule of God is contingent on people who "turn around and put faith in the good news." Suppliants who ask for healing come with a simple desire to be healed and the faith that, through Jesus or the disciples, God can heal them. They express their trust in observable actions: coming to Jesus, kneeling, pleading with Jesus, and asking for healing.[11]

Sometimes, friends or family bring the person to be healed: the paralyzed man, the deaf man, the blind man, and so on. Crowds also bring the sick and plead with Jesus to touch them. Others come in place of someone: Jairus and the Syrophoenician woman each come on behalf of a daughter. The active faith of all these surrogates counts for the faith or trust of those on whose behalf they come.

Suppliants show persistence and determination in their faith by overcoming obstacles: four men bypass a crowd to lower a paralyzed man through a roof;

Jairus perseveres in spite of his daughter's death; the Syrophoenician woman overcomes Jesus' unwillingness to heal Gentiles; and Bartimaeus gains Jesus' attention in spite of the efforts of the crowd to silence him.

For Mark, faith does not in itself restore the suppliant, for it is God alone who restores. However, because neither Jesus nor God forces healing, faith becomes essential as a way to release and to receive healing. Faith does not have to do with correct beliefs about Jesus. For Mark, faith is a matter of trusting that God will act through Jesus. Such faith gives people access to God's power, as illustrated by the power going out from Jesus to the woman with the flow of blood. Because everything is possible for God, everything may be possible for one who has faith. By faith, the suppliant is empowered to be a partner in the healing with God; so Jesus says to several suppliants, "Your faith has restored you." Where faith is present, people take the initiative to come to Jesus. Where faith is weak, as with the father of the demoniac boy, Jesus empowers it. Where faith in God to heal through Jesus is absent, as at Nazareth, only a few healings occur.[12]

Losing life, being least, and serving

In general, the minor characters show no concern to be great or to exert power or to acquire wealth, concerns that would inhibit their efforts to meet another's need. The poor widow is a paradigm for how to relinquish life—by giving "everything she had, her whole *living*." Her low status and the smallness of her gift suggest that she does not give for recognition or reward; in fact, she is unaware of being noticed. The Syrophoenician woman exemplifies being least. She cleverly accepts Jesus' reference to her as a dog in order to get her daughter exorcised. Bartimaeus the "beggar" exemplifies persistence in faith. Simon's mother-in-law exemplifies serving, as do the characters who bring someone for healing.

In the final scenes in Jerusalem, the minor characters especially exemplify the admonition to be "servant of all." Throughout the story, Jesus serves others in their need. So, in Jesus' time of need, others serve him: Simon the leper receives him in his house; a woman anoints Jesus on the head; Simon the Cyrenean takes up his cross; Joseph buries him; and the women from Galilee go to the grave to anoint him. The characters who perform these acts of service do so courageously, risking wealth or arrest or reputation to carry them out. These acts mirror the self-giving of Jesus and assure hearers that it is possible to follow him.

In their roles in the passion narrative, the narrator brings the minor characters to the fore by naming them. Earlier in the story, Jairus is the only positive minor character mentioned by name. In the Jerusalem episodes, however, Bartimaeus, Simon the leper, Simon the Cyrenean, Joseph from Arimathea, Mary the Magdalene, Mary the mother of James the lesser and of Joses, and Salome are all named. And the woman who anoints Jesus will have her deed recounted wherever the good news is proclaimed. This naming makes the minor characters personal and memorable to the audience, and it emphasizes that people achieve their full identity in acts of service.

Women

Many of the minor characters are women.[13] They are in the crowds. They are among Jesus' new family of mothers and sisters and brothers. As part of the crowd, they receive the invitation to renounce themselves and follow Jesus. Female characters generally typify the marginal status of the minor characters—sometimes in several ways.

Mark foregrounds a number of female characters. For the most part, the women exemplify the standards of the rule of God: the serving of Simon's mother-in-law, the faith of the woman with the flow of blood, the insight and clever wit of the Syrophoenician woman, the self-giving of the poor widow, and the prophetic act of the woman who anoints Jesus. Many show courage in flouting social expectations and religious customs—coming to Jesus in public, touching him in a state of impurity, or intruding on his privacy. The Syrophoenician woman succeeds in getting Jesus to change his mind about healing Gentiles. Jesus lifts up women as examples for the disciples to follow, such as the woman who anoints him and the poor widow.

Furthermore, the narrator tells us that "Mary the Magdalene, and Mary the mother of James the younger and of Joses, and Salome, along with many other women" had been serving Jesus, had followed him in Galilee, and had gone with him up to Jerusalem. Indeed, these women continue the discipleship character role. Apart from Jesus' mother Mary and Herodias, these are the only other women to be named and, like the twelve, they have an ongoing role in the narrative, albeit brief. They take risks by being at the crucifixion and by going to the grave, and they show their willingness to serve by buying spices and going to anoint Jesus. The women minor characters in particular exemplify the way of discipleship amid the failure and absence of the twelve.

Comparison and contrast with other characters

The minor characters serve as foils for the disciples in relation to the emerging standards in the story. In the first half of the story, the narrator implicitly contrasts the faith of the suppliants with the fear of the disciples. Then on the journey to Jerusalem and early in Jerusalem, Jesus explicitly corrects the disciples' behavior by contrasting them with minor characters—children, slaves, servants, a poor widow who gives out of her need, and a woman who anoints him—in order to show the disciples how to be least and to serve. In the final scenes, the minor characters take actions that the twelve fail to do—take down the body of Jesus, put him in a grave, and anoint him—the services of burial that John's disciples had done for their teacher.

Mark's story also contrasts the minor characters and the authorities: the woman who anoints Jesus with costly ointment contrasts with the authorities who give money to arrest him, and the poor widow who gives freely contrasts with the legal experts who exploit widows. In all the ways that the minor characters contrast with the disciples and the authorities, they are like Jesus, thus showing the audience more figures who live on "God's terms."

Ongoing discipleship

Whereas the disciples are expected to show an ongoing faithfulness to Jesus, the minor characters exemplify the standards of the story only on momentary occasions. What happens to the minor characters in the story after they encounter Jesus is generally not told. Some go out and proclaim (in spite of Jesus' command to the contrary), sowing seeds that "produce thirty and sixty and a hundred per measure." Others go back to their houses. Some receive Jesus and the disciples by hospitality, such as Simon the leper. Even people who give a cup of water to one who comes in the name of the anointed one "will definitely not lose their reward."

However, once ongoing discipleship involves threat of persecution, it may be a different matter. This may explain the surprising behavior of the three women at the grave. They are at the crucifixion, and they are prepared to anoint the body. But when they are confronted by the power of God, revealed by the empty grave, they too fail. They are to "go tell," but their reaction, like that of the disciples earlier, is fear and flight and silence. Everyone within the narrative fails to continue following. That role is left for the audience.

The crowds

In Mark's story, the people who flock to Jesus are "like sheep without a shepherd"—signifying that the leaders of the nation have not taken care of the sheepfold of Israel.[14] By contrast, Jesus has compassion for the crowds; he teaches them and twice feeds a throng in the desert. In general, the response of the crowds reveals their desire for a leader who will attend to their needs. They acclaim Jesus; they surround him in confined and open spaces alike and follow him in droves; they come from everywhere in and around Israel; they crowd into the villages; when the villages cannot hold them, they gather in the open spaces between villages; their presence in such large numbers protects Jesus from the threat of his family in Galilee and later from the threat of the authorities in Jerusalem.

The traits of the crowds are often similar to those of the suppliants. They come to Jesus wherever he is; they desire to be healed; and they press on him to touch him. Crowds bring people for healing and show persistence in getting to Jesus: one crowd runs after him from one town to the next; another follows his boat around the sea; and another stays with him for three days in the desert. They do not recognize him as the anointed one but think of him as John the baptizer or Elijah or a prophet. Nevertheless, the crowds are amazed by Jesus and praise God for these works of power. Such amazement usually reflects an openness to the transforming power of the rule of God. However, as we have said, amazement by itself is not a sufficient response to the rule of God.[15]

As long as Jesus is publicly accessible and the outcome of his activity is undetermined, the crowds follow him, respond to his compassion and power, acclaim him, and are "glad to hear him." However, as Jesus approaches Jerusalem, the crowds see him as one who will bring in "the coming rule of our father David" rather than the "rule of God." When Jesus is arrested, taken from the scene, and rendered powerless, they stop following. The crowd now becomes vulnerable to manipulation by the traditional authorities. The high priests, fearing and envying the support of Jesus by the people, stir up the crowd to ask Pilate to release Barabbas rather than Jesus. In the end, the crowd even calls for his crucifixion and joins the ridicule of Jesus. Like the disciples and the minor characters, the crowds too fail in following Jesus.

The audience and the minor characters

The people who originally heard Mark's story would have related to the marginal women and men in the story and been empowered by them. They would have celebrated the healings with the crowds. The stories of healing would have awakened hope for them and for others who shared the same conditions. And they would have identified with the minor characters who exemplify the values Jesus taught—and been assured that they did not have to be among the twelve in order to serve the rule of God.

By bringing minor characters to the fore, the narrator illustrates Jesus' assertion that "the least [will be] most important." For within the standards set by the story, these "little ones" are truly great. Just as Jesus puts forth children and servanthood as models for the disciples and later summons them to notice the self-giving of the poor widow, so the narrator puts forth the minor characters for the audience to notice and to learn from—so that they will be remembered wherever the good news is proclaimed. In fact, it is only by seeing the rule of God in the characters who are "least" that the audience has fully grasped the extent to which the rule of God turns the world upside down.

The minor characters also illustrate the way in which the seed falls "on the good soil" and produces "thirty, sixty, and a hundred per measure." Such responses are encouraging to audiences, who see that they will not be alone and that they too can receive the rule of God and be faithful in proclaiming and living out its values—"wherever the good news is proclaimed in the whole world."

Conclusion

What does Mark's characterization tell us overall about his view of human nature and the problems that constitute the human condition? Creation is awry, people are threatened by natural forces, nations dominate people, demons possess people, and many are ill, disabled, unclean, without direction, neglected, and oppressed. The rule of God brings healing and life to those who welcome it. The rule of God also brings challenges. Unfortunately, people are not easily given to taking risks. People tend to conform to their group, to the given values of their culture, and to actions that keep them safe. People are afraid and protect themselves and their group. Out of fear, the authorities try to protect themselves, their status, and their power. The disciples reflect the same values, despite their desire and partial success in doing otherwise. Perhaps because the minor characters have little access to power and glory, they are more willing to serve. Change is possible but very difficult, because the change involves breaking with values that protect one's self and one's group in order to become oriented to "others" for the rule of God.

Nevertheless, Mark's characters are open. The potential is there for a harvest. Jesus chooses to be obedient to God to the end. Many minor characters exemplify the rule of God. The gospel will still be proclaimed, and the response of the centurion offers hope for change among the Gentile nations, even Rome. The disciples' fates are open, and the audience hopes that they will yet prove to be faithful. The minor characters have appeared briefly, yet their future too is open. Most of all, the hearers' fate is now ready to be decided by their response to this story.

As we reflect on the hearers' initial impressions of Jesus, the authorities, the disciples, and the minor characters, we realize how the narrative enables audiences to see, through surprising twists and turns, just what discipleship entails. Can hearers of Mark's story discern the rule of God breaking in through Jesus' words and actions? Can hearers embrace a vision of the whole world under the rule of God? Can hearers have trust in the power of God in the present—the power to heal, to feed the hungry in the desert, to calm storms, to raise the dead? Can hearers love God "with your whole life" and "love your neighbor as yourself"? Can hearers be willing to live and die for the good news, trusting God enough to lose one's life for others? For this is what the Gospel of Mark is calling hearers to do.

The Audience

We have been focusing on the storytelling and the story. Now we focus on the hearers, or audiences, as they engage in the process of experiencing the story in performance. Like a reader, the audience responds to the story in a linear, temporal fashion from the first word to the last.[1] Unlike a reader, hearers cannot skip ahead, skim, or look back. What is the audience experiencing, and how is the audience being affected by that experience? Here we shift from asking what the story *means* to asking what the story does to the audience in the course of experiencing the story.

The Rhetoric

Rhetoric refers to the way in which an author writes so as to create certain effects on readers. When we are dealing with performances, rhetoric addresses the impact of the story on audiences. These effects are engendered by the narrative as a whole—*both* by the particular story being told (the settings, the dynamics of the plot, and the development of the characters) *and* by the way the story is composed. The rhetorical question is: How do all the dimensions of a narrative work together to affect an audience?

You may have read a novel that kept you in suspense. To ask about the rhetoric of that story is to ask: How did the story do that to you? You may respond to a film with greater compassion or perhaps with increased hostility or with a sense of personal courage you did not know that you had. To ask about the rhetoric of that film is to ask: How did the film lead you to react like that? Here we are asking about the rhetoric of Mark: What are the potential effects of Mark's story on audiences? And how does the story work to create that impact?

The Ideal Audience

Before we consider the responses of real audiences to Mark's story, we return to the concept of the *ideal audience*. Throughout this study, we have mentioned how the narrator has led hearers to respond in certain ways to various aspects of the story world. In most cases, this "audience" was not an actual audience, either ancient or modern, since it is not possible to predict the responses of actual audiences. Real audiences will engage Mark from different perspectives and with different reactions. Real audiences may already know about the fate of Jesus and the outcome of the disciples even before they hear the story. Real audiences may or may not understand the story. Real audiences may resist the story—be offended by the story or disagree with its standards of judgment. Rather, our audience has been a hypothetical "ideal audience"—an imagined audience with ideal responses to the rhetoric of the story inferred from the story itself.

Most literary criticism on this subject addresses the issue of rhetoric with the concept of the ideal *reader*, because most interpretations deal with written material that is being encountered in the act of reading. By contrast, since we understand that Mark was composed to be presented by storytellers and to be experienced aurally by gathered communities, we have throughout referred to Mark's ideal *hearers* or ideal *audience*. In actual performances, the storyteller brings out an interpretation of the story for the audience with voice inflection, volume, pace and emphasis, along with the use of gestures, facial expressions, postures, and bodily movements. In our study, we have not addressed physical and verbal aspects of performing Mark. Rather, we have focused on the rhetoric of the story itself and its implied ideal audience.

The ideal audience is the audience that the composer creates (has in mind to shape) in the course of telling the story—an imaginary audience with all the ideal responses *implied by* the narrative itself.[2] We could do a detailed analysis of an ideal audience by inferring from each line in the narrative how an audience is being led to respond and react. For there are responses implied for audiences in every line: filling gaps, identifying with characters, being held in suspense, anticipating later parts of the story, recalling earlier parts of the story, being drawn in by the narrator's asides and irony, having emotions aroused, having expectations raised and revised, experiencing resolution (or the lack of it), and so on.[3] However, for our purpose here, we will limit ourselves to giving a brief sketch of the overall experience of the implied ideal audience in the course of experiencing Mark's Gospel.[4]

Our overall conclusion is that *the story of Mark seeks to create ideal audiences who will receive the rule of God with faith and have the courage to follow Jesus whatever the consequences*. We have emphasized the arrival of the rule of God as the watershed event in Mark's story. The manifestations of the rule of God in the story world are designed to enable an audience to believe that the rule of God is also possible for the real world in which they live. As such, the story is like a process of enculturation into the rule of God. To enter the rule of God is to be in the world in a new way. The experience of the story by an ideal audience is an "apocalyptic" (world-ending) event in the here and now, an event that ends one way of being in the world for the audience and launches them into a new way of being in the world. The ideal audience will embrace the good news about the rule of God, understand its presence and dynamics, and live by its values and relationships.

The story of Mark seeks to transform audiences through three movements: The narrative leads audiences (1) to experience the powerful blessings of God's rule, enabling them to enter the new life of the rule of God; (2) to understand and embrace the expectations and costs of the rule of God; and (3) to be empowered to live for the good news in faithfulness and courage. These three movements correlate with the three main developments of Mark's Gospel: (1) experiencing the rule of God (in Galilee), (2) overcoming one's resistance to the rule of God (on the journey to Jerusalem), and (3) facing persecution and death in the service of God's rule (in Jerusalem). Last, we will deal with the impact of the ending of Mark.

The narrative guides the ideal audience to see and accept God's ways primarily by drawing audiences into the story world and leading them to follow Jesus through the story. The narrator seldom lets Jesus out of the audience's sight, allowing the audience to be present with Jesus, hearing his words and seeing his actions. The ideal audience identifies with the situation of Jesus' disciples in the story and learns from their positive and negative example. With the disciples, the audience follows Jesus in his travels, sides with Jesus in his conflicts with the authorities, and learns from his teaching. As the story progresses, of course, the ideal audience follows Jesus to Jerusalem and by experiencing his execution learns the full cost of what it might mean to follow him. And the ideal audience witnesses the empty grave.

Stage 1: Experiencing the rule of God

The opening announcement of Jesus guides the ideal audience to attend to the momentous events about to be described: "The rule of God has arrived." Throughout the first half of the story, the audience experiences the rule of God in healings, exorcisms, cleansings, pardon of sins, feeding of the hungry, authority over nature, hope for the outcasts, and challenges to all human oppression. Through the recounting of these events, the narrator invites the audience to embrace the joy, the amazement, and the exhilaration of this new reality and to "put faith in the good news."

From the start, the narrative leads the ideal audience to follow Jesus. Early on, this audience aligns with Jesus as the reliable protagonist of the story. As the story unfolds, the hearers are guided to identify with the favorable responses of the disciples and the approval of the crowds. Conversely, the hearers are distanced from those who oppose Jesus. These hearers especially identify with the disciples, because they have an ongoing relationship with Jesus and model the appropriate responses to his call to follow. Furthermore, the ideal audience is brought into the scenes in which Jesus teaches the disciples privately. The audience is drawn into the story in part because the audience has an advantage over the disciples. As we have suggested above, the ideal audience is given inside information in the opening words about Jesus' identify as "the anointed one, the son of God." Because of this, the ideal audience is led to adopt the narrator's point of view about Jesus and to be on the inside. When the disciples begin to stumble and are corrected by Jesus (about riddles, faith on the sea, faith in the desert), the ideal audience—from an advantaged position—sees what it means to be an ideal follower.

The ideal audience is led at times to experience puzzlement at Jesus' riddles and cryptic sayings. Nevertheless, by portraying a world in which many characters are blind to the rule of God, the narrative leads the hearers to want to see and to follow even more. The two-step progressions, the series of three, and the explanations of the riddles further entice the ideal hearers to keep trying to understand Jesus and the hidden presence of the rule of God—even when the hearers are sometimes kept off balance by new mysteries and more riddles.

Stage 2: Overcoming resistance to the rule of God

When Rock identifies Jesus as the anointed one, the ideal audience no longer has an advantage over the disciples, for both now know that Jesus is the anointed one. At this point, the audience experiences startling and difficult developments at the same time the disciples do, increasing the sympathetic identification with the disciples. As Jesus predicts his execution and resurrection three times and teaches the disciples the costs and demands of following, the audience is present with the disciples to grapple with Jesus' challenges to their human-centered beliefs and values.

This stage of the story brings the audience into "seeing" the rule of God in greater depth—the second step of the two-step progression. As the blind man is touched twice, so also the ideal audience is invited to be touched twice to see clearly, to take a second and a more profound look. Along with the disciples, the hearers must revise and expand their expectations. Ideal hearers learn not only that Jesus will be handed over and executed but also that they too, like the disciples in the story, must be prepared for persecution and death. And they learn that the rule of God requires them to give up the quest for status, power, and wealth and to embrace leastness, service, and self-giving. In part, the strategy of the narrator is to teach by the negative example and misunderstanding of the disciples. The narrative leads the audience not only to identify sympathetically with the struggles of the disciples but also, and at the same time, to see that, by Jesus' standards, the disciples are wrong. At every point where the disciples resist or oppose or fail to understand, the audience hears Jesus telling them the right way to follow—giving them models such as children and servants, and admonishing them not to be like rulers who lord over people or like the wealthy who refuse to give up their wealth or like James and John who ask for glory in the age to come.

As the ideal audience sees the disciples' resistance and hears Jesus' teaching, they work through their own resistance and they strengthen their allegiance to Jesus—measuring their own commitment against that of the disciples. As hearers react to the failures of the disciples, the hearers are able to come to grips with their own failures and to desire even more to succeed in following Jesus.

In the process, the narrative invites the hearers into a deeper experience of faith. Thus, on the journey, the audience is called to make a further step in faith: if God can heal and drive out demons, then God can also raise one to life and salvation in the new age. In this section, the audience hears Jesus announce the coming of the rule of God in power and promise eternal life in the new age to those who follow him faithfully. The audience is led to grasp this insight: faith in a future salvation results neither in complacency nor in passive security but in the courage to bring God's rule to others even if it results in loss and death.

Stage 3: Facing persecution and execution in Jerusalem

The audience continues to be with Jesus in Jerusalem. Here the ideal audience overhears Jesus prepare four disciples by warning them about the Judean and Roman opposition and persecution they will encounter in proclaiming the good news to all the Gentile nations—arrests, beatings, witnessing before governors and kings—and the promise to be supported by the holy spirit. The ideal audience knows that Jesus is speaking about them too, in so far as they will be faithful to follow Jesus and the rule of God. This is made explicit when Jesus concludes the speech by telling the disciples to "stay awake" and to "keep watch"—and then adds, "And what I say to you I say to everyone. Keep watch!" So the ideal audience watches to see if the disciples do indeed stay awake.

At Gethsemane, the disciples fail when Jesus tells them to "keep watch." As the disciples fail to keep watch, fall asleep, and then flee, the audience remains awake and stays with Jesus. When Rock denies him, the audience follows Jesus to Golgatha. The audience is led to empathize with the disciples and take heart that Jesus knows the "flesh is weak." Yet at the same time, the audience judges the disciples for their failure to pray or to remain faithful.

In this section, irony is the primary means the narrative employs to bring the audience on the inside. Dramatic irony leads the audience to see the truth that the characters within the story do not see. At the entry to Jerusalem, because of Jesus' earlier teaching about not lording over, the ideal hearers know that it is not the rule

of David that is coming but the rule of God. In the narrative of Jesus' death, ironies heap up one on top of another. The soldiers ridicule the idea that Jesus is the
king of the Judeans, but he really is. The authorities ridiculing Jesus at the cross
unwittingly attest to the truth that Jesus "restored others but he cannot save himself." The authorities cannot see how an executed person could be king of Israel,
but the audience sees. Irony gives the hearers an inside perspective that leads them
to embrace the narrator's point of view about the crucifixion. And such irony creates community, as the audience shares the insider knowledge with the narrator.

The audience is led to see revealed in this executed man the embodiment
of God's idea of true greatness—the willingness to risk security, status, power,
and life itself in the service of the rule of God. The ideal hearer no longer judges
greatness by human standards but by God's standards. Because the narrative has
led the hearer to accept these standards, the hearer can accept the crucifixion of
the anointed one.

Furthermore, the narrative enables the ideal hearer to address the fear of following Jesus. Like the disciples, the hearer now knows the cost of following Jesus.
However, unlike the disciples, who flee, the hearer goes all the way through this
story with Jesus. In so doing, the ideal hearer faces vicariously the experience of
Jesus' abandonment, rejection, mocking, physical suffering, and death. By going
through Jesus' death in the experience of the narrative, the audience has a chance
to face with courage the fears of persecution and death that might otherwise para-
lyze them. Thus Mark empowers the audience not so much to believe something
about Jesus as to be *like* Jesus, faithful to the rule of God.

As presented by Mark, Jesus' faithfulness empowers the ideal hearers to have
the same kind of courage to be faithful. The narrative distances hearers from the
Judean and the Roman authorities, because they will destroy others to save themselves. The narrative distances hearers from the disciples, because they flee to
save themselves. So the audience looks to Jesus as the one faithful figure in the
story. Jesus is afraid and does not want to die; nevertheless, he is willing to live
life on God's terms. Thus the ideal hearer identifies with Jesus and comes away
from the story saying, "I too want to be faithful to God even in the face of death."

The example of Jesus' life for others in the face of death helps to free hearers
from the tenacious grip of self-centeredness and self-preservation, so that they too
may live for others, even in the face of persecution. The narrative seeks to create
ideal hearers who will establish solidarity with others who share the same values
and commitments, in order to shape relationships and communities of mutual
serving marked by faithfulness to the rule of God.

The ending[5]

We have said that the narrative works to invite the ideal audience to become faithful followers of Jesus through the experience of the story. By staying with the

story, the audience remains faithful to the end, following the women to the grave. At the grave comes the announcement the hearers have come to hope for and expect: "He was raised!" God has the last word on Jesus' conflict with the authorities, and the victory is God's. This last word can become a first word for the ideal audience, who will now follow.

The brief statement of the young man to the women at the grave—"You are seeking Jesus, the Nazarene who was crucified"—recalls for the audience the whole life of this man who was raised. Not just anyone, but the one who did these things and who died in this way, *this* is the one who was raised. And if this is the person God raised, then God will also raise those who associate with him, who follow him, who live for the good news as he did, and who are willing to face the persecution that comes, as he did. Thus the resurrection of Jesus affirms for the ideal hearers that the way Jesus lived is the way for all humans to live. And the ultimate consequence of living the standards of the rule of God is resurrection and eternal life in the rule of God in the coming age.

The ending also provides hope for the ideal hearer in terms of the identification with the disciples. The young man's announcement that Jesus "is going ahead of you to Galilee" means that Jesus is still going ahead of them and calling them to follow, including Rock—despite the flight and denial of the disciples. If the women did not convey this assurance to the disciples, nevertheless, the audience has heard it. The ideal hearer is assured that whatever their own fear and flight and silence might have been or might yet be, nevertheless, Jesus will still be calling them to follow him. The ending of Mark points the hearers to a new beginning—back to the beginning of the story, back to Galilee, to begin again the quest to follow Jesus faithfully.

However, at this point the narrative gives the final ironic twist—the women flee in fear and silence! The ideal audience expects the grave to be empty, but they do not expect the flight and silence of the women. All through the story, Jesus told people to be quiet and they proclaimed anyhow. Now the young man at the grave tells the women to "go tell," but they "said nothing to anyone at all"! This abrupt and shocking ending aborts the message to the disciples, cuts off any news about the resurrection, and ends the story in fear and silence. It is at this point that the story turns upon the audience, for there is no satisfying ending, no resolution, no closure to this story.

For those of us who are used to stories with a resolution, it is tempting to dull the shock of this ending by adding what we know from other Gospels or the history of the Christian movement. But imagine reading a story or seeing a film in which virtually everything is left up in the air, unresolved at the end. Mark's story is such a story: it is not resolved. It cries out for a resolution, cries out for the hope that people—the women, the disciples, anyone—will proclaim the good news. And who is left at the end of the story to do this? Not Jesus. Not the disciples. Not the women who fled the grave. Only the audience is left to complete the story!

So the ideal hearers are called to finish the story, to proclaim what happened. The hearers alone have remained faithful to the last and are now left with the choice to flee with the women or to proclaim boldly in spite of fear and the threat of death. And the ideal hearers will choose to proclaim! When all the characters in the story have failed, the ideal hearers will be the faithful. The ideal hearers have followed Jesus faithfully—received the rule of God, understood the costs and demands of following, and been empowered to proclaim. At the end, the ideal hearers are committed, in Jesus' absence, to live a life like Jesus lived, by faith in God, until Jesus returns.

Hypothetical First-Century Audiences

Of course, when the story of Mark was composed, the composer had actual first-century people in mind as his audience. But we do not know from the story itself who these people might have been. We can perhaps infer that they were mostly Judeans who followed Jesus, who were peasants in predominantly rural areas, and who were facing persecution. Such people likely had prior knowledge about Jesus, the outcome of the twelve disciples, and the beginnings of the Jesus movement.[6] They would have come from a particular place in society. And they would have come with a particular perspective and probably with a disposition to delight in the story and respond positively to it. They also would have struggled with their own fears and failures in seeking to be faithful followers of Jesus.

Mark may have had multiple audiences in mind, particularly if he expected the story to be told from place to place in public gatherings at meals or in synagogue gatherings or in village market areas. We can imagine how different groups might have responded to the story—people with ailments, widows, women in general, upper-class Judeans, Pharisees, or Roman soldiers. Each probably would have reacted quite differently. Surely the story was told to some people who were already followers of Jesus and already knew about Jesus and his disciples. Other hearers may never have heard about Jesus. Some may have rejected the story outright. Others may have agreed with some parts but resisted other parts. A sympathetic hearer, however, would have responded to the story in much the same way as the ideal audience and would have had additional responses in light of the historical situation of the time.

Mark's rhetoric seeks to enable real hearers to become ideal hearers and followers. And the rhetoric of Mark's narrative is compelling in large part because first-century hearers understand it to be based on real events and related to their real world. The power of Mark's narrative was rooted in the conviction that the rule of God had actually arrived, that the anointed messiah had come, been killed, and been raised, and that people even now were being called to proclaim and to follow, because the culmination of the rule of God was coming soon. The telling of the Gospel is itself the offer of the rule of God about to be established fully—with all its possibilities for restoration in the present, its dynamics of serving others, and its call to live and die for the good news.

Hence the rhetoric of Mark presents a way of understanding the world that challenges the way the hearers have constructed their world—with an end to their old way of living in the world and the onset of God's world here and now, in anticipation of the final and full arrival of the rule of God. The narrative draws the audience into the rule of God in the story world and then leads them to transfer their experience of the story to their real world. Hence, the story does not just *tell them about* the rule of God. The story itself actually *bears the reality* to them through the proclaiming of the good news. If the audience experienced their world under the dominion of Satan—with illnesses, demonic possession, threats of nature, and the tyranny of human rulers—they would be led to see and embrace the new world of possibilities opened up by the presence of the rule of God in their midst.

If the real hearers were outside the boundaries of society, treated as unclean or shunned as sinners, they would be invited to enter into this realm of God's rule. If hearers ordered their world by purity and avoided the ill, demoniacs, tax collectors, sinners, unclean food, and Gentiles, they would be challenged to remove these barriers and reach out with the power of the spirit to spread wholeness. If the audience saw in their own world the same standards embraced by the authorities in the story, they would be led to question and challenge the quest for public honor, the accumulation of wealth, and the use of power to dominate, and to embrace lives of serving and self-giving for others.[7] If hearers had recently experienced the devastation of the Roman-Judean War, they would have been drawn into Mark's vision of a world that renounces domination and exploitation. In all of these responses, the narrative of Mark seeks to shape not only individuals but also communities, by leading hearers to create relationships that will embody the values of the rule of God.

As we have indicated, Mark's Gospel was probably written around the year 70 CE, at the end of a four-year war between Israel and the Roman Empire during which time the Roman armies defeated Israel, destroyed Jerusalem, and leveled the temple.[8] At this time, some forty years after the death of Jesus, Judean and Gentile followers of Jesus alike were troubled by this catastrophic event. Some followers of Jesus expected Jesus to return and may have expected him to appear at the temple in Jerusalem. They would have wondered what it meant that God's city and temple were destroyed and that Jesus had not yet returned. Perhaps Jesus had not really been the anointed one. Perhaps he would not return, as they had hoped, to establish the rule of God in power within the generation.

The audience would be reassured by this story in which they hear the Markan Jesus predict all that has happened up to the time of the real hearers—famines, wars, persecutions, the horrible desecration and destruction of the temple, and the appearance of false prophets and anointed ones. Because these predictions of Jesus had already been fulfilled in the real world, the hearer would tend to trust the Markan Jesus when he says that the final establishment of God's rule and the return of Jesus were to occur, not at the time of the war or the desecration of the temple, but very soon after—before that generation had died out.[9] Furthermore, the narrative points the followers' hopes for Jesus' return away from Jerusalem toward Galilee and the Gentile nations.

The rhetoric of Mark's story makes most sense addressing followers who are under the threat of persecution, with reason to fear for their lives because of their association with Jesus.[10] These people would have listened to this story with intense involvement, because the story would be about them, about their loyalties, and about their hopes and fears. The first-century audience would know the very real threats to any who would follow Jesus: rejection by family, misunderstanding from Judean compatriots, trials before local Judean courts, and trials before Gentile governors and kings. To Judeans who engaged in war, the followers of Jesus who renounced violence and who opposed the war would have been viewed as traitors. And to the Romans, the followers of Jesus were suspected of revolution because their leader was executed as a revolutionary by a Roman procurator. Thus, if the hearers of Mark were to act as the story suggests, they would face persecution. In short, as Mark's Jesus predicted, "You will be hated by everyone because of my name."

The overall impact of the story might lead a sympathetic first-century audience, like the ideal audience, to face squarely the possibility of persecution and death and thus be better prepared to testify for Jesus and to bear to others the powerful acts of the good news of the rule of God. Followers who heard the story together in a gathering of the faithful would be empowered by the story. They would experience a solidarity with Jesus as one who had gone through everything they might have to endure and yet had remained faithful. They would experience support from each other, knowing that their trusting efforts to live the values of the rule of God would be just as misunderstood by and hidden from the world as Jesus' faithfulness was. But they would act in the conviction that very soon what is now hidden will be revealed and the son of humanity will come in glory to gather the chosen ones—including themselves—and finally establish God's rule over all creation.

Case Study: A Performance Scenario

Although we think Mark's story was composed for performances before many different audiences, in what follows we imagine one example of an early presentation of the oral composition of Mark. We imagine a peasant storyteller, a skilled oral performer, perhaps a nonliterate person, shortly after the Roman-Judean War of 66–70 CE. We imagine this person telling this story of Jesus in its entirety in the marketplace or after a meal of gathered followers in a village or small town, perhaps in northern Galilee or southern Syria, to a predominantly peasant audience of mostly Judeans and some Gentiles, not all of whom may be followers of Jesus. The narrative does not yet present itself as a "Christian" story distinct from Judaism. It is a story rooted in Judaism and reaching out to Gentiles.

This concrete performance scenario highlights three key aspects of the context: first, the political empire of Rome and its Judean agents in Israel; second, the cultural context of core values as expressed by opponents in the narrative world; and third, the specific historical context of the aftermath of the Roman-Judean war of 66 to 70 CE. When these three aspects are taken into account, Mark may be seen as a Gospel that is more radical—radical in the deepest sense of the word—than we have often considered it to be.

The reign of God and the empire of Rome

First, the Markan focus on the cosmic dimensions of God's reign magnifies the contrast between the reign of God and the empire of Rome. Consider the following contrasts *within* the story world of Mark's Gospel: Rome works from the center out; God's reign begins at the margins, in the wilderness, initiating a new sociopolitical order. Rome works from the top down; God's reign starts from the bottom up, a peasant movement spreading like invasive mustard plants. Rome secures the strongest of its people and exploits the weak; God's reign restores the weakest and most vulnerable. Rome occupies the land and the people much like a demon possesses a human being; God's reign liberates people from dominating demonic forces. The Judean authorities collaborating with Rome's empire in Israel establish boundaries of purity that exclude and marginalize; under God's reign, agents cross boundaries to restore the unclean to wholeness. The Judean collaborators of the Roman Empire in Israel use laws to control and marginalize; in God's reign, laws are interpreted or disregarded in order to bring life to people. Agents of the Roman Empire lord over people and exert authority over them; agents of God's reign serve and bring good news. Agents of the Roman Empire accumulate wealth ("acquire the whole world"), seek greatness, and acquire power to protect and aggrandize themselves; agents of God's reign are to relinquish wealth to the poor, be least, and use power to serve. The Roman Empire inflicts cruel and shameful death; the agents of God's reign are called to be faithful to the rule of God despite persecution and humiliation. Because these features of the Roman Empire existed in the lived world of the audience, the hearers could not help being aware of these contrasts. A performance imagined in the actual context of Roman power makes clear that the story offers a "world without empire," and the performer seeks to draw audiences into this new world.

The culture of the rule of God

Second, when we take into account the cultural context in which Mark's Gospel would have been first performed, we see that Jesus challenges core cultural values and practices within Israel as it is portrayed within the story world, many of which were also common values and practices throughout the ancient Mediterranean region as a whole. The reign of God reverses the direction of purity: instead of withdrawing for fear of defilement, its agents are to spread holiness and whole-ness through the holy spirit. Instead of fear of external contact with food and people and places considered to be unclean, followers are now to guard against internal uncleanness in their hearts resulting in actions harmful to others. The reign of God breaks the patronage cycle: Jesus does not seek followers who are beholden to him; so, instead of seeking honor for healing, Jesus tells suppliants to be quiet and go home. The rule of God subverts the core value of wealth: instead of wealth seen as a blessing, people are to relinquish their wealth to the poor. Kinship is reordered: instead of families ordered by patriarchy, the metaphorical kinship relations of the realm of God are structured so that no one serves as father and all are to function as servants to each other. The core value of honor is rede-fined: instead of seeking honor in the eyes of others as a mark of status, people are to choose to be least as a means to avoid the destructiveness of competition and to raise others up. The core definition of power is reconfigured: instead of using authority to dominate for one's advantage, people are to limit their power and use it to be servants to others. Even the visceral human drive for survival is challenged: instead of securing life at the expense of others, people are to risk their lives to bring the life-giving words and actions of God's reign to others. In experiencing a performance, those gathered to hear this story would not escape the challenge to certain values and taken-for-granted ways of life in so far as they were evident in their actual cultural context.

In the aftermath of the Roman-Judean War

Third, when we place this Gospel in the context of the Roman-Judean War of 66–70 CE, we are able to see Mark's story in sharper relief. The war involved a widespread peasant rebellion within Israel, both against the Roman Empire and against the prevailing Judean leadership under the Romans, which led to a four-year war that decimated the Galilean and Judean countrysides and that ended in the destruction of the city of Jerusalem and the burning and dismantling of the massive temple that served as the center of Judaism. If, as we have suggested, the Gospel of Mark was composed in the immediate aftermath of this war and if it was performed in or around Israel/Palestine at that time, then this war becomes the most compelling historical context in which to interpret Mark's Gospel.

It is not adequate to see Mark simply as a response to the *fact* of the war. Rather, Mark provided a response to the *dynamics* of this war—to the specific course, motives, and causes of that war. Mark told this story of Jesus who lived before the war as a way to address the war and offer to audiences another way. For example, imagine the hearers of Mark living in a village in northern Galilee that had already been devastated by Roman armies, with vivid memories of lost loved ones, dashed hopes, and the sounds of war still fresh in their minds. Now imagine how much the announcement of "good news," the declaration of an "anointed one" who was "son of God," the preparation of the "way" of the "Lord," the announcement of the arrival of the "empire" *of God*, and the call for fealty to or faith in this new rule of God—imagine how all of this may have echoed and yet contrasted with the entrance of the Roman armies into Palestine from the north with their trumpets and shouts and clash of arms. As the Roman general Vespasian moved south, he waged a scorched-earth campaign of domination and destruction of cities and villages throughout Galilee and the surrounding regions. By contrast, the Markan Gospel portrays Jesus waging a campaign in Galilee also, but a campaign against Satan and other manifestations of evil and ill-fortune as a means to bring restoration and healing—driving out demons where the Romans had acted like demons, restoring wholeness where the Romans had maimed, bringing life where the Romans had brought death, providing bread where the Romans had burned the supplies and fields of grain, and calming storms on the Sea of Galilee that the Romans had turned bloodred.

The Gospel of Mark presents an ironic and alternative "empire"—a grass-roots movement that involved "fishing" and "sowing seeds" of words and deeds that restore life, and trusting God for the harvest. As the narrative progresses, the journey to Jerusalem continues to provide a contrast to Roman conquest. Along that journey, Jesus teaches that disciples are not to lord over anyone "as the Gentile nations do" but to be servants and slaves to the needs of others. The subsequent entrance to Jerusalem shows that the Markan Jesus is no conqueror who will usher in a Davidic kingdom, as the crowds hope, but a royal figure who comes in peace and humility on a donkey. In Jerusalem, more contrasts occur: Jesus clears the temple of "brigands"; he prophesies the downfall of the temple and offers prayer and faith as an alternative; he warns against false prophets; the insurrectionist Barabbas is chosen over Jesus; an innocent Jesus is executed with two revolutionaries; and God splits the temple curtain in two and leaves the temple to its destruction. Hearers of this story would clearly experience these and many other sayings and events of the narrative in light of the cataclysmic war that was so recently in their midst and in their memories.

Opposing the Judean revolutionaries

In rejecting Jesus as a Davidic warrior-messiah, Mark presents the rule of God as a stark contrast not only to the Roman Empire and the rulers within Israel but also to the hopes and actions of the Judean people who fought against the Romans.

Jesus' instruction to his followers to be servants and slaves must have been bitter to hear in the situation where so many of those Judean people who were not killed in the war were forced into slavery by the Romans. In the narrative, the crucifixion of Jesus reveals the crushing power of the Roman Empire, abetted by the Judean leadership that cooperated with them. It also reveals Jesus' commitment to the reign of God as an absolute commitment not to use force over others. Again, the call of the Markan Jesus to take up the cross and the depiction of Jesus' crucifixion must have recalled for the audience the horror of the many public crucifixions that came at the beginning, during, and end of the war. And here is Jesus telling them to *choose* to take up the cross, not as an act of revolution but as a commitment to live peacefully for the reign of God even if it means dying for it. In the Gospel, Jesus is most explicitly contrasted with the revolutionaries when the crowd chooses Barabbas, who had committed murder in the insurrection. Despite being executed with two revolutionary brigands, Jesus was, in the view of Mark, the true "king of the Judeans." In Mark, Jesus resists the call to replace one empire of domination with another; he seeks the end of imperial domination as such.

As a political figure, the Markan Jesus lived in the service of the rulership of God. But it was not politics as usual. He chose twelve peasants as core disciples to be agents to spread liberation and healing in the villages of Galilee. He considered human need to be the legal imperative for applying the law. He did not seek wealth and status and power. He refused to use force. He confronted oppression without himself becoming an oppressor. He acted for the good of the society and trusted God for the rest. The audience of this performance in the village in Galilee was invited to renounce all that the social and political order had to offer that was contrary to this and to live for Jesus and the rule of God.

Call to commitment

We might imagine that such a radical understanding of Mark founders on the fact that the Markan Gospel expects the world to end within the generation. When the audience overhears Jesus tell his disciples that the son of humanity will return before all who are alive have died, we may suppose the audience might think that action and agency are unnecessary. Perhaps people are simply to stay put and hold out to the end. On the contrary, the entire narrative of Mark is oriented to overcoming quietism and to generating agency—an agency that dislodges disciples from their secure worlds of family and place and sends them out to act on behalf of God's reign in the face of resistance, rejection, even death.

In the Gospel of Mark, fear is the opposite of faith or trust in God's rule. It is the major obstacle to the embrace of the rule of God and its values. Fear is what leads people to save their lives rather than lose them. Fear is what leads the authorities to secure their position at whatever cost to others. Fear is the paralyzing emotion that stops even the most determined followers of Jesus from living their commitments. The Gospel of Mark takes fear very seriously. It seeks nothing less than to break the grip of the powerful protective interest people have for themselves and their own groups so that the audience can embrace the paradox: "All who will lose their lives for me and the good news will save them." The whole narrative urges hearers to get to a point at the end of the story when they are led to say: "Even if the authorities are determined to destroy us, even if the disciples flee in terror, even if the women flee in awe and fear from the empty grave, we will be faithful."

Hence, the Gospel of Mark moves the audience toward mission, the mission to bring liberation, healing, forgiveness, wholeness, food, and much more to as many individuals and communities as possible and with a commitment to resist oppression. In this narrative, the expectation of an imminent end does not stifle agency. Quite the opposite. The assurance that God will establish the rule of God fully and soon provides the springboard for the capacity to take whatever risks might come—"for the good news must first be proclaimed to all the Gentile nations." The audience for this performance of Mark would have heard the call directed to them.

A new world

Mark's *good news* is a positive vision for life in which people live "the things of God." As such, Mark is more than an "alternative" to the Judean culture or the Roman Empire. Mark's real thrust is much more than a negative critique of the imperial status quo or a call to national reformation. Rather, the Gospel of Mark positively and exuberantly presents a different world to its hearers, a world with exquisite attention to personal needs of impoverished people. As we have suggested, the Gospel is apocalyptic in its hearing. To embrace this narrative represents the end of one way of being in the world and the onset of another way, already in the lived experience of the hearers. As such, the experience of the story is an experience of enculturation into a new world, a new cosmos, a reordering of creation, a new grasp of power, a new set of relationships, a new ethos of values, and a new release from self-orientation to orientation for others—new wine for new wineskins.

The performance event generates resocialization at the most basic level, designed not only to change individuals but more importantly to create new communal relationships, new cultural values, a new vision of what it means to be the nation of Israel, and a profoundly humane political order—the realm of the rule of God. What is the world like when God reigns and people are open to it and loyal to it? And what is it like for people who enter this realm of God when the rest of the world has not yet changed and the rule of God has not come fully? That is what the Gospel is about. The audience who experienced Mark in a peasant village of first-century Galilee would have been left at the end of the story to make the choice to embrace God's rule or to reject it.

Contemporary Readers

In one sense, the time limits of the story world do not account for real hearers or readers beyond the generation of Jesus, because the story assumes that the rule of God will be fully established shortly after the temple is destroyed. Nevertheless, we modern readers, having entered the story world and participated in it, can in many ways see our own society and our own lives reflected in the story, though from quite different perspectives.[11]

Readers and listeners in the twenty-first century may be troubled by many aspects of the ancient story of Mark: The world is flat and filled with demons; paralysis may be caused by sin; everything is possible if one only has faith; people will be healed if they touch the master's garment; women do not play major and active roles in the narrative; the narrative comes dangerously close to suggesting that martyrdom is redemptive; people will be judged and thrown into Gehenna to be destroyed; in the end, God will forcibly put Christ's enemies down under his feet; and the expected apocalyptic end never came. We have to be honest about these problems, honest about what they say about Mark, and honest about the dangers they may have presented to audiences then and the dangers they may present to readers of today.

At the same time, we believe today's readers need also to hear the radical, and we mean *radical*, call to a personal lifestyle, a communal formation, and a societal order that enthrones service to those in need above the securing of wealth, status, and power. We need to hear that living such a life may well risk resistance and rejection as much in today's world as it did in the first century. For in this world presented by Mark, we too have experienced the radical new order called for in God's rule, the astounding figure of Jesus, the possibilities of faith in God, the call to serve, the deep resistance to relinquishing security and privilege for one's self and one's group, the destructiveness of dominating others, the vision of communities of mutual service, the power and difficulty of steadfastness in the face of opposition, and much more. Having experienced this story world, contemporary readers may be able to think anew about the meaning of life, its purpose, its possibilities, and its outcome—to see and struggle with the real world in new ways and perhaps be better prepared to live more faithful and humane lives.

Reading as a Dialogue:
The Ethics of Reading

Ancient audiences interacted with performers; performers would adapt performances to the interests and situation of their audiences. Modern readers cannot affect the printed text in direct interaction, but they can think of reading as a dialogue—a meaningful exchange between the story and the reader.[1] Each partner has power over what happens in the dialogue. On the one hand, a story seeks to influence readers—to affect them for good or for ill, to change people, and to shape communities. On the other hand, a reader also has influence in the dialogue. A reader can take a story seriously and be changed by it or be indifferent to the story and even dismiss it as irrelevant. A reader can embrace the story or be resistant and take strong objections to some part or all of the story. A reader can even increase the effect of the story by quoting it in ways that may help or harm others. The story attempts to influence the reader; the reader in turn must ethically judge the story according to his or her values or standards of judgment.

To judge a story, one must first listen to it attentively in order to understand what the story is saying on its own terms. It is important to assume that what the story says will be different from what we expect or want or fear. In this dialogue with a story, the reader has the responsibility to treat the story with respect, to seek to read it without imposing alien ideas and images onto the story, and to be eager and open to learn from it.[2] This process is especially challenging when the story is from a different culture in an ancient time or has gained canonical authority, both of which are true of Mark. In this dialogue between story and reader, the reader has the advantage. A story cannot explain itself; it can only repeat. Therefore, the reader needs to be an active reader, reading carefully—over and over—in order to let the story speak for itself. Readers need to employ literary, sociological, and other relevant methods to get at the meaning in context, to use knowledge of the first century to understand the story in light of its cultural and political context, and to test interpretations.

In this book, we have encouraged today's readers of Mark to be faithful to the story on its own terms—to see Mark's story as a whole and to enter empathetically into its world. We have tried to make sense of the parts by interpreting them in light of the whole story. We have tried to use some helpful background information from the cultural and social context to see the Gospel as a story in its own time. Of course, ours is only one interpretation in a range of faithful interpretations.[3]

One way to help us avoid reading our own ideas into a story is to be aware of our limited and relative perspective.[4] We cannot help bringing presuppositions to our reading experience. First, we bring the ideas and assumptions of our culture and society. If we come from the West, we bring the assumptions of our individualistic, psychological, postindustrial, electronic age.

Second, we read from a particular social place within a culture, in terms of gender, race, ethnic group, social class, political affiliation, health, legal status, among others. Third, we each come with personal experiences, as well as with our particular beliefs and ethical commitments.[5] All these shape the way we read— how we see a story through the lens of our experiences. Explicitly acknowledging our own values and beliefs may help us to avoid making the story conform to our own views and to pay attention to the challenges posed by the story that we might prefer to soften or ignore.[6]

We can see our own social location more clearly by noting the contrast with the social location of the ancient composition we are studying. In the case of Mark, we can name its peasant perspective in a preindustrial agrarian society with its sharp differences in gender roles, one's purity rating, the honor held in the community, religio-ethnic identity as Judean or Gentile, ancient village or city location, and so on. When we see how different the ancient society was from our modern world in the West, we become more aware of our own particularity.

Also, we can address the limitations of our own social locations by interpreting with others who come from different social locations.[7] Each social location has its own angle of vision that may enhance understanding. Women will see things about Mark's story that men are unlikely to notice. People who are ill or disabled will see dynamics in Mark that others may take for granted. Oppressed groups from a low socioeconomic place in society will understand things about Mark that others with more social and economic standing do not grasp.[8] People who come from contexts of persecution will relate to the story in ways different from people who carry out their religious and ethical commitments with little resistance from their societies. People from diverse societies—such as an honor/shame culture or a society based on purity and defilement or a society defined by economic achievements—will bring experiences to the story that will enhance understanding.

People from each social location will have insights as well as limitations when reading a story, because each will see things from a place in society different from others. By reading together at a roundtable in which no perspective is privileged and no perspective is marginalized, we can see more clearly how we may distort or fail to understand the story on its own terms and what parts we may be ignoring.[9]

Hence, given the nature of stories and the limitations of reader perspectives, it is not possible to provide one correct and objective understanding of a story. The goal is to be as faithful as possible and to learn from other interpretations as well.

Once we have allowed Mark's Gospel to address us on its own terms to the best of our ability, the dialogue can begin to move to the readers' side of the equation—how the story relates to our various contemporary lives. We can move in this direction because we have become aware that the Gospel of Mark is not addressed to us in any direct way and that we are experiencing a composition from a different culture and time. Conscious of the differences, we nevertheless see analogies to our own context.

On the one hand, we may feel the impact of Mark's story and be deeply affected and even transformed by it. We may see ourselves and our society in new ways and be empowered to change or to persevere in times of hardship. Despite this, we may also resist many of the ideas Mark seems to present. We will disagree with his view of a flat earth and an end-time that was to come within that generation. We may or may not have trouble with his view of demons and exorcisms, angels and voices of God, or of walking on water and multiplying bread, all things that first-century people assumed were real or possible.

We may also object to some of Mark's portrayals as contrary to our values and beliefs.[10] For example, readers may object to Mark's stereotypical portrayal of Judean leaders as figures who abuse power. Along with other New Testament writings, Mark's portrayal has fed into the subsequent horrors of antisemitism. Others may object that, despite the favorable view of women in Mark (his antipatriarchal stance and his putting women forward as examples of the rule of God), the limited speaking and acting roles given to women—roles noticeably more limited than the roles women likely played in the actual life of Jesus—contribute to the continuing marginalization of women in many Christian settings today.

In addition, readers may object to the ways in which the Gospel has been *misused*. Mark's view that faith is needed for *God* to heal has led some to believe that faith itself causes the healing and thus to blame themselves and others for sicknesses when they are not healed. Also, Mark's insistence that persecution is simply the lot of those who follow the rule of God in this age has led some to believe that suffering *in itself* is good or redemptive—despite the fact that Jesus tells the disciples to pray that they *not* come to a testing. It becomes especially important when a narrative carries the authority of Scripture to be aware of how the narrative may function to oppress some people in certain circumstances. Because of the potential harm to people, some may be even reluctant to promote the Gospel at all.

Others, ourselves included, find the values of the narrative's portrayal of the rule of God and its fundamental opposition to oppression to be so overwhelmingly positive that we want not only to retain the narrative but also to promote it—even while remaining responsible for denouncing any use or misuse of the story or any parts of the story that oppress people.

Thus, if reading or hearing is to be a genuine dialogue, we need to be open to being transformed by the story.[11] Real dialogue involves risk, the possibility of being changed by our encounter. The story offers a powerful call to a new vision of life characterized by healing, forgiveness, access to God's power, and an invitation to share God's power and love. It calls for a willingness to serve others, a willingness to take risks in serving, and a refusal to let money or power or status or position define our lives. We can be open to the kind of community and world Mark seeks to foster: having compassion for the weak, reaching out to outcasts, opposing oppression, creating social relationships of mutual serving, being of service particularly to those with less power, providing laws and institutions that bring life—even if our actions result in personal criticism, social rejection, damaging economic consequences, and even persecution.

We modern readers can enter this storyworld in imagination, and by such immersion we can allow the story to work its magic on us. And having entered the Markan story world and participated in it, we may choose to proclaim this story to others.

Afterword

MARK ALLAN POWELL

In 1980, while serving as a parish pastor in southeast Texas, I talked with a director of theological education about the possibility of pursuing a PhD in New Testament. He encouraged the postgraduate study, but not my choice of fields. "Every verse of that poor book," he told me, "has been so thoroughly analyzed, that there is just nothing more to say. Unless something new comes along . . ."

This was disappointing. I wanted to study the New Testament, but I did not want to devote my career to research that would be regarded as redundant or superfluous. But then, two years later, *Mark as Story* was published. I read it cover-to-cover in a matter of days and, the next week, sent applications to half a dozen graduate schools, applying for programs in New Testament. Something new *had* come along!

No one seemed ready for this, and few knew what to make of it. Conservatives worried that Rhoads and Michie thought Mark's Gospel was just fiction—and, if they didn't, why would they, or anyone else, want to read it as though it were? Liberals suspected an end run around truly critical scholarship—what's up with proposing the *a priori* acceptance of the final, canonical form of the text?

What *was* this book? Demythologizing on steroids? Or Sunday school curriculum in disguise? In any case, whether one thought this new approach wasn't "historical" or whether one thought it wasn't "critical," it clearly was *not* an application of "the historical critical method." But in 1982, the historical critical method was pretty much the only game in town. Indeed, to be more precise, at that time the reigning methodology in Gospel studies was redaction criticism. This approach, still popular, attempts to determine the particular intentions of Gospel authors by analyzing how they arranged and edited their source materials; the goal is to understand the historically referential meaning that a Gospel would have had within a reconstructed original context. By contrast, Rhoads and Michie advocated understanding Mark on its own terms as a narrative, by reading the Gospel as story rather than as history.

In the hallowed halls of academia, of course, there were many scholars working along the lines that Rhoads and Michie proposed: Thomas Boomershine, Alan Culpepper, Joanna Dewey (who would later join Rhoads and Michie in preparing the second edition of their work), Werner Kelber, Norman Petersen, Vernon Robbins, Robert Tannehill, and Mary Ann Tolbert leap to mind. But it was *Mark as Story* that introduced "narrative criticism" to the world and simultaneously demonstrated the effectiveness of the approach with an application that remains unequaled to this day.

In the years that followed, biblical studies would embrace a wide variety of literary critical methods, and academic discussions would come to focus increasingly on literary *theory*—on the epistemological and hermeneutical underpinnings for whatever approaches were adopted. Though complicated, these discussions were often interesting and sometimes fruitful. Still, the attraction and charm of *Mark as Story* may lie in its fundamental simplicity.

Let me make a bold statement followed by an explanation.

The Gospel of Mark is, by all accounts, one of the most important books ever written. And *Mark as Story*, better than any volume known to me, reveals the meaning of the Gospel of Mark in a way that comes pretty close to what most people, most of the time, mean when they talk about the meaning of a story.

The concept of *meaning* is, of course, very complicated—but what do most people usually mean when they talk about the meaning of a story? What do they mean when they say that they *understand* a story, that they "get it"? Generally speaking, what do most people think qualifies as sufficient understanding of a story to legitimize having opinions about that story or responses to it?

Consider a non-biblical work such as *Gulliver's Travels*. I would suggest that there are different levels of appreciation or understanding of the story related in that narrative.

First, many people—almost everyone in our culture—would possess a degree of vague familiarity with the story. At the very least, they know it tells about a man traveling to an island and getting tied up by tiny, little people. But I do not think that very many people would count such vague familiarity as truly understanding *Gulliver's Travels* or as having grasped what the story means. Most people, I suspect would think that understanding the story involves reading the entire book, knowing what happens in the narrative, and having some appreciation for how what happens is reported: for example, is the encounter with the little people told in a way that is funny—or scary—or something else?

Gulliver's Travels is also studied by academics who know that its author, Jonathan Swift, had motives for producing the book that might not be apparent to general readers. Some of the characters in the book are actually based on real people whom Swift wanted to satirize. Some of the events correspond, roughly, to actual occurrences that Swift considered worthy of mockery. Swift's political views can be discerned with increased acuity when one is well informed about the context and circumstances of this book's composition. But is such historical, academic analysis necessary to understand the story and grasp its basic meaning? Some would say yes, but most would say no. Without dismissing the significance of such investigation, most people would say that if you have read the book, know what happens, and have some appreciation for how the story is told, then you understand the story: your responses to it have legitimacy even if they do not correspond precisely to the specific goals that an academic, historical investigation might reveal the author intended to produce. Not very many people in our world today would claim someone has failed to understand *Gulliver's Travels* because, after reading the book, they still do not think ill of some (now historically distant) individual whom Swift intended to disparage.

So what about the Gospel of Mark? There is a great deal of casual familiarity regarding this book: people have heard about Jesus walking on water and being crucified. There are also many people who approach the book with historical, academic understanding of its context and of the circumstances of its composition. But what about that in-between level of meaning—knowing what happens in the story and having some appreciation for how the story is told? Does *that* count as understanding the Gospel of Mark in a way that legitimates responses?

The Gospel of Mark relates a story that, like other stories, can be understood and appreciated at many different levels. What Rhoads and Michie's *Mark as Story* accomplished better than any other book of which I am aware is simply this: it explains what happens in the story (the plot, the characters, the settings) and how the story is told (the tone, the rhetoric, and the role of the narrator). It reveals the basic *meaning* of the Gospel of Mark in a manner that corresponds quite closely to what most people, most of the time, mean when they talk about "the meaning of a story." This is at least interesting, and it is hard to imagine how anyone could consider it not worthwhile to have a basic understanding of one of most important books ever written.

In the years between the first and second editions of *Mark as Story*, narrative criticism would be adapted to serve different ends and would be employed by interpreters with diverse hermeneutical assumptions. I describe this development as the emergence of what were essentially three different approaches, all of which appealed to the principles and procedures of narrative critical analysis:

Interpreters who operated with an *author-oriented hermeneutic* tended to use narrative criticism with the belief that expectations attributable to the implied audience probably reflect the historical intentions of the work's actual author or can at least be used as an "index" of that author's intentions. This approach to interpretation (exemplified, I think, by Ernest Best, John Paul Heil, and Petri

Merenlahti) has often been accompanied by a hermeneutical understanding that defines a story's legitimate meaning in terms of the meaning intended by the story's author.

Interpreters who operate with a *text-oriented hermeneutic* tend to use narrative criticism for its own sake, ascribing normative value to whatever understanding can be attributed to the implied or ideal audience and declaring other understandings to be intrinsically invalid. This perspective (evident, I think, in the work of Donald Juel, Jack Dean Kingsbury, and Elizabeth Struthers Malbon) usually seems to be informed by a hermeneutic that locates meaning in "the text itself." Such a hermeneutic typically assumes or asserts that the legitimate, normative meaning of a story can be equated with "what the story means for people who receive it in the manner expected of them" rather than with "what the author of the story intended for it to mean to people."

Finally, interpreters who operate with a *reader-oriented hermeneutic* tend to use narrative criticism as a base method to guide them in discerning and understanding disparate and polyvalent responses. By gaining a general idea of how an audience is expected to respond to a story, interpreters are able to identify more readily the points at which individuals or communities adopt various strategies of reception and, so, are able to probe the processes that determine these different receptions. This approach (exemplified, I think, by Robert Fowler and Mary Ann Tolbert) tends to be adopted by people whose hermeneutic locates meaning in the process of readers or audiences engaging texts. Meaning is best understood here as the product of such engagement and so will be legitimately different for each recipient.

The second edition of *Mark as Story* by Rhoads, Michie, and Joanna Dewey revealed a deeper appreciation for this third incarnation of the method. This is noteworthy because the first edition had established a definitive paradigm for *text*-oriented interpretation, with some allowance for *author*-orientation in the concluding speculation as to what sort of first-century reader "would have responded to the story in much the same way as the implied reader" (see the section on "Hypothetical First-Century Audiences" in the conclusion to this third edition). The second edition, however, added a new section on "reading as a dialogue," which invited contemporary readers to compare their own responses to Mark's story with what the book suggested might be expected of an implied reader. The second edition also allowed that resistance to such expectations might sometimes constitute an ethically faithful response. Thus, the two editions of *Mark as Story* managed to cover all three of the interpretive interests I've just described, exemplifying how narrative criticism might be employed in service of distinct hermeneutical goals.

This third edition continues in that vein by pushing the implications of this fundamentally text-oriented approach further in both directions. We are now invited to imagine the story being performed and heard within a particular social-cultural context and to imagine the nuances the story would acquire within that setting (for example, for people who associated power with tyranny, wealth with blessing, and honor with the enhancement of one's own social status). Scholars and other readers who favor an author-oriented hermeneutic will be delighted by this move because it takes us closer to discerning how an historically situated first-century author would have wanted the book to be understood. In essence, Rhoads, Dewey, and Michie are now using narrative-critical method to fulfill the goals of redaction criticism. They do so, I think, in a manner that is certainly no more speculative than the traditional approach, which calls for reconstruction of possible sources followed by discernment of possible adjustments that the author might have made to those hypothetical sources. The irony of this accomplishment should not go unnoticed. When *Mark as Story* first appeared, narrative criticism was disparaged by redaction critics because it did not seem interested in pursuing redaction-critical goals (and because, apparently, no other worthwhile interpretive goals could be envisioned). Now, as it turns out, narrative criticism might provide a more effective method for accomplishing redaction-critical goals than redaction criticism itself.

But this move toward imagining what the story would mean when received within one particular context (first-century oral performance) has implications that also move in the opposite direction. By linking meaning to reception, Rhoads, Dewey, and Michie encourage us to recognize the role that readers or audiences inevitably play in the production of meaning. The imagined first-century performer and his or her audience make the story meaningful for *their* context; in a similar fashion, contemporary readers must find the meaning for their own setting, one in which the acquired nuances may differ.

Potential flexibility of application is part of what has made narrative criticism more than a passing fad. In terms of nuts and bolts, the method itself is simply useful, providing an effective means for obtaining information about a Gospel's plot, characters, settings, and rhetoric. What one *does* with such useful information—what level of engagement with the story, if any, one decides to deem normative, authoritative, or inspired—depends, of course, upon the user. In any case, such information is definitely helpful for knowing what happens in the story and for appreciating how the story is told—and that is what most people, most of the time, think it means to understand a story.

So the theological advisor who warned me that New Testament studies was a fatigued branch of scholarship, on its last legs, now sounds a bit like the Decca Records executive who passed on signing The Beatles because he thought bands with guitars were on the way out. In retrospect, narrative criticism was just one small part of a renaissance in biblical studies. The field would also be enriched by the advent of social-scientific approaches, by feminist, womanist, and postcolonial criticism, and by the revival of historical Jesus studies, to name but a few of the more exciting trajectories in the last thirty years of this discipline. Furthermore, despite all the innovations and talk of paradigm shifts, the tried-but-true historical critical method is still alive and doing well.

Nevertheless, today, most New Testament scholars who work in *any* of the aforementioned sub-disciplines would have some awareness and some appreciation for how an implied reader or ideal audience would be likely to understand the narrative of Mark's Gospel. The primary reason for that fact is the book that inspired me to go to doctoral school: *Mark as Story*, first published by Rhoads and Michie in 1982, revised by David Rhoads and Joanna Dewey in 1999, and now appearing in this welcome third edition by all three authors.

Exercises for an Overall Narrative Analysis of Mark

1. Experience the Story

One: Read, listen to, or see (on DVD) the whole Gospel of Mark.

Two: What was your experience of the "story world" of Mark's Gospel? What were your initial impressions of this story of Jesus?

Three: Were you able to respect the limits of this story and not bring with you information from the other Gospels?

2. Point of View

One: Choose three people to take the point of view of the disciples and three to take the point of view of the authorities.

Two: Staying imaginatively within the story world of Mark, debate the differing views of Jesus, the arrival of the rule of God, and the values of the rule of God.

3. Stylistic Features

One: Choose one of the narrative patterns or stylistic devices discussed in chapter 2. Read through Mark looking for its occurrence, taking notes as you find it.

Two: What does this device contribute to the meaning and impact of the story?

4. Analysis of Settings

One: Choose a recurring setting in Mark. Read Mark, looking for each instance in which that setting occurs.

Two: As you read, take notes on the following questions. What are the characteristics of the setting? What is the relationship of the setting to the conflicts that occur there? How do the characters interact with the setting? What mood is evoked?

Three: Are there associations between this setting and a setting in stories from Israel's past? How do these associations inform the experience of the setting?

Four: In light of the above, what is the role of this setting in the overall story?

5. Analysis of Conflicts

One: Choose a conflict that runs through the story (Jesus and the cosmic forces of evil; Jesus and the authorities; Jesus and the disciples).

Two: Read through Mark, tracing this conflict:

- Who/what initiates the conflict and how does it escalate?
- What is the conflict about and what is at stake?
- What are the tactics of each side?
- How is the conflict resolved/unresolved?
- What are the consequences?

Three: How does this conflict relate to the other conflicts that run through the story? What is the role of this conflict in the establishment of God's rule in the story?

6. Analysis of Characters: Part I

One: Choose one of the following characters or character groups: Jesus, the disciples (including Rock), Rock, the authorities, the minor characters who favor Jesus.

Two: Turn blank pages sideways and make three columns. In each column make separate brief notes (not quotes) in the following categories.

- What the character *says* that illuminates her or his character
- What the character *does* that illuminates her or his character
- What *others say* to or about them that illuminates their character

Three: Review your notes, comparing and contrasting the columns. List the insights you gained into the character from this exercise.

7. Analysis of Characters: Part II

One: Choose a character or character group (as above).

Two: Read Mark, taking notes on the following questions:

- What are the traits of the character?
- What drives the character as motivations or goals?
- How does the character relate to other characters?
- Does the character change?

Three: Review your notes and consider what factors about the character predominate. From this review, give a brief profile of the traits of the character.

8. Analysis of Rhetoric

One: Again, read, hear, or see (on DVD) the whole Gospel of Mark. This time, focus on the responses you are having while experiencing Mark's Gospel.

Two: Discuss the feelings, thoughts, emotions, and challenges you experienced while encountering the story. How did your responses change as the story went along? What was your reaction to the ending?

Three: What new insights did you get about the story by focusing on what Mark's story does to readers/hearers? What new insights did you get about yourself in experiencing the story?

Exercises for a Narrative Analysis of Episodes

We have been encouraging you to read Mark as a whole and to interpret each line and episode in the context of the whole. The following exercises are meant to give you practice in narrative analysis with exercises on a brief portion of the story. Learning to apply narrative critical tools to a single episode can help in applying them to the whole narrative.

These exercises for analyzing an episode can be done individually, in pairs, or in groups. Not all exercises apply to every episode, and some are repetitious. Therefore, select a limited number of the most appropriate ones. An individual or team might do all exercises on a single episode in preparation for a paper or a performance.[1]

1. Getting to Know the Episode

One:

- Pair off and both read/study the episode silently.
- Both close books, then the first person recounts to the other what he or she read, as faithfully as possible (word for word is the goal).
- Both now look at the episode and see which details were accurately remembered and which were omitted, added, or changed in telling.

Two:

- Both reread/study the episode silently.
- Both close books, and the other person recounts the episode as faithfully as possible.
- Both check to see what was omitted, added, or changed in telling.

Three:

- Both go line by line asking questions for clarification (without trying to answer them), based on what you noticed in steps one and two.

2. Noticing the Narrator

One:

- Read or hear the episode, paying attention to the way in which the narrator guides the reading experience. Identify the role of the narrator.

Two: Pose the following questions:

- With what tone or attitude does the narrator address the audience? What do you notice about the narrator's style and choice of words?
- What does the narrator say that gains the trust of the audience? How does the narrator lead you to identify with some characters and be distant from others?
- What emotions does the narrator evoke? How?
- What insights does the narrator give into the thoughts and feelings of the characters?
- What explanatory asides does the narrator give to the audience?
- How does the narrator guide the audience's attitude toward different characters?

3. The Points of View of Different Characters

One: Choose a character in the episode and retell the story from that character's point of view. That is, change the pronouns to the first person for the character you have chosen, and tell the episode as if you were that person.

Two: Address the following questions:

- What did you learn of the character's point of view? Relation to others?
- Did you identity with the character? What emotions were involved?
- How did this telling or reading change the emphasis of the story?
- What group does the character represent, and how might that affect her or his point of view?

Three: Now do the same process for other characters in the episode.

4. Identifying Stylistic Features

One: Identify the rhetorical features in your episode:

- Explanations introduced by "for"
- Repetitions of words and lines

- Foreshadowings and retrospections
- Two-step progressions
- Similarity to other episodes in the Gospel, such as type scenes
- One episode sandwiching another episode within it
- Similar episodes that frame a larger section
- Lines or episodes in a concentric or chiasmatic pattern
- Episodes in a series of three
- Types of questions
- Riddles or parables
- Quotations from and allusions to "the writings"
- Prophecy and fulfillment
- Irony
- Other

Two: Ask questions:

- How does the awareness of a particular stylistic device enable you to understand better the characters, conflicts, and settings of this episode?
- What effect does the use of this stylistic technique have on the reader of this episode?
- Create and tell a brief story of your own using one or more of these stylistic devices.

5. Questions about Settings

One: Identify all the settings of time, place, and cultural milieu in this episode. What are the relevant items/details within the setting?

Two: Ask questions:

- What atmosphere is conveyed by the setting (bleakness, urgency, restriction, and so on)?
- What is the larger cosmological context that informs the dynamics of this episode?
- What, if any, associations in Israel's history illuminate the setting here?
- How does the setting relate to conflicts, events, and problems in this episode? (Does it cause a problem, create tension, provide commentary, and so on?)
- What does the setting reveal about the characters in the episode? (Does it bring out fear, courage, isolation, and so on?) What are their differing attitudes toward the setting?
- How does this setting relate directly or indirectly to Israel under the Roman Empire?
- What part does this setting play in the overall structure of the Gospel?

6. Tracing the Story

One: Read the episode line by line and try to identify the relationship between one line and the next. How does each line follow from the one preceding it? Why does this action or event happen next? Why is this dialogue of a character said in response to that? Is there a clear connection? What is it? Be sure to determine your answers from clues in the episode itself.

Two: What insights have you gained? Explore the places where you had trouble understanding why one thing followed another.

Three: Now ask how this episode is related to the episode that precedes it and the one that follows it. Is this episode a part of a larger pattern of episodes? Concentric pattern? Episodes in a series of three? Type-scenes? Foreshadowing or retrospection? Prophecy or fulfillment? Other? How do these connections illuminate the episode you are studying?

Four: Is this episode a turning point or breakthrough in the larger plot of the Gospel? How so?

7. Analysis of Conflicts

One: Identify the conflicts in this episode:

- Inner (within a person)
- Between people
- With nature
- With society or authorities
- With supernatural beings

Two: Trace the progress of the conflict:

- What is the source of the conflict?
- Who initiates it?
- How does it escalate?
- Is it resolved? How? Is anything left unresolved?
- Does the resolution lead to further conflict?
- With what words would you characterize the nature of the conflict?

Three: Assess the conflict:

- State in one sentence what is at stake in the conflict.
- Now identify the beliefs and values of each party in the conflict.
- In what way does this conflict further the establishment of the rule of God or hinder it?

8. Analysis of Characters

One: Name the characters in the episode (human and nonhuman)

Two: Choose a character and, with as much detail as possible, note:

- What the character says
- What the character does
- What others say (including the narrator) about the character
- How the character interacts with other characters

Three: Based on the details noted in step two, *identify the traits* of the character.

Four: Ask questions:

- What drives or motivates the character? What is the character's desire or purpose? What are the beliefs and values of the character?
- What is the place of the character in the social order? How does that illuminate interactions with other characters?
- Does the character develop? Change?
- Is this character illuminated by comparison or contrast with other characters?
- How does this episode fit into the role this character plays in the whole Gospel?

9. Identifying Standards of Judgment

Standards of judgment are those norms (beliefs, attitudes, values, actions) that are implicit or explicit in the narrative by which an audience is led to evaluate the characters. Note that the positive standards have corresponding negative standards.

One: On what bases are the standards of judgment identified in this episode? The narrator's words? The words and actions of reliable characters? God's words? Scripture? Negative words/actions of unreliable characters (showing what not to do)? Other?

Two: Based on the analysis of step one, identify the implicit and explicit standards in the episode.

Three: Evaluate the characters in the episode by the standards of judgment you identified in step two. What characters embody the positive standards? The negative standards?

Four: How do the standards in this episode fit into the larger (dualistic) standards of the whole Gospel? How do they relate to the cosmic realities of the story and to the political authority and power of Israel and the Roman Empire?

10. The Rhetorical Impact: Then and Now

One: Based on your study of this episode, identify the effect(s) that this passage might have had on original hearers. Did it amaze, evoke faith, convict, expose hypocrisy, offer hope, impel to action, and so on?

Two: What kinds of relationships in community does the story foster?

Thre: Think of a contemporary story (personal experience, anecdote, film, or novel) or create a story that might have a similar impact on hearers today.

Four: Tell the story to someone and see what effect it has.

11. Questions on the Ethics of Reading

One: What influence does this episode have on your values and beliefs?

Two: How has your particular place in your particular society shaped your understanding of this episode? For example, gender, education, place of origin, ethnic and racial identity, religion, occupation, political persuasion, family, economic level, among others.

Three: How might your understanding be enhanced or changed in dialogue with people from different places in society?

Four: What do you resist about the values and beliefs of this episode? Why?

Five: Could this episode have a negative effect on someone? How? What is your responsibility in such a circumstance?

Six: If you took the episode seriously, how might it change your life and commitments?

APPENDIX 3

Exercises for Learning and Telling Episodes

We have emphasized that the Gospel of Mark is performance literature; that is, it was composed in order to be performed orally before gathered groups. A contemporary experience of performing Mark enables us to understand better the oral dynamics of Mark's story. An experience of presenting one of the stories or teachings from Mark in a modern language involves a change of medium from a print to an oral/aural experience. The medium shift is twofold: the performer becomes the narrative voice of the story, and the listeners become the audience and hearers of the story.

There are several ways that performances of Markan stories can be done with a group. (1) Participants can be invited to learn an episode of their choice and present it to the group; (2) Participants can learn and perform a series of episodes in a row, such as the opening stories of the Gospel or the journey to Jerusalem or the execution narrative. (3) The whole Gospel can be divided into sections according to the number of participants for performing or for reading. Then set aside two and a half to three hours for experiencing the Gospel in its entirety with opportunity for discussion afterward. (4) One of the first three choices can be done as a presentation for a community beyond the group, such as a school, a church, or a worshiping community.

Some individuals or groups will memorize the stories word for word from a translation. Others will learn the story well enough and with enough details to get across the gist of the story without verbatim memorizing. Still others will learn how to read the story aloud to a group in meaningful and engaging ways. Learning a story enables us to embrace Scripture by heart—to make it our own and to tell it to others.

The goals of the following exercises are (1) to experience the Gospel in a new medium, its original oral medium; (2) to increase understanding of the Gospel and its potential impacts; and (3) to have a powerful encounter with the story as a contemporary experience.

1. Become familiar with the story. Make use of the exercises in Appendix 2 as means to know the episode well. Here are the key steps.

One: In pairs (or adapting to individual use) do the following exercise:

- Read the passage silently and study it. Then have one of your pair tell the story as closely as possible to the wording while the other person listens without following the text. Then look and see what details you missed.
- Repeat the above, but reversing roles.
- Ask questions line by line without answering them.

Two: Tell the story from the point of view of each character by changing the relevant pronouns. For example, if you are telling the story as a blind man who was healed, change the pronouns and references to reflect that first person telling. Invest yourself in the feelings and tone of each character. This exercise will help the performer say the dialogue and understand the reactions of characters to each other.

Three: Follow the story, line by line, for causation and connection from one action and/or dialogue to the next. Ask how and why each detail follows the previous one. This exercise will help you remember what comes next.

Four: Imagine the progression within the single episode as a series of brief moments of action and dialogue. For example, (1) a leper comes to Jesus; (2) then he pleads with Jesus; (3) Jesus responds to his plea; and so on. Imagine where the characters will stand as they act and speak. This exercise will help you visualize the story as you tell it—so you can, in a sense, tell/show the audience "what you have seen."

Five: Act out the story. Remember that you are embodying the story with your whole self. This exercise will help you remember the story with your entire body.

2. Learn the story by heart.

- Learn each line one after the other by repeating each line five times without looking. Keep checking to see what you may have added, omitted, or changed. After you know the first line, do the second one five times. Then do the first two lines together and so on to the end.

- Repeat the whole episode often until you know it by heart. Carry a printed copy of the story with you so you can relearn parts you may have forgotten.
- Find your own way to learn the story—telling others, making and listening repeatedly to an audio tape, acting it out, or setting it out on paper in patterns that will help you learn it.
- Once you know it well, you can slow down and concentrate on *how* you will tell it.

3. Tell it.

- Tell it to a friend in a natural way appropriate to the nature of the story. Do this apart from a "performance" setting. You may want to tell it in a plain and straightforward way. Or tell what you have "seen" with the appropriate animation and emotion.
- Now do it as a presentation to a group, as you did it with the friend, as if you were addressing just one or two persons. The goal is to tell the story in ways that most appropriately and naturally convey its meaning and potential impact.
- Experiment with how you will tell it. How will you stand? What will your gestures be? How will you inflect the dialogue of the characters? Where and how will you place the emphasis? How will you pace the story?

4. Performance Exercises.

There are many ways to tell a story. The tone and inflection of your voice, the volume and pace of the telling, your gestures and facial expressions, as well as your body posture and movement all contribute to a distinctive way to share the story. The goal is to gain an understanding of the passage and its potential impact, and then seek to find ways to present it that are faithful to that interpretation. You are "performing" the passage. However, think of yourself less as an actor and more as a storyteller. After you have learned the story well, here are some exercises that may help you refine and stretch your experience of performing the passage.

Voice: In your telling, think about tone of voice, inflection, volume, and pace. The "subtext" is the message you give by *how* you say a line. You can convey joy, amazement, seriousness, sarcasm, puzzlement, and so on simply by the way you deliver a line. As an exercise, take each line and say it in different ways. Then settle on the most effective way you can say it so as to convey the meaning you think it has and the impact you want it to make.

Facial expressions and gestures: These are not meant to be add-ons, as if to find a gesture to match every line. Be sparing. Use gestures in a suggestive rather than a dramatic way. Gestures and facial expressions are an integral part of conveying the meaning and impact of a line.

Physical movement: You may want to move around the performance space to convey some change of scenery or move closer or further from the audience to manifest some aspect or impact of the story. Again, make this movement integral to the telling rather than something that is wooden or mechanical.

Characterizations: You may want to provide slightly different presentations of yourself for each of the characters when you, as the narrator, switch to saying their lines.

- Determine the goal and purpose of the character speaking and give the appropriate inflection.
- As you portray dialogue, do not try to turn 180 degrees to the right and then to the left as you imagine dialogue between two people. Rather, turn very slightly to the right and left to convey two different characters in dialogue.
- You may want to direct all lines, including the characters you portray, *offstage* to the audience. Or, when you give the dialogue line of a character, you may want to direct it *onstage* to the imaginary character or characters you are addressing.

Emotions: Feelings may range from urgency to amazement to laughter. Express emotions in ways that are appropriate to the story or teaching you are telling.

Tips: Do stretching and relaxation exercises before you practice and perform your passage. Keep a copy of the text nearby and consult it if needed. Consult a storytelling guide or a performance manual as a way to increase your ability as a storyteller.

5. Reflection questions for discussion.

For the performers:
- What was your process of learning the story and how did it work?
- What did you learn about the passage and the Gospel of Mark? Did your views change?
- What was it like being the narrator and taking the role of different characters?
- What did you understand to be the potential impact(s) of the passage on the audience?

For the hearers:
- In what ways is it different to hear the passage in contrast to reading it?
- What did you understand in a new way about the passage and the Gospel of Mark?

- What feelings did you have while listening? And what was it about the story and the way it was told that evoked these emotions?

For performers and hearers:
- In what ways does this experience change the way you think about the origins of the Gospels (and the New Testament) in the predominantly oral cultures of the first century?
- Were there aspects of the story that you found profoundly meaningful or that you resisted?
- How does this experience lead you to think differently about your relationship to Scripture? Do you want to experience the Bible this way more often?

For information about audio and video recordings and live performances of the Gospel of Mark and other biblical writings, as well as guides to learning and performing biblical selections, explore the following websites: www.biblical performancecriticism.org and www.nbsint.org.

Notes

Introduction: The Gospel of Mark as Story

1. The mention of women disciples only at the very end of the narrative suggests that the author was male, and we will refer to the author as "he."

2. For the traditions about Mark, see C. Clifton Black, *Mark: Images of an Apostolic Interpreter* (Columbia: University of South Carolina Press, 1994).

3. See 1 Pet. 3:19 and Acts 12:12.

4. For the Roman location, see, for example, Martin Hengel, *Studies in the Gospel of Mark*, trans. John Bowden (Philadelphia: Fortress Press, 1985); Donald Senior, "'With Swords and Clubs . . .'— The Setting of Mark's Gospel and His Critique of Abusive Power," *Biblical Theology Bulletin* 17 (1987): 10–20; and John R. Donahue, "Windows and Mirrors: The Setting of Mark's Gospel," *Catholic Biblical Quarterly* 57 (1995): 1–26.

5. For the Palestinian location, see, for example, Howard C. Kee, *Community of the New Age: Studies in Mark's Gospel* (Philadelphia: Westminster Press, 1977); Gerd Theissen, *The Gospels in Context: Social and Political History of the Synoptic Tradition*, trans. Linda Maloney (Minneapolis: Fortress Press, 1991); and Joel Marcus, "The Jewish War and the Sitz im Leben of Mark," *Journal of Biblical Literature* 111 (1992): 441–62. See also P. J. J. Botha, "The Historical Setting of Mark's Gospel: Problems and Possibilities," *Journal for the Study of the New Testament* 51 (1993): 27–55, who wisely cautions against claims to certainty.

6. For an analysis of the social location of Mark's Gospel, see Richard L. Rohrbaugh, "The Social Location of the Marcan Audience," *Interpretation* 47 (1993): 380–95.

7. For a survey of various literary analogues for Mark, see Kee, *Community*, 14–30, and the literature cited there. On the importance of genre for analysis, see Mary Ann Tolbert, *Sowing the Gospel: Mark's World in Literary-Historical Perspective* (Minneapolis: Fortress Press, 1989), 48–79.

8. See Frank Kermode, *The Genesis of Secrecy: On Interpretation in Narrative* (Cambridge: Cambridge University Press, 1979), and Stephen Moore, "Are the Gospel Narratives Unified?" in *Society of Biblical Literature 1987 Seminar Papers*, ed. Kent H. Richards (Atlanta: Scholars, 1987), 443–58.

9. Other scholars have also found Mark's narrative to be coherent. See Norman R. Petersen, "'Point of View' in Mark's Narrative," *Semeia* 12 (1978): 97–121, and Robert C. Tannehill, "The Gospel of Mark as Narrative Christology," *Semeia* 16 (1979): 57–95.

10. For the fugue analogy, see Kee, *Community*, 75. On the tapestry metaphor, see Joanna Dewey, "Mark as Interwoven Tapestry: Forecasts and Echoes for a Listening Audience," *Catholic Biblical Quarterly* 52 (1991): 224.

11. Norman R. Petersen considers it a "referential fallacy" to view the statements expressed or implied in the text as a direct representation of the earlier historical events of Jesus' day, in *Literary Criticism for New Testament Critics* (Philadelphia: Fortress Press, 1978), 38.

12. See Hans Frei, *The Eclipse of Biblical Narrative: A Study in Eighteenth and Nineteenth Century Hermeneutics* (New Haven: Yale University Press, 1984), and Thomas E. Boomershine, "Mark the Storyteller: A Rhetorical-Critical Investigation of Mark's Passion and Resurrection Narrative" (PhD diss., Union Theological Seminary, 1984).

Chapter 1. The Gospel of Mark

1. For the reader's convenience, we include on each page the chapter and verse designations for the portion of Mark on that page.

2. Early Greek manuscripts had no punctuation, no paragraph designations, no episode headings, no spaces between words or sentences, and no chapter and verse designations.

3. See the text that appears in Matthew Black et al., eds., *The Greek New Testament*, 4th ed. (New York: United Bible Societies, 1994), and Erwin Nestle, Kurt Aland, et al., eds., *Novum Testamentum Graece*, 27th ed. (Stuttgart: Deutsche Bibelgesellschaft, 1994).

4. For example, see the NRSV and the NIV. For a textual analysis of the endings, see Bruce Metzger, *A Textual Commentary on the Greek New Testament* (New York: United Bible Societies, 1971), 122–26. On recent work, see S. L. Cox, *A History and Critique of Scholarship Concerning the Markan Endings* (Lewiston: Mellen Biblical Press, 1993), and Paul Danove, *The End of Mark's Gospel: A Methodological Study* (Leiden: E. J. Brill, 1993), 119–31.

5. For a translation of dynamic equivalence, see the Scholars Version Translation in Daryl Schmidt, ed., *The Gospel of Mark* (Sonoma, CA: Polebridge, 1990). Reynolds Price has captured Mark's spare, running style in *Three Gospels* (New York: Scribner, 1996), 37–124.

6. We follow this principle except in a few cases where the meaning would be distorted. For example, we use "restore" and "save" to translate the single Greek word *sōzō*. Also, we have translated *kyrios* the same throughout, but distinguished it by uppercase (God as "Lord") and lowercase (Jesus as "lord").

7. On the translation "Judeans" as a means to avoid anti-Judaism, see David Rhoads, *The Challenge of Diversity: The Witness of Paul and the Gospels* (Minneapolis: Fortress Press, 1996), 35–36, 82–83. See also John Pilch, "No Jews or Christians in the Bible," *Explorations* 12 (1998): 3.

8. We have not, however, retained Mark's irregular use of the Greek historical present, which employs the present tense to recount past events in a vivid way.

9. See, however, the Afterword below, which deals with the ethics involved in reading Mark.

Chapter 2. The Narrator

1. On narrators and features of narration, see Mieke Bal, *Narratology: Introduction to the Theory of Narrative*, trans. Christine van Boheemen (Toronto: University of Toronto Press, 1985), 119–48; Wayne Booth, *The Rhetoric of Fiction*, 2nd ed. (Chicago: University of Chicago Press, 1983); Seymour Chatman, *Story and Discourse* (Ithaca: Cornell University Press, 1978), 146–260; Shlomith Rimmon-Kenan, *Narrative Fiction: Contemporary Poetics* (New York: Methuen, 1983), 86–116.

2. On the narrator in Mark's story, see the groundbreaking works by Norman R. Petersen, "'Point of View' in Mark's Narrative," *Semeia* 12 (1978): 97–121, and Thomas E. Boomershine, "Mark the Storyteller" diss., Union Theological Seminary, 1984 (PhD). For a comprehensive treatment of the issues of narration in Mark dealt with in this chapter, see Robert M. Fowler, *Let the Reader Understand: Reader-Response Criticism and the Gospel of Mark* (Minneapolis: Fortress Press, 1991).

3. It should be stressed that the reliability of the narrator of a story does not refer to the historical accuracy of the narrative. Rather, reliability here is a literary concept used to identify whether the author has created a narrator who is trustworthy in contrast to an unreliable narrator who, for purposes of irony and interest, misleads and misinforms the reader in relation to the story the narrator is narrating.

4. This sense of immediacy is enhanced by the use of the historical present tense throughout Mark. See above, ch. 1, note 8.

5. On the use of inside views as a way for the narrator to control distance, see Boomershine, "Mark the Storyteller," 284–314, and Booth, *Rhetoric*.

6. For the many levels and complexities of point of view in literature, see Boris Uspenski, *Poetics of Composition* (Berkeley: University of California Press, 1973); and Susan Snaider Lanser, *The Narrative Act: Point of View in Prose Fiction* (Princeton: Princeton University Press, 1981).

7. Booth shows that the implied author's beliefs and judgments are always present in every aspect of a work, evident to anyone who knows how to look for them (*Rhetoric*, 20).

8. On Markan ethics, see also Frank Matera, "Ethics for the Kingdom of God: The Gospel according to Mark," *Louvain Studies* 20 (1995): 187–200; the chapter on Mark in Richard Hayes, *The Moral Vision of the New Testament: A Contemporary Introduction to New Testament Ethics* (San Francisco: HarperSanFrancisco, 1996); and Dan O. Via Jr., *The Ethics of Mark's Gospel: In the Middle of Time* (Philadelphia: Fortress Press, 1985).

9. On biblical style of narration typical of Mark, see Erich Auerbach, *Mimesis: The Representation of Reality in Western Literature*, trans. Willard Trask (Princeton: Princeton University Press, 1953).

10. On rhythm in narrative, see Gérard Gennette, *Narrative Discourse: An Essay in Method*, trans. Jane Lewin (Ithaca: Cornell University Press, 1980), 86–112, and Bal, *Narratology*, 68–77.

11. Joanna Dewey, "The Gospel of Mark as an Oral-Aural Event: Implications for Interpretation," in *The New Literary Criticism and the New Testament*, ed. Edgar McKnight and Elizabeth Struthers Malbon (Valley Forge, PA: Trinity Press International, 1994), 145–63.

12. For bibliography of literary and biblical studies about repetition in narrative, see Janice Capel Anderson, *Matthew's Narrative Web: Over, and Over, and Over Again* (Sheffield: JSOT Press, 1994). For the notion of enrichment by repetition with variation, see Robert C. Tannehill, "The Disciples in Mark: The Function of a Narrative Role," *Journal of Religion* 57 (1977): 396.

13. See Joanna Dewey, "Mark as Interwoven Tapestry: Forecasts and Echoes for a Listening Audience," *Catholic Biblical Quarterly* 52 (1991): 221–36.

14. On types of repetitive patterns in Mark, see Joanna Dewey, *Markan Public Debate: Literary Technique, Concentric Structure and Theology in Mark 2:1 to 3:6*, SBLDS 48 (Chico, CA: Scholars, 1980).

15. On verbal threads in Mark, see Boomershine, "Mark the Storyteller," 264–69. On motifs in literature, see William Freedman, "The Literary Motif: A Definition and Evaluation," *Novel* 4 (1971): 123–31.

16. Norman R. Petersen, *Literary Criticism for New Testament Critics* (Philadelphia: Fortress Press, 1978); Dewey, "Interwoven Tapestry," 221–36; and Elizabeth Struthers Malbon, "Echoes and Foreshadowings in Mark 4–8: Reading and Rereading," *Journal of Biblical Literature* 112 (1993): 211–30.

17. For an extensive treatment of this narrative pattern, see Frans Neirynck, *Duality in Mark: Contributions to the Study of Markan Redaction* (Louvain, Bel.: Louvain University Press, 1972). On the suspense related to such narrative patterns, see Eric Rabkin, *Narrative Suspense: "When Slim Turned Sideways. . . ."* (Ann Arbor: University of Michigan Press, 1973), 7–70.

18. For the twofold answer to the two-part question, see David Noble, "An Examination of the Structure of Mark's Gospel" (PhD diss., Edinburgh University, 1972).

19. See, for example, James Edwards, "Markan Sandwiches: The Significance of Interpolations in Markan Narratives," *Novum Testamentum* 31 (1989): 193–216, and Tom Shepherd, "The Narrative Function of Markan Intercalation," *New Testament Studies* 41 (1995): 522–40; and Kermode, *Secrecy*, 128–34.

20. For an analysis of concentric structures in Mark and the analysis of Mark 2:1—3:6, see Joanna Dewey, *Markan Public Debate*.

21. See also Vernon K. Robbins, "Summons and Outline in Mark: The Three Step Progression," in *New Boundaries in Old Territory: Form and Social Rhetoric in Mark* (New York: Peter Lang, 1994), 119–36.

22. In other Gospels, the parables are not always allegories, but in Mark, the parables function primarily as allegory. See Mary Ann Tolbert, *Sowing the Gospel* (Minneapolis: Fortress Press, 1989), 121–24; Mikeal Parsons, "'Allegorizing Allegory': Narrative Analysis and Parable Interpretation," *Perspectives in Religious Studies* 15 (1988): 147–64; and John R. Donahue, *The Gospel in Parable:*

Metaphor, Narrative, and Theology in the Synoptic Gospels (Philadelphia: Fortress Press, 1988), 28–62. On the function of parables in Mark, see Mary Ann Beavis, *Mark's Audience: The Literary and Social Setting of Mark 4:11-12* (Sheffield: JSOT Press, 1989).

23. This may be a typical Semitic saying that treats the result of an action as its purpose.

24. On the role of intertextuality in biblical interpretation, see Dana Nolan Fewell, ed., *Reading between Texts: Intertextuality and the Hebrew Bible* (Louisville: Westminster John Knox, 1992); Sipke Draisma, *Intertextuality in Biblical Writings: Essays in Honor of Bas van Iersel* (Kampen, Netherlands: J. K. Kok, 1989); and Richard Hays, *Echoes of Scripture in the Letters of Paul* (New Haven: Yale University Press, 1989).

25. See Howard C. Kee, "The Function of Scriptural Quotations and Allusions in Mark 11-16," in *Jesus and Paulus*, ed. E. Grasser and E. E. Ellis (Göttingen: Vandenhoeck & Ruprecht, 1975), 165–88; and Joel Marcus, *The Way of the Lord: Christological Exegesis of the Old Testament in the Gospel of Mark* (Louisville: Westminster John Knox, 1992). For a comprehensive listing of possible parallels to the Hebrew Bible in Mark, see Dale Miller and Patricia Miller, *The Gospel of Mark as Midrash on Earlier Jewish and New Testament Literature* (Lewiston: Mellen Biblical Press, 1990).

26. Of course, the arrangements of lines on a page would not be apparent to a listening audience!

27. Petersen, *Literary Criticism*.

28. On irony in literature, see Wayne Booth, *A Rhetoric of Irony* (Chicago: University of Chicago Press, 1974); D. C. Muecke, *The Compass of Irony* (London: Methuen, 1970); and Muecke, *Irony: The Critical Idiom* (London: Methuen, 1970). On irony in Mark, see Fowler, *Let the Reader*, and Jerry Camery-Hoggatt, *Irony in Mark's Gospel: Text and Subtext* (Cambridge: Cambridge University Press, 1992).

Chapter 3. The Settings

1. On setting in literature, see Seymour Chatman, *Story and Discourse* (Ithaca: Cornell University Press, 1978), 62–107; Mieke Bal, *Narratology* (Toronto: University of Toronto Press, 1985), 43–45 and 93–99; Wesley A. Kort, *Narrative Elements and Religious Meaning* (Philadelphia: Fortress Press, 1975), 20–39; and Shlomith Rimmon-Kenan, *Narrative Fiction* (New York: Methuen, 1983), 66–70.

2. For settings in Mark, see Werner Kelber, *The Kingdom in Mark: A New Time and A New Place* (Philadelphia: Fortress Press, 1974); Elizabeth Struthers Malbon, *Narrative Space and Mythic Meaning in Mark* (San Francisco: Harper & Row, 1986); Mark Allan Powell, *What Is Narrative Criticism?* (Minneapolis: Fortress Press, 1990), 69–83; Brenda Deen Schildgen, *Crisis and Continuity: Time in the Gospel of Mark* (Sheffield: Sheffield Academic, 1998); and Stephen Smith, *A Lion with Wings: A Narrative-Critical Approach to Mark's Gospel* (Sheffield: Sheffield Academic, 1996), 124–65.

3. See Malbon, *Narrative Space*, and James Robinson, *The Problem of History in Mark and Other Markan Studies* (1957; repr., Philadelphia: Fortress Press, 1982).

4. For an interesting view of the relation between time and ethics in Mark, see Dan O. Via Jr., *The Ethics of Mark's Gospel: In the Middle of Time* (Philadelphia: Fortress Press, 1985), 25–66. On the ways in which a projected outcome can be the organizing principle for a narrative, see Frank Kermode, *The Sense of an Ending: Studies in the Theory of Fiction* (New York: Oxford University Press, 1967).

5. For a sociological description of this setting in relation to Mark, see Ched Myers, *Binding the Strong Man: A Political Reading of Mark's Story of Jesus* (Maryknoll: Orbis, 1986); H. Waetjen, *A Reordering of Power: A Socio-Political Reading of Mark's Gospel* (Minneapolis: Fortress Press, 1989), 4–12; and Richard L. Rohrbaugh, "The Social Location of the Marcan Audience," *Interpretation* 47 (1993): 380–95.

6. Kort, *Story*, 44–45.

7. On the significance of the temple in Mark, see Donald Juel, *Messiah and Temple: The Trial of Jesus in the Gospel of Mark*, SBLDS 31 (Missoula: Scholars, 1977).

8. Willard M. Swartley, *Israel's Scripture Traditions and the Synoptic Gospels: Story Shaping Story* (Peabody, MA: Hendrickson, 1994).

Chapter 4. The Plot

1. On plot in literature, see Wesley A. Kort, *Narrative Elements and Religious Meaning* (Philadelphia: Fortress Press, 1975), 59–85; Kort, *Story, Text, and Scripture* (University Park: Pennsylvania State University Press, 1988), 24–29, 52–61; Seymour Chatman, *Story and Discourse* (Ithaca: Cornell University Press, 1978), 43–95; Shlomith Rimmon-Kenan, *Narrative Fiction* (New York: Methuen, 1983), 6–28, 43–58; Mieke Bal, *Narratology* (Toronto: University of Toronto Press, 1985), 11–25, 49–79; Frank Kermode, *The Sense of an Ending* (New York: Oxford University Press, 1967); Peter Brooks, *Reading for Plot: Design and Intention in Narrative* (New York: Vintage, 1985); Norman Friedman, "Forms of the Plot," in *The Theory of the Novel*, ed. Philip Stevick (New York: Free, 1967), 145–66; Elizabeth Dipple, *Plot*, The Critical Idiom 12 (London: Methuen, 1970); and Robert Scholes and Robert Kellogg, *The Nature of Narrative* (New York: Oxford University Press, 1966).

2. For the distinction between key events (called *kernels*) and related events (called *satellites*), see Chatman, *Story*, 53–56.

3. Aristotle, *Poetics*, trans. Stephen Halliwell, Loeb Classical Library, Aristotle 23 (Cambridge, MA: Harvard University Press, 1995), 28–141.

4. Gerard Genette, *Narrative Discourse* (Ithaca: Cornell University Press, 1980), 33–85, and Menakhem Perry, "Literary Dynamics: How the Order of a Text Creates Its Meanings," *Poetics Today* 1, no. 1 (1979): 35–64 and 311–61.

5. See Robert C. Tannehill, "The Gospel of Mark as Narrative Christology," *Semeia* 16 (1975): 57–95.

6. On the analysis of Mark as a tragedy, see Gilbert Bilezikian, *The Liberated Gospel: A Comparison of the Gospel of Mark and Greek Tragedy* (Grand Rapids: Baker, 1977); and Stephen Smith, *A Lion with Wings* (Sheffield: Sheffield Academic, 1996): 112–23.

7. On conflict analysis in literature, see Laurence Perrine, *Story and Structure*, 2nd ed. (New York: Harcourt, Brace, and World, 1959), 58–65.

8 Our goal here is to trace the main conflicts as they develop through the narrative. To analyze individual episodes in detail, see the set of exercises in appendix 2.

9. On the role of God in Mark, see John R. Donahue, "The Neglected Factor in Markan Studies," *Journal of Biblical Literature* 101 (1982): 563–94.

10. See Jerome H. Neyrey, "The Idea of Purity in Mark's Gospel," *Semeia* 35 (1986): 91–128; and David Rhoads, "The Social Study of Mark: Crossing Boundaries," in *Mark and Method*, ed. Janice Capel Anderson and Stephen Moore (Minneapolis: Fortress Press, 1992), 135–61.

11. For a comprehensive look at the nature of the Jesus movement as depicted in Mark's narrative, see David Rhoads, "Mission in the Gospel of Mark," *Currents in Theology and Mission* 22 (1995): 340–55.

12. On the messianic secret and other dimensions of hiddenness in Mark, see the collection of essays in Christopher Tucket, ed., *The Messianic Secret* (Philadelphia: Fortress Press, 1983); Heikki Räisänen, The "Messianic Secret," in *Mark*, trans. Christopher Tucket (Edinburgh: T & T Clark, 1990); and Joel Marcus, *The Mystery of the Kingdom of God*, SBLDS 90 (Atlanta: Scholars, 1986).

13. See Jack D. Kingsbury, *The Christology of Mark's Gospel* (Minneapolis: Fortress Press, 1983).

14. Historically Jesus had both women and men disciples in the circle around him, and Mark provides some historical evidence for this. However, in Mark's narrative, the inner circle around Jesus is portrayed as twelve males.

Chapter 5. The Characters I: Jesus

1. On characterization in contemporary literature, see Mieke Bal, *Narratology* (Toronto: University of Toronto Press, 1985), 25–36, 79–92; Seymour Chatman, *Story and Discourse* (Ithaca: Cornell University Press, 1978), 96–145; Thomas Docherty, *Reading (Absent) Character: Towards a Theory of Characterization in Literature* (New York: Oxford University Press, 1983); B. Hochman, *Character in Literature* (Ithaca: Cornell University Press, 1985); Wesley A. Kort, *Narrative Elements and*

Religious Meaning (Philadelphia: Fortress Press, 1975), 40–58; and Shlomith Rimmon-Kenan, *Narrative Fiction* (New York: Methuen, 1983), 29–42, 59–70.

2. There are minor characters whom we will not treat: John the baptist, Herodias and her daughter, the young man who flees naked, and the maid of the high priest.

3. On characterization in Mark, see Mary Ann Tolbert, "How the Gospel of Mark Builds Character," *Interpretation* 47 (1993): 347–57; Elizabeth Struthers Malbon, "Disciples/Crowds/Whatever: Markan Characters and Readers," *Novum Testamentum* 28 (1986): 104–30, and "Narrative Criticism: How Does the Story Mean?" in *Mark and Method*, ed. Janice Capel Anderson and Stephen Moore (Minneapolis: Fortress Press, 1992), 23–49; Stephen Smith, *A Lion with Wings* (Sheffield: Sheffield Academic, 1996), 52–81; and Mark Allan Powell, *What Is Narrative Criticism?* (Minneapolis: Fortress Press, 1990), 51–67. See also Elizabeth Struthers Malbon and Adele Berlin, eds., *Characterization in Biblical Literature* (*Semeia* 63; Atlanta: Scholars, 1983); Fred Burnett, "Characterization and Reader Construction of Characters in the Gospels," in *Listening to the Word of God*, ed. B. L. Callen (Anderson, IN: Warner, 1990), 69–90; John Darr, *On Character Building: The Reader and the Rhetoric of Characterization in Luke-Acts* (Louisville: Westminster John Knox, 1992); and Kari Syreeni and David Rhoads, eds., *Character in the Gospels: Rethinking Narrative Criticism* (Sheffield: Sheffield Academic, 1999).

4. See Bruce J. Malina, *The New Testament World*, rev. ed. (Louisville: Westminster John Knox, 1993), 63–89 and related bibliography.

5. See Mary Ann Tolbert, *Sowing the Gospel* (Minneapolis: Fortress Press, 1989), 121–230.

6. See Elizabeth Struthers Malbon, "Fallible Followers: Women and Men in the Gospel of Mark," *Semeia* 28 (1983): 29–48.

7. See Chatman, *Story*, 121–34, and Bal, *Narratology*, 85–93.

8. For a comprehensive list of such contrasts, see Hochman, *Character*.

9. For these categories of analysis, see E. M. Forster, *Aspects of the Novel* (New York: Harcourt Brace, 1927), 54–84.

10. On distance and identification, see Wayne Booth, *The Rhetoric of Fiction* (Chicago: University of Chicago Press, 1983), 155–59, 243–66; and Hans Robert Jauss, "Levels of Identification of Hero and Audience," *New Literary History* 5 (1974): 283–317.

11. For treatments of the character of Jesus, see Robert C. Tannehill, "The Gospel of Mark as Narrative Christology," *Semeia* 16 (1975): 57–95; John R. Donahue, "Jesus as Parable in the Gospel of Mark," *Interpretation* 32 (1978): 369–86; Jack D. Kingsbury, *Conflict in Mark* (Minneapolis: Fortress Press, 1989), 31–61; Vernon K. Robbins, *Jesus the Teacher: A Socio-Rhetorical Interpretation of Mark*, 2nd ed. (Minneapolis: Fortress Press, 1991); Edwin Broadhead, *Miracles and Christology in the Gospel of Mark*, JSNT supp. 74 (Sheffield: Sheffield Academic, 1992); and Tolbert, *Sowing*. On the temptations of Jesus throughout the narrative of Mark, see Susan Garrett, *The Temptations of Jesus in Mark's Gospel* (Grand Rapids: Eerdmans, 1998), and Jeffrey Gibson, *The Temptations of Jesus in Early Christianity* (Sheffield: JSOT Press, 1995).

12. On healing in Mark, see, for example, Adela Yarbro Collins, *The Beginning of the Gospel* (Minneapolis: Fortress Press, 1992), 39–72, and Frank Matera, "'He Saved Others; He Cannot Save Himself': A Literary Critical Perspective on the Markan Miracles," *Interpretation* 47 (1993): 15–26.

13. On the passion narrative, see E. K. Broadhead, *Prophet, Son, Messiah: Narrative Form and Function in Mark 14–16* (Sheffield: JSOT Press, 1994); Frank Matera, *Passion Narratives and Gospel Theologies* (Mahwah, NJ: Paulist, 1986), 12–79; George W. E. Nickelsburg, "The Genre and Function of the Markan Passion Narrative," *Harvard Theological Review* 73 (1980): 153–84; and Donald Senior, *The Passion of Jesus in the Gospel of Mark* (Wilmington, DE: Michael Glazier, 1984).

14. On the various interpretations of Jesus' death in Mark, see Adela Yarbro Collins, "From Noble Death to Crucified Messiah," *New Testament Studies* 40 (1994): 481–503; D. J. Harrington, "What and Why Did Jesus Suffer according to Mark?" *Chicago Studies* 34 (1995): 32–41; Morna Hooker, *Not Ashamed of the Gospel: New Testament Interpretations of the Death of Christ* (Grand Rapids: Eerdmans, 1994), 47–67; Jack D. Kingsbury, "The Significance of the Cross within Mark's Story," *Interpretation* 47 (1993): 370–79; David Lull, "Interpreting Mark's Story of Jesus' Death: Toward a Theology of Suffering," in *Society of Biblical Literature Seminar Papers*, ed. Kent H. Richards

(Atlanta: Scholars, 1985), 1–13; M. S. Medley, "Emancipatory Solidarity: The Redemptive Significance of Jesus in Mark," *Perspectives in Religious Studies* 21 (1994): 5–22; and John Pilch, "Death
with Honor: The Mediterranean Style Death of Jesus in Mark," *Biblical Theology Bulletin* 25 (1995):
65–70.

15. On this point, see Burton L. Mack, *A Myth of Innocence: Mark and Christian Origins* (Philadelphia: Fortress Press, 1988).

16. For a comprehensive view of Mark based on Jesus' resurrection, see Hugh Humphrey, *He Is
Risen! A New Reading of Mark's Gospel* (Mahwah, NJ: Paulist, 1992).

Chapter 6. The Characters II: The Authorities, the Disciples, and the People

1. On the opponents in Mark, see Terence Keegan, "The Parable of the Sower and Mark's Jewish
Leaders," *Catholic Biblical Quarterly* 56 (1994): 501–18; Jack D. Kingsbury, "The Religious Leaders
in the Gospel of Mark: A Literary Critical Study," *New Testament Studies* 36 (1990): 42–65; Elizabeth
Struthers Malbon, "The Religious Leaders in the Gospel of Mark: A Literary Study of Markan Charac-
terization," *Journal of Biblical Literature* 108 (1989): 259–81; Mark Allan Powell, *What Is Narrative
Criticism?* (Minneapolis: Fortress Press, 1990), 58–72; Anthony Saldarini, "The Social Class of the
Pharisees in Mark," in *The Social World of Formative Christianity and Judaism: Essays in Tribute
to Howard Clark Kee,* ed. Jacob Neusner et al. (Philadelphia: Fortress Press, 1988), 69–77; Stephen
Smith, "The Role of Jesus' Opponents in the Markan Drama," *New Testament Studies* 35 (1989):
161–82.

2. On the problem of the heart or mind of the authorities, see Mary Ann Tolbert, *Sowing the
Gospel* (Minneapolis: Fortress Press, 1989), 185, and elsewhere; and Dan O. Via Jr., *The Ethics of
Mark's Gospel* (Philadelphia: Fortress Press, 1989), 88–98, 116–21.

3. See also Tolbert, *Sowing.*

4. On unbelief in Mark, see Christopher Marshall, *Faith as a Theme in Mark's Gospel* (Cambridge: Cambridge University Press, 1989); and Mary Ann Thompson, *The Role of Disbelief in Mark:
A New Approach to the Second Gospel* (Mahwah, NJ: Paulist, 1989).

5. Marshall, *Faith,* 200–208.

6. On the disciples in Mark, see Ernest Best, *Following Jesus: Discipleship in the Gospel of Mark*
(Sheffield: JSOT Press, 1981), and Best, *Disciples and Discipleship: Studies in the Gospel According
to Mark* (Edinburgh: T & T Clark, 1986); Joanna Dewey, *Disciples of the Way: Mark on Discipleship*
(Women's Division, Board of Global Ministries; United Methodist Church, 1976); Jack D. Kingsbury,
Conflict in Mark (Minneapolis: Fortress Press, 1989), 89–117; Elizabeth Struthers Malbon, "Text and
Context: Interpreting the Disciples in Mark," *Semeia* 62 (1993): 81–102; Whitney Shiner, *Follow Me!
Disciples in the Markan Rhetoric,* SBLDS 145 (Atlanta: Scholars, 1995); and Robert C. Tannehill,
"The Disciples in Mark: The Function of a Narrative Role," *Journal of Religion* 57 (1977): 386–405.

7. See Stephen C. Barton, *Discipleship and Family Ties in Mark and Matthew* (Cambridge: Cambridge University Press, 1994).

8. For a different approach to this issue, see Burton L. Mack, *A Myth of Innocence: Mark and
Christian Origins* (Philadelphia: Fortress Press, 1988).

9. On the role of Peter in Mark, see Thomas E. Boomershine, "Peter's Denial as Polemic or
Confession: The Implications of Media Criticism for Biblical Hermeneutics," *Semeia* 39 (1987):
47–68; and Willem Vorster, "The Characterization of Peter in the Gospel of Mark," *Neotestamentica*
21 (1987): 57–76.

10. On the minor characters in Mark, see Elizabeth Struthers Malbon, "The Major Importance of
the Minor Characters in Mark," in *The New Literary Criticism and the New Testament,* ed. E. McK-
night and E. S. Malbon (Valley Forge, PA: Trinity Press International, 1994): 58–86; David Rhoads,
"The Syrophoenician Woman in Mark: A Narrative-Critical Study," *Journal of the American Academy
of Religion* 62 (1994): 342–75; Robert C. Tannehill, "The Gospel of Mark as Narrative Christology,"
Semeia 16 (1979): 57–95; Tolbert, *Sowing;* Joel Williams, *Other Followers of Jesus: Minor Characters as Major Figures in Mark's Gospel* (Sheffield: JSOT Press, 1994).

11. On faith in Mark, see Sharyn Echols Dowd, *Prayer, Power, and the Problem of Suffering*
(Atlanta: Scholars, 1988); Marshall, *Faith;* Eduard Schweizer, "The Portrayal of the Life of Faith in

the Gospel of Mark," *Interpretation* 32 (1978): 387–99; Robert C. Tannehill, *A Mirror for Disciples* (Nashville: Discipleship Resources, 1977); and Tolbert, *Sowing*, 176–230.

12. Rita Nakashima Brock, *Journeys by Heart: A Christology of Erotic Power* (New York: Crossroad, 1992).

13. As noted earlier, there is historical evidence, implied even by Mark, that women were more important in Jesus' ministry than the Gospel portrays. On women in Markan characterization, see Janice Capel Anderson, "Feminist Criticism: The Dancing Daughter," in *Mark and Method*, ed. Janice Capel Anderson and Stephen Moore (Minneapolis: Fortress Press, 1992), 103–34; Joanna Dewey, "The Gospel of Mark," in *Searching the Scriptures: A Feminist-Ecumenical Commentary*, ed. Elizabeth Schüssler Fiorenza (New York: Crossroad, 1994) 2:470–509; Hisako Kinukawa, *Women and Jesus in Mark: A Japanese Feminist Perspective* (Maryknoll: Orbis, 1994); Elizabeth Struthers Malbon, "Fallible Followers: Women and Men in the Gospel of Mark," *Semeia* 28 (1983): 29–48; Mary Ann Tolbert, "Mark" in *The Women's Bible Commentary*, ed. Carol A. Newsom and Sharon H. Ringe (Louisville: Westminster John Knox, 1992), 263–67.

14. On the crowds, see Elizabeth Struthers Malbon, "Disciples/Crowds/Whatever: Markan Characters and Readers," *Novum Testamentum* 28 (1986): 104–30.

15. Timothy Dwyer, *The Motif of Wonder in the Gospel of Mark* (Sheffield: Sheffield Academic, 1996).

Conclusion: The Audience

1. For an introduction to reader-response criticism, see Susan Sulieman and Ingrid Crossman, eds., *The Reader in the Text: Essays on Audience and Interpretation* (Princeton: Princeton University Press, 1980); Jane Thompkins, ed., *Reader Response Criticism: From Formalism to Post-Structuralism* (Baltimore: Johns Hopkins University Press, 1980); and Elizabeth Freund, *The Return of the Reader* (New York: Methuen, 1987); as well as works by theorists Wayne Booth, Stanley Fish, Umberto Eco, and Wolfgang Iser.

2. On the notion of the ideal or implied reader, see Wayne Booth, *The Rhetoric of Fiction* (Chicago: University of Chicago Press, 1983). On reader participation in the construction of texts, see Stephen Moore, "Doing Gospel Criticism as/with a Reader," *Biblical Theology Bulletin* 19 (1989): 85–93, and Temma Berg, "Reading In/To Mark," *Semeia* 48 (1989): 187–206.

3. Reader-response criticism of Mark has focused most fully on the way the story shapes the reader. See Robert M. Fowler, *Let the Reader Understand* (Minneapolis: Fortress Press, 1991); and Mark Allan Powell, *What Is Narrative Criticism?* (Minneapolis: Fortress Press, 1990), 11–22.

4. Of course, there are many different ways in which interpreters may understand the implications of this narrative and construct Mark's ideal audience. Our effort at understanding the implied, ideal audience is therefore only one way in which it can be faithfully constructed. See, for example, Fowler, *Let the Reader*; Bas van Iersel, *Reading Mark*, trans. W. H. Bisscheroux (Edinburgh: T & T Clark, 1989); John Paul Heil, *The Gospel of Mark as a Model for Action: A Reader-Response Commentary* (Mahwah, NJ: Paulist, 1992); and W. R. Tate, *Reading Mark from the Outside: Eco and Iser Leave Their Marks* (Bethesda, MD: Christian Universities Press, 1995). For illustrations of how Mark draws the reader into the story world, see J. G. Cook, *The Structure and Persuasive Power of Mark: A Linguistic Approach* (Atlanta: Scholars, 1995).

5. On the ending, see Thomas E. Boomershine, "Mark 16:8 and the Apostolic Commission," *Journal of Biblical Literature* (1981): 225–39; Boomershine and Gilbert Bartholomew, "The Narrative Technique of Mark 16:8," *Journal of Biblical Literature* 100 (1981): 213–23; Paul Danove, *The End of Mark's Gospel: A Methodological Study* (Leiden: E. J. Brill, 1993); J. David Hester, "Dramatic Inconclusion: Irony in the Narrative Rhetoric in the Ending of Mark," *Journal for the Study of the New Testament* 57 (1995): 61–86; Andrew T. Lincoln, "The Promise and the Failure," *Journal of Biblical Literature* 108 (1989): 283–300; Lee Magness, *Sense and Absence: Structure and Suspension in the Ending of Mark's Gospel* (Atlanta: Scholars, 1986); Robert C. Tannehill, "The Disciples in Mark," *Journal of Religion* 57 (1977) 386–405; and Mary Ann Tolbert, *Sowing the Gospel* (Minneapolis: Fortress Press, 1989), 288–99.

6. See Werner Kelber, *Mark's Story of Jesus* (Philadelphia: Fortress Press, 1979).

7. See also Mark Wegener, *Cruciformed: The Literary Impact of Mark's Story of Jesus and the Disciples* (Lanham, MD: University Press of America, 1995).

8. For an analysis of Mark's stance vis-à-vis the Roman-Judean War, see Ched Myers, *Binding the Strong Man: A Political Reading of Mark's Story of Jesus* (Maryknoll: Orbis, 1988), 413–47.

9. See Timothy Geddert, *Watchwords: Mark 13 in Markan Eschatology* (Sheffield: JSOT Press, 1989).

10. For a different view of Mark's audience, see Donald Juel, *A Master of Surprises: Mark Interpreted* (Minneapolis: Fortress Press, 1994).

11. For efforts to relate the Gospel of Mark to the contemporary world, see Bryan Blount, *Go Preach! Mark's Kingdom Message and the Black Church Today* (Maryknoll: Orbis, 1998), Ched Myers, *Who Will Role Away the Stone? Discipleship Queries for First World Christians* (Maryknoll: Orbis, 1994); Myers et al., *"Say to This Mountain": Mark's Story of Discipleship* (Maryknoll: Orbis, 1996); Mitzi Minor, *The Spirituality of Mark: Responding to God* (Louisville: Westminster John Knox, 1996); and Jack Nelson-Pallmeyer, *Brave New World: Must We Pledge Allegiance?* (Maryknoll: Orbis, 1992), ch. 8.

Epilogue: Reading as a Dialogue: The Ethics of Reading

1. Hans-Georg Gadamer, *Truth and Method*, rev. ed., trans. Joel Weinsheimer and Donald Marshall (New York: Crossroad, 1989). See also Anthony Thistleton, *New Horizons in Hermeneutics* (London: HarperCollins, 1992).

2. On the ethics of reading in literary studies, see, J. Hillis Miller, *The Ethics of Reading: Kant, de Man, Eliot, Trollope, James, and Benjamin* (New York: Columbia University Press, 1987); and Wayne Booth, *The Company We Keep: The Ethics of Fiction* (Berkeley: University of California Press, 1988). In biblical studies, see Elisabeth Schüssler Fiorenza, "The Ethics of Interpretation: De-Centering Biblical Theology," *Journal of Biblical Literature* 107 (1988): 3–17; D. J. Smit, "The Ethics of Interpretation: New Voices from the USA," *Scriptura* 33 (1990): 16–28; J. Botha, "The Ethics of New Testament Interpretation," *Neotestamentica* 26 (1992): 169–74; Gary Phillips, "The Ethics of Reading Deconstructively," in *New Literary Criticism and the New Testament*, ed. E. McKnight and E. S. Malbon (Valley Forge, PA: Trinity Press International, 1994), 283–325; Daniel Patte, *Ethics of Biblical Interpretation: A Reevaluation* (Louisville: Westminster John Knox, 1995); and Danna Nolan Fewell and Gary Phillips, "Bible and Ethics of Reading," *Semeia* 77 (1997).

3. Recent studies that emphasize the multivalent dimensions of Scripture include Daniel Patte, *Discipleship according to the Sermon on the Mount: Four Legitimate Readings, Four Plausible Views of Discipleship and Their Relevant Values* (Valley Forge, PA: Trinity Press International, 1996); Fernando Segovia, ed., *What Is John? Readers and Readings of the Fourth Gospel* (Atlanta: Scholars, 1996); and Charles Cosgrove, *Elusive Israel: The Puzzle of Election in Romans* (Louisville: Westminster John Knox, 1997).

4. The importance of these dynamics was first promoted by feminist critics. See, for example, Elisabeth Schüssler Fiorenza, *In Memory of Her: A Feminist Theological Reconstruction of Christian Origins* (New York: Crossroad, 1983). The concern has been broadened by recent critics who employ ideological criticism. See the collection of articles in *Ideological Criticism of Biblical Texts*, ed. David Jobling and Tina Pippin (*Semeia* 59; Atlanta: Scholars, 1992), and "Ideological Criticism," in *The Postmodern Bible*, ed. G. Aichele et al. (New Haven: Yale University Press, 1995), 272–308.

5. Janice Capel Anderson and Jeffrey L. Staley, "Taking it Personally," *Semeia* 72 (1995).

6. We ourselves are from white, middle-class, Protestant, American culture.

7. For an understanding of the way our social location affects interpretation, see the two volumes edited by Fernando Segovia and Mary Ann Tolbert, *Reading from This Place* (Minneapolis: Fortress Press, 1994, 1995); Brian Blount, *Cultural Interpretation* (Minneapolis: Fortress Press, 1995); and Daniel Smith-Christopher, ed., *Text and Experience: Towards a Cultural Exegesis of the Bible: Reorienting New Testament Criticism* (Sheffield: Sheffield Academic, 1995); M. Brett, *Ethnicity and the Bible* (Leiden: Brill, 1996); and Cain Hope Felder, ed., *Stony the Road We Trod: African-American Biblical Interpretation* (Minneapolis: Fortress Press, 1991).

8. "Postcolonialism and Scriptural Reading," ed. Laura Donaldson, *Semeia* 75 (1996); and *The Postcolonial Bible*, ed. R. S. Sugirtharajah (Sheffield: Sheffield Academic, 1998).

9. On the image of the roundtable, see Justo Gonzalez, *Out of Every Tribe and Nation: Christian Theology at the Ethnic Roundtable* (Nashville: Abingdon, 1992). For readings from a diversity of social locations, see, for example, Hisako Kinukawa, *Women and Jesus in Mark: A Japanese Feminist Perspective* (Maryknoll: Orbis, 1994) and John Keenan, *The Gospel of Mark: A Mahayana Reading* (Maryknoll: Orbis, 1995). ,

10. See Judy Fetterly, *The Resisting Reader: A Feminist Approach to American Literature* (Bloomington: Indiana University Press, 1978).

11. Wesley A. Kort argues that it is precisely this willingness to risk in reading that defines our attitude toward a writing as Scripture, in *"Take, Read": Texts as Scripture: Scripture, Textuality, and Cultural Practice* (University Park: Pennsylvania State University Press, 1996).

Appendix 2

1. For an example of a comprehensive analysis of a single episode in Mark, see David Rhoads, "The Syrophoenician Woman in Mark: A Narrative-Critical Study," *Journal of the American Academy of Religion* 62 (1994): 342–75. For other exercises and questions, see Mark Allan Powell, *What Is Narrative Criticism?* (Minneapolis: Fortress Press, 1990), 103–5.

Selected Bibliography
for the Third Edition

Anderson, Janice Capel, and Stephen D. Moore, eds. *Mark and Method: New Approaches in Biblical Studies*. 2nd ed. Minneapolis: Fortress Press, 2008.

Bolt, Peter G. *Jesus' Defeat of Death: Persuading Mark's Early Readers*. New York: Cambridge University Press, 2004.

Boring, M. Eugene. *Mark: A Commentary*. Louisville: Westminster John Knox, 2006.

Blount, Brian. *Go Preach! Mark's Kingdom Message and the Black Church Today*. Maryknoll: Orbis, 1998.

Broadhead, Edwin K. *Mark*. Sheffield: Sheffield Academic, 2001.

Byrne, Brendan. *A Costly Freedom: A Theological Reading of Mark's Gospel*. Collegeville: Liturgical, 2008.

Carter, Warren. *The Roman Empire and the New Testament: An Essential Guide*. Nashville: Abingdon, 2006.

Collins, Adela Yarbro. *Mark: A Commentary*. Minneapolis: Fortress Press, 2007.

Culpepper, R. Alan. *Mark*. Macon, GA: Smyth & Helwys, 2007.

Danove, Paul L. *The Rhetoric of Characterization of God, Jesus, and Jesus' Disciples in the Gospel of Mark*. New York: T & T Clark, 2005.

Donahue, John R., and Daniel J. Harrington. *The Gospel of Mark*. Collegeville: Liturgical, 2002.

Driggers, Ira Brent. *Following God Through Mark: Theological Tension in the Second Gospel*. Louisville: Westminster John Knox, 2007.

Duran, Nicole Wilkinson, Teresa Okure, and Daniel Patte, eds. *Mark*. Minneapolis: Fortress Press, 2011.

Gray, Timothy C. *The Temple in the Gospel of Mark: A Study in its Narrative Role*. Tübingen: Mohr Siebeck, 2008.

Hanson, James S. *The Endangered Promises: Conflict in Mark*. Atlanta: Scholars, 2000.

Hartman, Lars. *Mark for the Nations: A Text- and Reader-Oriented Commentary.* Eugene: Wipf and Stock, 2010.

Hearon, Holly E., and Philip Ruge-Jones, eds. *The Bible in Ancient and Modern Media: Story and Performance.* Eugene: Wipf and Stock, 2009.

Henderson, Suzanne Watts. *Christology and Discipleship in the Gospel of Mark.* Cambridge: Cambridge University Press, 2006.

Hooker, Morna D. *Endings: Invitations to Discipleship.* Peabody, MA: Hendrickson, 2003.

Horsley, Richard. *Hearing the Whole Story: The Politics of Plot in Mark's Gospel.* Louisville: Westminster John Knox, 2002.

Horsley, Richard A., Jonathan A. Draper, and John Miles Foley, eds. *Performing the Gospel: Orality, Memory, and Mark: Essays Dedicated to Werner Kelber.* Minneapolis: Fortress Press, 2006.

Iverson, Kelly R., and Christopher W. Skinner, eds. *Mark as Story: Retrospect and Prospect.* Atlanta: Society of Biblical Literature, 2011.

Kaminouchi, Alberto de Mingo. *But It Is Not So among You: Echoes of Power in Mark 10:32-45.* London: T & T Clark International, 2003.

Kim, Seong Lee. *Mark, Women, and Empire: A Korean Postcolonial Perspective.* Sheffield: Phoenix, 2010.

Levine, Amy-Jill, and Marianne Blickenstaff, eds. *A Feminist Companion to Mark.* Sheffield: Sheffield Academic, 2001.

Liew, Tat-seong Benny. *Politics of Parousia: Reading Mark Inter(con)textually.* Leiden: Brill, 1999.

Malbon, Elizabeth Struthers, ed. *Between Author and Audience in Mark: Narration, Characterization, Interpretation.* Sheffield: Phoenix, 2009.

Malbon, Elizabeth Struthers. *Mark's Jesus: Characterization as Narrative Christology.* Waco: Baylor University Press, 2009.

Malbon, Elizabeth. *In the Company of Jesus.* Louisville: Westminster John Knox, 2000.

Maloney, Elliott C. *Jesus' Urgent Message for Today: The Kingdom of God in Mark's Gospel.* New York: Continuum, 2004.

Marcus, Joel. *Mark: A New Translation with Introduction and Commentary.* New York: Doubleday, 2000–2009.

Merenlahti, Petri. *Poetics for the Gospels? Rethinking Narrative Criticism.* London: T & T Clark, 2002.

Moloney, Francis J. *The Gospel of Mark: A Commentary.* Peabody, MA: Hendrickson, 2002.

Moloney, Francis J. *Mark: Storyteller, Interpreter, Evangelist.* Peabody, MA: Hendrickson, 2004.

Moore, Stephen. *Empire and Apocalypse: Postcolonialism and the New Testament.* Sheffield: Phoenix, 2006.

Painter, John. *Mark's Gospel: Worlds in Conflict*. London: Routledge, 1997.

Resseguie, James. *Narrative Criticism and the New Testament: An Introduction*. Grand Rapids: Baker Academic, 2005.

Rhoads, David. *Reading Mark, Engaging the Gospel*. Minneapolis: Fortress Press, 2004.

Rhoads, David, and Kari Syreeni, eds. *Characterization in the Gospels: Reconceiving Narrative Criticism*. New York: T&T Clark, 1999.

Sabin, Marie Noonan. *Reopening the Word: Reading Mark as Theology in the Context of Early Judaism*. New York: Oxford University Press, 2002.

Samuel, Simon. *A Postcolonial Reading of Mark's Story of Jesus*. London: T & T Clark, 2007.

Schildgen, Brenda Deen. *Crisis and Continuity: Time in the Gospel of Mark*. Sheffield: Sheffield Academic, 1998.

Shiell, William. *Delivering from Memory: The Effect of Performance on the Early Christian Audience*. Eugene: Wipf and Stock, 2011.

Shiner, Whitney. *Proclaiming the Gospel: First-Century Performance of Mark*. Harrisburg, PA: Trinity Press International, 2003.

St. Claire, Raquel. *Call and Consequence: A Womanist Reading of Mark*. Minneapolis: Fortress Press, 2008.

Stewart, Eric C. *Gathered around Jesus: An Alternative Spatial Practice in the Gospel of Mark*. Eugene: Wipf and Stock, 2009.

Swanson, Richard. *Provoking the Gospel of Mark: A Storyteller's Commentary*. Cleveland: Pilgrim, 2005.

Thatcher, Tom, and Stephen Moore, eds. *Anatomies of Narrative Criticism: The Past, Present, and Futures of the Fourth Gospel as Literature*. Atlanta: Society of Biblical Literature, 2008.

Upton, Bridget Gilfillan. *Hearing Mark's Endings: Listening to Ancient Popular Texts through Speech Act Theory*. Leiden: Brill, 2006.

van Iersel, Bas M. F. *Mark: A Reader-Response Commentary*. Translated by W. H. Bisscheroux. Sheffield: Sheffield Academic, 1998.

Watson, David F. *Honor among Christians: The Cultural Key to the Messianic Secret*. Minneapolis: Fortress Press, 2010.

Watts, Rikki. *Isaiah's New Exodus and Mark*. Tübingen: Mohr-Siebeck, 1997.

Witherington, Ben, III. *The Gospel of Mark: A Socio-Rhetorical Commentary*. Grand Rapids: Eerdmans, 2001.

Yamasaki, Gary. *Watching a Biblical Narrative: Point of View in Biblical Exegesis*. London: T&T Clark, 2007.